Bread
Making

A HOME COURSE

Bread Making

Crafting the Perfect Loaf

from Crust to Crumb

Lauren Chattman

Storey Publishing

The mission of Storey Publishing is to serve our customers by
publishing practical information that encourages
personal independence in harmony with the environment.

Edited by Margaret Sutherland and Molly Jackel
Art direction and book design by Dan O. Williams

Cover and interior photography by Dan O. Williams, except for back cover; author's photo-
graph; and © Darren Brode/iStockphoto.com: 51 bottom; © Donald Erickson/iStockphoto.
com: 47 bottom right; © Homiel/iStockphoto.com: 50 second from top; © Labazele/iStock-
photo.com: 51 middle; © Robin Maby/iStockphoto.com: 43 top, 44; © Andrey Parfenov/
iStockphoto.com: 55 bottom; © Lauri Patterson/iStockphoto.com: 56 second from bottom;
© Sinankocaslan/iStockphoto.com: 46 bottom left, 56 third from top; © EddWestmacott/
iStockphoto.com: 55 top, 58 top
Illustrations by Alison Kolesar

Indexed by Christine R. Lindemer, Boston Road Communications

Storey Publishing
210 MASS MoCA Way
North Adams, MA 01247
www.storey.com

Printed in the United States by Malloy
10 9 8 7 6 5 4 3 2 1

Library of Congress Cataloging-in-Publication Data

Chattman, Lauren.
Bread making : a home course / by Lauren Chattman.
   p. cm.
Includes index.
ISBN 978-1-60342-791-3 (pbk. : alk. paper)
1. Bread. I. Title.
TX769.C4166 2011
641.8'15—dc22
            2010050577

Contents

Part One

GETTING STARTED

WHEN COMMERCIAL PRODUCTION of bread began in the midnineteenth century, our ancestors gladly shrugged off the responsibility of making bread for their households in favor of purchasing loaves from a local baker. Why not buy bread that was just as good as what could be made at home for the same price? There were more similarities than differences in the recipes of home and professional bakers at that point in our history.

As commercial baking grew into a mass industry, every innovation seemed to take bread further from its origins as a wholesome, homemade food. The industrialization of milling resulted in the removal of valuable nutrients from flour. Superheating the grain to speed up the process also damaged the starches to the point where they couldn't feed yeast as efficiently as before. The mechanization of mixing, kneading, and shaping bread dough required a certain kind of dough — extensible so it could be extruded through a machine and quick-rising to speed up production. None of these changes were good for bread.

Most people have nothing against progress. Even the most avid homemakers are not nostalgic for the days of beating dirty laundry against a rock or building a fire to cook every meal. But many of us who grew up with preservative-packed sliced bread have welcomed the resurgence of old-fashioned bread baking. Artisan bakers have set up shop across the country, producing all-natural breads that haven't been processed to within an inch of their nutritional lives. After tasting these beautiful and delicious breads, many home bakers have grown more interested in making quality bread at home. If you are among them, there is nothing to stop you from achieving and surpassing this modest goal. Flour with integrity is available in most supermarkets. Foolproof yeast sits near it in the baking aisle. But unless your parents run a bakery, you probably haven't learned to bake bread from them. You have the will and access to good ingredients. You just need some tutoring in the basics of the craft.

Wine and Cheese Are Difficult. Bread Is Easy.

Like wine and cheese, bread is fermented. All three rely on the activity of yeast to transform a foundational ingredient — grape juice, milk, flour — into an entirely different and much more delicious food. Not all wine and cheese are artisanal — there are plenty of mass-produced examples of both that rival Wonder bread in their banality. But there are many transcendent examples: a Lafite Bordeaux, a Montgomery cheddar. Bread experts argue that fine breads exhibit a complexity akin to these.

However, there is an important difference. While making a palatable wine or cheese can take hundreds of tries, and homemade wine and cheese rarely if ever achieve the excellence of a Lafite Bordeaux or a Montgomery cheddar, making great bread takes just a little knowledge of the basics of the process and a little experience to get a feel for bread dough. It is not inconceivable that after a few tries your bread will be as good as, or better than, anything you can buy at your local bakery. With some study and effort, you may even be able to bake breads that rival the loaves sold by Acme Bread Company in San Francisco, Amy's Bread in New York, and even the legendary Poilâne in Paris.

Becoming a Bread Baker

The wonderful thing about bread baking is that you can be as casual or serious as you like about it. This book is organized to help you find an entry point and to guide you to other places when you are ready. Maybe you just want to take some baby steps, because someone's given you a bread machine as a holiday gift. Rather than just follow the recipes in the machine's manual, spend a little time learning about the basics of bread baking, and you will be able to use your machine to craft exemplary loaves. Even if you make them start to finish in the machine, if you make them with knowledge and care they will have some artisanal flavor.

You may want to stop there, and that's fine. But I am betting that you will be so intrigued by what has occurred inside your machine that you will want to take the next step: mixing a simple straight dough, kneading it by machine or even by hand, and seeing what happens.

Maybe you've let that dough ferment overnight and are impressed by the dramatic improvement in your bread's texture and flavor that has resulted from this simple technique. This may get you thinking about something you read about extended fermentation. You might take a look at a bread recipe made in two stages, with a simple sponge, and give it a try.

Then you think that it was so easy to mix that sponge a few hours before mixing the dough itself. You perhaps wonder what your two-stage dough would have been like if it had been raised with sourdough instead of a starter made with commercial yeast.

The next thing you know, you will be mixing together some rye flour and water, hoping to encourage wild yeast to grow in a bowl on your kitchen counter. Maybe you'll never get to the place where passionate-amateur-turned-sourdough-entrepreneur Dr. Ed Wood was when he volunteered to capture wild yeast and cultivate an authentic Egyptian sourdough as part of a scholarly expedition sponsored by the National Geographic Society; he went so far as to plant heirloom grain, mill it in the ancient Egyptian way, and bake some bread using his yeast and flour in a replica of a New Kingdom oven. But you just might order some of Dr. Wood's sourdough online to see what he got so excited about.

I hope you'll use this book to discover the many ways to bake bread at home. As you read and bake, take notes alongside the recipes you try, recording your successes and disappointments. At a certain point, your own experience will guide you as much as what you've read here, helping you to get where you want to be as a home bread baker.

Chapter 1
Ingredients

PEOPLE WHO HAVE never baked bread tend to focus on the mysterious aspects of the process: the invisible activity of the yeast that makes dough rise; the complex routines of kneading, deflating, turning, and shaping the dough that are necessary to form the perfect baguette or boule; the seemingly magical oven spring that dough achieves when it hits a pre-heated baking stone. It is complicated enough to scare you a little, and maybe make you want to walk away from the whole idea of baking a loaf at home.

But the first thing you notice when you actually confront a recipe is how familiar and simple the ingredient list is. The vast majority of bread recipes, from the most basic sandwich loaves to the most complex sour-dough artisan breads, are made from flour, yeast, water, salt, and not much else. If you come at bread baking from this standpoint, remembering that for thousands of years people have been baking bread successfully at home with these same ingredients, it's easy to feel confident about a suc-cessful outcome even if you are an absolute beginner. In this chapter, you will learn all you need to know about these ingredients — how they work in a bread recipe, how to shop for the right ones, how to store and handle them — in order to use them in the recipes in this book and beyond.

Essential Ingredients

The following ingredients are essential to most bread recipes. Shop for them wisely and handle them carefully and you will have taken impor-tant steps toward achieving great homemade bread.

Wheat Flour

No matter how inexperienced you are at baking, you probably have a bag of wheat flour in your pantry. Perhaps you've used it to make cookies or muffins or a coffee cake. Knowing a little bit about this pantry staple, which happens to be the primary ingredient in most breads, will help you choose the best flour for bread baking and also help you get the best results from it.

PROTEIN AND FLOUR

Throughout recorded history and in all parts of the world, leavened bread has been made primarily with flour milled from wheat. This is no coincidence. Bakers through the ages discovered independently, through trial and error, that wheat, more than any other grain, produces the best well-risen loaf.

Food scientists have come to understand in molecular terms what bakers in ancient Egypt and medieval Europe knew intuitively. Wheat flour is particularly suited to bread baking because it contains two types of protein, gliadin and glutenin, which, when exposed to water, bond with each other to form a stretchy, elastic protein web called gluten. This gluten web, which is further developed and strengthened during mixing, kneading, and fermentation, provides the structural support (like the steel beams that hold up a building) for dough as it rises. Without sufficient gluten, bread dough won't have the ability to trap and hold the gases that are a by-product of yeast. Nor will it have the ability to expand, balloonlike, as these gases proliferate. A dough with too little gluten or an insufficiently developed gluten web will either collapse or fail to rise altogether. This is why breads made with low- or no-gluten flour milled from other grains, such as rye, corn, or buckwheat, are generally denser and less well-risen than breads made from 100 percent wheat flour.

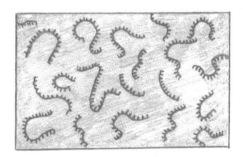 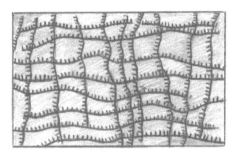

When exposed to water, the proteins in wheat flour bond to form a stretchy, elastic web, which is strengthened during mixing and kneading.

In the United States, the flour available to consumers in supermarkets is classified in general terms according to how much protein it contains. The standard level of protein in American bread flour is between 11 and 13 percent. This type of flour will form the strongest gluten web and can produce crusty, high-rising breads with an open, bubbly crumb in the European artisan style. All-purpose flour has between 8 and 10 percent protein. It can be used to make a softer, less chewy style of bread. Cake flour, which is used primarily to make tender cakes and pastries that don't require a high rise or thick crust, has a mere 6 to 8 percent protein level. In general it isn't used to bake breads, although it can be mixed with all-purpose or bread flour to produce soft breads with a tight crumb, such as Parker House rolls or Danish pastry.

It should be noted that as home bread baking has gained in popularity over the past decade or so, it has become more difficult to identify the protein content of a type of flour simply by its *bread, all-purpose,* or *cake* label. For example, King Arthur unbleached all-purpose flour, which is marketed to baking enthusiasts and sold online and by catalog as well as in supermarkets, has considerably more protein, 11.7 percent, than national

brands such as Gold Medal or Pillsbury all-purpose flour, which have a protein content of only 10.5 percent. Its higher protein content makes it suitable for bread baking, even though it is labeled *all-purpose*. While Pillsbury bread flour has a protein content of between 11.5 and 12.5 percent, King Arthur bread flour is 12.7 percent protein. Keep this in mind as you choose a bread recipe and shop for flour, taking care to buy a flour with a protein content that will help you achieve the result you desire.

THE TWO TYPES OF WHEAT FLOUR

Wheat flour is milled from wheat kernels, each one consisting of three parts: the bran, the germ, and the endosperm. The bran is the tough outer layer, made up mostly of fiber. The germ is the core, packed with protein, healthy oil, and vitamins and minerals. The endosperm is the largest part of the kernel, made up mostly of starch and proteins, and containing abundant minerals as well, especially in the part nearest to the bran.

Flour that retains the bran and germ during milling, giving it a speckled brown and off-white appearance, is called whole wheat. When the bran and germ are removed during milling, the resulting flour, without any flecks of bran and germ, is called white.

What is the difference between these two types of wheat flour in terms of how they are used in bread baking? First, there is the difference in appearance. Breads made with whole-wheat flour have a darker, more speckled appearance, because of the presence of wheat bran, than breads made with white flour. There is also a difference in flavor. Whereas white flour has a mild, wheaty flavor, whole-wheat flour lends a nutty, toasted taste and aroma to bread.

White flour and whole-wheat flour also have different nutritional values. Whole-wheat flour retains the wheat kernel's bran, which consists of fiber and minerals. White flour, stripped of this bran, lacks these nutritionally valuable components.

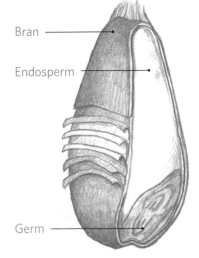

Bran

Endosperm

Germ

A wheat kernel

But the most significant difference in terms of successful baking is in the relative ability of the two types of flour to absorb water. Because whole-wheat flour is more absorbent, it requires longer and more vigorous kneading and longer fermentation time to get a good rise. Unless special care is taken in handling whole-wheat dough, the result will be a less lofty, heavier bread than is desirable. Often, bakers will use a

How Wheat Becomes Flour

It is a long way from the fields of Nebraska to the supermarket shelf. And not every crop of wheat travels the same path to get there. As you knead your dough, you might think about all that has gone into producing your flour, to put your own labor into perspective!

Sweating. After wheat is harvested, it must be set aside for six weeks or so, during which it is allowed to dry out slightly, making it easier to grind.

Tempering. Next, the wheat is sifted to remove sticks and stones and other foreign matter before being soaked in chlorinated water. This is called tempering, and it accomplishes two things. The chlorine kills any microorganisms that might feed on the wheat. The water also toughens the outer bran layer, making it easier to remove from the endosperm later in the milling process. At large commercial flour mills in the United States, where time is of the essence, just a few hours are devoted to tempering before the wheat is milled. In European mills, the wheat berries can be tempered for up to 48 hours. What difference does tempering time make? The longer the wheat berries soak, the easier it is to crush the wheat, meaning the starches and proteins in the endosperm are minimally damaged — enough to encourage the enzymatic action needed for fermentation, but not enough to compromise the flour's ability to develop gluten. That's why artisan bakers in this country obtain their flour from small mills sensitive to their needs, where a European schedule of tempering is followed.

Milling. Most flour sold in the United States has been milled at large factories, where the grain is put through a series of rollers to crush it and separate the bran and germ from the endosperm. As it is repeatedly sifted and ground, the maximum amount of endosperm is extracted from the wheat berries. To produce whole-wheat flour, some of the combination of the two to get the benefit of white flour's relatively quick and reliable gluten development and of whole-wheat flour's fiber, minerals, and healthy oil. This is not to say that you can't make bread from 100 percent whole-wheat flour or that these breads won't be as good as breads made with a mixture of white and whole-wheat flour or breads made entirely with white flour. It is simply a reminder that the qualities

bran and germ is mixed back into the refined flour. Excess bran and germ is then sold to manufacturers of food for livestock or pets. The whole process is designed for the maximum extraction of the valuable endosperm in the least amount of time, rather than to produce the best flour for bread.

Increasingly, artisan bakers and home bakers interested in making artisan-style breads are seeking out flour from smaller mills, some of which use alternative milling methods such as hammer milling or stone grinding, which are less efficient but also less damaging to the grain. Or they buy flour from mills like the highly regarded Giusto's, where roller technology is used, but in conjunction with an air-cooling system designed to preserve the grain's vitamins and minerals as it is processed.

Aging. Flour is not ready for baking immediately after it has been milled. It must be "aged." Aging involves exposing the flour to oxygen, allowing certain parts of the protein molecules to exchange their sulfur for oxygen. This swap makes the protein molecules better able to bond with each other and to stretch, so that they can form a strong and elastic gluten web in bread dough.

Aging can be accomplished either chemically, in a matter of minutes or the old-fashioned way, over time. To chemically age flour, bleach or potassium bromate is added. But the same effect can be accomplished naturally by exposing flour to air over the course of several months. During this time, flour will become naturally bleached and strengthened (although "unbleached flour," as this type is labeled, will never be as snowy white as bleached flour). Most bakers today prefer naturally aged flour for two reasons. Additives can leave a bitter aftertaste in flour, affecting the flavor of bread. Additionally, potassium bromate is a suspected carcinogen that has long been outlawed in Europe and has lost favor with American producers in recent years. Be sure you are baking with unbleached and unbromated flour by buying a product that is specifically labeled as such.

of these two types of wheat flours differ, and choosing one or the other or a blend of the two will determine the flavor and texture of the bread you bake.

A WORD ABOUT STARCH

Discussions among bakers about flour tend to focus on protein or bran, but keep in mind that wheat flour consists of between 68 and 72 percent starch, all of it originating in the endosperm of the wheat kernel. While protein gives bread dough structure as it ferments, starch provides the food necessary for this fermentation to occur. Starch molecules, damaged during milling and kneading, are converted into sugars, which provide food for yeast. As the yeast in bread dough feeds on these sugars, it proliferates, producing the gases that inflate the gluten cell structure developed during kneading. So the relative amount of starch in flour will affect a dough's rise just as much as the amount of protein.

Dough made with whole-wheat flour, which contains relatively less starch than white flour, will be slower to rise than dough made with white flour, because it provides less food for yeast. In contrast, dough made with rye flour, which has much less protein and much more starch than wheat flour, provides a sugar feast for yeast, and it must be watched carefully so that it doesn't rise to a point at which its more fragile protein structure can't support it.

ORGANIC FLOUR

Certified organic flour is more widely available to home bakers than ever. You may be wondering what distinguishes it from regular flour and whether it is worth the higher price tag.

Certified organic flour is milled from pesticide-free grain grown in soil fertilized only by natural substances. The harvested grain is stored without fumigants or irradiation. Some bakers believe that organic flour produces better-tasting baked goods. But even those who can't detect a difference between a loaf baked with certified organic flour and one baked with a standard supermarket brand worry that pesticides and other synthetic agents may enter the wheat plants and be retained in flour, presenting a health risk over the course of years of ingestion. And many people buy organic flour to support organic farming and its gentle impact on our environment. If you fall into one or more of these camps, then by all means splurge on organic flour. The difference in cost may at first seem significant: A 5-pound bag of King Arthur unbleached all-purpose flour retails for about $4.75, while King Arthur organic all-purpose flour costs $7.95. But when you think about how many loaves of bread you can bake from a single bag (2 to 3 baguettes per pound), even organic flour seems like a bargain compared to the price of this many loaves from the local bakery.

HARD, SOFT, SPRING, WINTER, RED, WHITE:
WHEAT CLASSIFICATIONS AND THE HOME BAKER

Farmers, millers, and professional bakers understand wheat in terms of several classifications, which affect the type of flour it becomes when milled and the type of bread that flour becomes when baked. If you order from a specialty flour source (see Resources, page 273), you may be able to choose with some specificity the type of flour you buy, as professional bakers do. But even if you buy your flour at the supermarket, it's interesting to know what type of grain it comes from and the qualities that your particular grain, or blend of grains, will bring to your bread.

Hard and *soft* describe two basic types of cultivated wheat. Put simply, hard wheat has a harder kernel, and thus more protein, than soft wheat. Bread flour and most all-purpose flour sold in the United States are milled from hard wheat. Cake and pastry flour, and some all-purpose Southern flours (which are traditionally softer than Northern brands) are milled from soft wheat.

Spring and *winter* refer to the season in which the wheat is grown and harvested. Spring wheat is planted in the spring and harvested in late summer. Winter wheat is planted in the fall, grows through the winter, and is harvested in the spring. In general, spring wheat is grown in colder climates — the Great Plains, Minnesota, Canada. Winter wheat is grown where it is warmer in the winter — Kansas, Nebraska, and the Carolinas.

Hard wheat is grown in both spring and winter, but the hard wheat grown in spring tends to have a higher level of protein than hard wheat grown in winter. This doesn't necessarily make hard spring wheat flour

Extra Credit: Understanding Ash Content

Artisan bakers often discuss the quality of flour in relation to its ash content. What does this mean?

Most of the minerals in a wheat berry reside in the outer layers of the endosperm, the parts closest to the bran. These minerals lend flavor and an increased fermentation capability to bread dough. To determine the mineral content of a particular batch of flour, a miller will incinerate a small sample from that batch and analyze the ashes. The term *ash content* derives from this test, and flour with a high ash content is desirable. White flour that is minimally milled, so that every trace of bran hasn't been sifted from it, will contain more minerals than a commercial white flour milled with superefficient rollers. Although ash content is rarely advertised on the packaging of flour marketed to consumers, you can be pretty sure you have purchased flour with a relatively high ash content if it comes from a specialty mill that uses European milling techniques. Compare it to a supermarket brand and it should be a little darker because of the bran particles (and minerals) it contains.

best for bread, since all protein is not created equal. The gluten in dough made from hard spring wheat flour is of a lesser quality, tending to break down during long fermentation periods. Artisan bakers who make long-fermenting white breads tend to favor hard winter wheat, which has a lower percentage of protein but whose protein is of a higher quality, to give a good rise without the risk of deflation. If they use spring wheat flour, it is usually in a relatively small percentage, as a gluten supplement in whole-wheat and multigrain breads.

Finally, there is the issue of color. Hard white wheat has a recessive gene for bran color, giving it a lighter shade than red wheat. The lighter wheat also has a milder flavor than red wheat. Traditionally, American farmers have tended toward red wheat, which won't sprout in wet weather the way white wheat can. And, traditionally, artisan bakers have primarily used flour milled from hard red winter wheat because, of available flours, it was the best choice for bread in terms of protein quality and quantity. But new strains of white wheat that resist the tendency to sprout have been developed during the past 20 years, and have made farmers take a second look at white wheat. With more white wheat available in the marketplace, bakers have more choices than ever. Now, many artisan bakers have the option of choosing blends of red and white wheat to customize the flavor of their breads.

Until recently, these distinctions wouldn't mean much for home bakers shopping for flour. The choices were bread flour, all-purpose flour, and whole-wheat flour, all milled from hard red winter wheat. To get an idea of how our choices have grown, take a look at what is offered through the King Arthur Flour website: white whole-wheat flour made from hard white spring wheat, high-gluten flour made from hard red spring wheat, European-style bread flour made from a mixture of spring and winter wheats, and more. Rather than becoming overwhelmed by these choices, keep in mind the differences between hard and soft, winter and spring, and red and white, and you will be able to buy just what you need.

THE BOTTOM LINE ON BUYING FLOUR FOR BREAD

With this knowledge in hand, you may be more confused than you were before about what kind of flour to buy to bake a loaf of bread! Because home bakers have more options than ever before, there's no simple answer, but here is my advice:

Always start by reading your recipe carefully. Baking books written in the past five years or so will often specify the protein content of the flour used to develop a particular recipe or even specify a specific brand. Make sure the flour you have has a similar protein content, no matter how it is labeled.

If you are working from an older recipe, it may simply call for *all-purpose* or *bread* flour. But nowadays choosing the right flour isn't as easy as grabbing any bag with this designation. If no guidelines about protein content are given, assume that *all-purpose* means a protein content of 8 to 12 percent, while *bread* designates a higher protein content, 11.5 to 13 percent. Remember that many brands of all-purpose flour will fall into the higher range (King Arthur all-purpose flour is 11.7 percent protein), while some bread flours may have a little more protein than you might want (King Arthur bread flour, made from 100 percent hard red spring wheat with a protein content of 12.7 percent, is quite hard). Then check to make sure that the flour you have falls within the proper range, no matter how it is labeled.

Protein Content of Popular Flour Brands

Having trouble finding the protein content on your flour? Not every packager includes this vital information.

Here are the protein contents, gathered by Rose Levy Beranbaum for her book *The Bread Bible* and by Shirley Corriher for her book *BakeWise* (see Suggested Reading, page 275), for the country's most popular brands of flour. I've included softer flours such as Swans Down and White Lily, since the bread baker will occasionally find a use for a lower-protein flour. Keep in mind that the protein content of any brand of flour will change slightly from season to season and from year to year, due to the variability of wheat crops. That said, large mills and flour packagers maintain a high level of consistency through careful testing and blending:

Gold Medal unbleached all-purpose flour: 10 to 12 percent

Gold Medal bread flour: 12.1 to 12.6 percent

Gold Medal Harvest King Better for Bread flour: 11.7 to 12.3 percent

Hecker's unbleached all-purpose flour: 11 to 12 percent

King Arthur unbleached all-purpose flour: 11.7 percent

King Arthur European-style artisan flour: 11.7 percent

King Arthur bread flour: 12.7 percent

King Arthur high-gluten flour: 14 percent

Martha White bleached all-purpose flour: 7.5 to 9.5 percent

Pillsbury unbleached all-purpose flour: 10.5 to 11.5 percent

Pillsbury bread flour: 11.5 to 12.5 percent

Robin Hood unbleached all-purpose flour: 11 to 12 percent

Softasilk cake flour: 7.5 to 8.5 percent

Swans Down cake flour: 7.5 to 8.5 percent

White Lily bleached all-purpose flour: 7.5 to 9.5 percent

If you are working from a recipe that you've made before, you may want to play with the type of flour you are using, to modify the result. Say you made whole-wheat bread with 30 percent whole-wheat flour and 70 percent bread flour and were a little disappointed with its rise and slightly flabby crust. You might want to try some high-gluten white flour (which has a protein content of 14 percent) in place of a portion of the regular bread flour, to make your dough stronger and to give your crust some chew. Or say you used bread flour to make a crisp and chewy pizza dough, but now you'd like a pizza with a more yielding, thinner crust. You might try all-purpose flour this time around. There is no end to the experimenting you can do with flour once you understand how one type of flour works in a particular recipe.

STORING FLOUR

You have plunged into home bread baking, purchasing sacks of unbleached all-purpose flour, higher-gluten bread flour, and stone-ground whole-wheat flour. How do you keep them in good condition until you are ready to bake?

When stored properly, white flour has a shelf life of about one year. After this amount of time, it will lose some of its strength and its potential to form a strong gluten structure. To keep it in good baking shape, place the flour, still in its paper sack, inside a large resealable plastic bag and squeeze the air out of the bag as you seal it. Or dump the contents into an airtight plastic container. It is very important that flour be stored in an airtight bag or container, because if it isn't it will either absorb moisture from the humid air or give up its own moisture to the dry air, affecting its flavor and performance in baking.

Whole-wheat and other whole-grain flours won't keep for as long as white flour because they contain oils that will go rancid over time. If you are planning on using these flours within three months, you can store them the same way you would white flour, in an airtight container or bag on a cool, dark pantry shelf. But to preserve their freshness for up to a year, keep them in the freezer.

Flours Milled from Other Grains

Although wheat flour gives yeast breads their characteristic structure, there is a growing interest among professional and home bakers in using flours milled from other grains to give bread flavor and boost its nutritional value. Here is some information on the most commonly used flours, to help you successfully incorporate them into your baking if you'd like. Since these flours contain more natural oils than white flour, they should be stored in an airtight container in the freezer, rather than in the pantry, to preserve their freshness for up to six months.

Buckwheat flour is made by grinding seeds from buckwheat, a plant in the rhubarb family. It has a distinctive gray color and an earthy flavor. Because it has no gluten at all and won't become a well-risen bread on its own (its most famous use, after all, is in blini, which are very flat), it must be used in combination with wheat flour in bread. You can safely substitute buckwheat flour for one-third of the wheat flour in a white bread recipe and still obtain a reasonable rise. More than this and you risk baking a buckwheat flatbread.

Oat flour is well tolerated by many people who are sensitive to wheat. To make a lower-gluten bread, substitute no more than 30 percent oat flour for the white flour in your recipe. Flour made from ground oats has about 17 percent protein, but it's not the type of protein that will form an effective gluten structure.

Rye flour, compared to wheat, is high in starch and low in gluten-forming proteins. It is possible to make 100 percent rye bread (there are many examples of these breads in northern and eastern Europe, where rye has been a staple grain for centuries), but most rye breads are made with a percentage of wheat flour to help them rise sufficiently and to give them the less starchy, less sticky texture that appeals to American palates.

Spelt flour is made from spelt, an ancient grain genetically related to wheat. Spelt flour has a similar flavor to wheat flour, but with a much lower gluten content. Many people with wheat sensitivity can tolerate spelt, and as sensitivity to wheat seems to be on the rise, so is spelt's popularity as a wheat flour substitute in all sorts of baked goods. It is possible to make a bread with 100 percent spelt flour, but there are some pitfalls on the road to success.

Spelt does contain protein, but it has less protein than wheat flour and the protein that it does contain forms a more fragile gluten web. Underkneading the bread will result in a heavy, underrisen bread. At the same time, overkneading the dough can break down the strands of gluten that have been developed, also resulting in a heavy, underrisen bread. It takes practice to get this step just right. Although wheat is superabsorbent and with sufficient kneading will accept a remarkable amount of liquid while still becoming a silky-smooth dough, spelt is not so absorbent. If you add too much water, your dough will be sticky and difficult to work with, and you'll run the risk of overkneading as you try to make the dough cohere. But underhydrating the dough is also a mistake, because the proteins in spelt flour must be fully hydrated to develop the necessary amount of gluten to allow the dough to rise.

Soy flour, made from ground dried soybeans, is very high in protein, but not the kind that creates gluten. Its flavor ranges from slightly grassy to nutty, depending on how it is processed. If you'd like to make a higher-protein bread, substitute up to 30 percent soy flour for white flour in your recipe. Using a higher proportion than this will compromise the bread's structure and its rise and may impart a stronger flavor than you'd like.

Water

It is possible to make bread without salt or packaged yeast (sourdough breads have no added yeast; they are raised with the yeast already present in air and flour). But it is not possible to make bread without water, which is essential for transforming flour into dough. Only in the presence of water will flour's proteins link together to form the gluten web that characterizes leavened bread.

The wonderful thing about this ingredient is that it comes straight from the tap. There's no need to go to a specialty market or shop online for the best water. Even water that is heavily chlorinated can be used successfully in bread recipes. Chlorine has no effect on the chemistry of the dough and will dissipate as the bread bakes, leaving no traces of its distinctive flavor. If this assurance doesn't satisfy you, you can always let your water sit on the counter for a few hours before using it, giving the chlorine time to dissipate into the air.

Minerals in water are generally good for bread. They provide food for yeast and thus aid in fermentation. If your water is exceptionally soft, meaning its mineral content is very low, then your yeast might perform sluggishly, resulting in a slack and sticky dough. If your water is exceptionally hard, the excess minerals will tighten the gluten strands, resulting in a dough that is too tough to expand sufficiently. Most tap water is neither too hard nor too soft, but if you suspect that yours falls outside the acceptable range, substitute bottled spring water and you will be fine. Don't use distilled water, which has no minerals at all and is not suitable for bread baking.

So You Want to Mill Your Own Flour

Among the most passionate home bakers, there is a small group that swears by home-milled flour. Home milling isn't for everybody. In fact, it isn't for most bakers, who, if not satisfied with the flour selection at the supermarket, have access to an ever-increasing selection of boutique and specialty flours online. But it isn't just for survivalists and others desiring to live off the grid, either. For people who are truly passionate about baking with the freshest flour possible, it is the natural next step.

If you are new to home milling and just want to try it out, there are a number of inexpensive mills that will give you a taste of what milling is like. A small hand-cranked model that grinds wheat berries into fine whole-wheat flour can be had for less than $100. Or you could buy a milling attachment for your KitchenAid mixer. An electric Nutrimill will set you back about $300. Then there are the more expensive, semiprofessional machines that cost closer to $2,000 and will grind much larger quantities of grain.

Choose a mill with the features that you'll need, and take care to choose one that promises not to overheat the grain. And of course, you'll need to seek out a source for the freshest grain (see Resources, page 273, for farm-fresh and ready-to-grind wheat, rye, and other grains) in order to get the most out of the milling experience.

There are a few questions you should ask yourself before you spend even a few dollars, in order to pinpoint the kind of mill you'll need:

When cultivating a sourdough starter from scratch, you should use bottled spring water rather than tap water. The reason is that the chlorine, minerals, and harmless bacteria present in some tap water can discourage the growth of natural yeast before it has a chance to really thrive. (If you are using packaged yeast, you will be adding it to your dough in a sufficient quantity — it is estimated that one gram of packaged yeast contains approximately 20 billion yeast cells — that the sheer number will guarantee a healthy proliferation of yeast no matter what the makeup of your tap water.) Once your culture is well established, you can feed it with tap water with no ill effects, but until you are sure that your culture is alive and well, use bottled spring water to be safe.

- How much flour will you want to mill at a time? Enough for two loaves, or enough for a dozen?

- What kind of grain will you be milling? Will you limit yourself to wheat and rye? Or will you be milling beans as well as grain? Will you want to mill smaller grain, such as millet?

- Will you need a variety of settings, from coarse (for grits) to fine (for pastry flour)?

- Will you need a mill that sifts and re-mills, to produce white flour?

Hand-cranked (left) and electric home flour mills

Yeast

Yeast, a single-celled microorganism that is a member of the fungus family, feeds on the simple sugars in bread dough, producing carbon dioxide and alcohol as by-products. The carbon dioxide causes the dough to inflate. The alcohol, as it heats up and evaporates during the first few minutes of baking, further inflates the dough, a phenomenon known as *oven spring*. This sounds plausible, but because individual yeast cells are invisible and the granules of yeast called for in most recipes are apparently inert, inexperienced bakers often have trouble accepting the idea that yeast will actually work. If you lack faith, some more details about yeast may ease your fears as you develop your bread-baking skills.

COMMERCIAL YEAST

Thousands of strains of yeast exist in nature, and there are probably dozens, if not hundreds, that exist in the air in your kitchen, on the skins of the fruit sitting on your countertop, and on the leaves and bark of the trees outside your window right now. Before the production of commercial baking yeast in the late nineteenth century, bakers cultivated these strains of natural yeast in sourdough cultures, which they then used to raise breads. Although it is not difficult to cultivate a natural yeast starter (in fact, it is hard not to cultivate one if you simply mix flour and water together and let it stand for a few days), it is quicker and more convenient to use commercial yeast, especially if you only bake bread occasionally and not on schedule every day or once a week.

Commercial yeast is available in several forms:

Fresh compressed yeast (or baker's yeast) can sometimes be found in the refrigerator section of the supermarket, although it is becoming more and more rare as time goes by. Long the choice of professional bakers, it has fallen out of favor recently because it must be kept wrapped and refrigerated to maintain its freshness and will dry out and lose its ability to raise bread in a matter of days once its packaging has been opened.

Active dry yeast has been around for years, sold in supermarkets in little packages of three or in small glass jars. Kept in an airtight container in the refrigerator or in a cool, dry pantry, it will keep for months or even years (although as a hedge against failure, each package has an expiration date). To become activated, it must be combined with warm water and rehydrated for 10 minutes or so before being added to flour. Insufficient soaking, as well as soaking in cold rather than warm water, may compromise its ability to raise dough.

Rapid-rise yeast is dry yeast that has been packaged with enzymes and other yeast foods in order to hasten fermentation. It was first developed to save time and money for commercial bakers, who could use it to hasten the bread-making process. Bread doughs mixed with rapid-rise yeast rise so quickly that they require only one rise instead of the conventional two. There is no need for a period of bulk fermentation after kneading. Kneaded doughs can be shaped directly, proofed briefly, and then baked, considerably cutting down on the time spent making bread from start to finish. But if you've decided to bake your own bread at home, I assume that your primary goal is not to produce it as quickly as possible. And since it is widely agreed among artisan bakers that longer fermentation produces better-tasting bread, I recommend that you stay away from rapid-rise yeast in your pursuit of breads with character and complexity.

Instant yeast is relatively new to the market. It is similar to active dry yeast, but since it is air-dried rather than oven-dried it is quicker and easier to activate. It can be added directly to the flour without first being hydrated, without worry that it won't come alive. Don't confuse it with rapid-rise yeast, which has been packaged with yeast food to encourage dough to rise quickly. "Instant" refers to the fact that you can mix the yeast directly with the dough ingredients without rehydrating it in water first, as you must with active dry yeast.

The recipes in this book call for instant yeast, which is easy to use, readily available, and keeps in the refrigerator in an airtight container for months or even years without losing its ability to raise bread. But in case you want to use active dry yeast or fresh compressed yeast, use the following conversions:

1 teaspoon instant yeast = 1½ teaspoons active dry yeast =
1½ packed teaspoons fresh compressed yeast

WILD YEAST

Growing your own yeast is an option that you might consider once you've had a few successes with packaged yeast. Baking with wild yeast in a sourdough culture is necessarily a more time-consuming process. Aside from the extra time it takes to grow the culture itself, wild yeast isn't as efficient at fermenting dough as commercial yeast, which is bred for its quickness and predictability. But artisan bakers would argue that longer fermentation times result in better bread. The longer a bread takes to ferment, the more opportunity there is for lactobacilli, harmless bacteria that coexist with yeast, to produce flavorful acids that give long-fermenting breads their great taste. Because these acids take between eight and twelve hours to produce, only doughs that ferment for this length of time will reap the flavor benefits that lactobacilli can confer.

What Is a Dough Conditioner, and Do I Need One?

Commercial bakers often add chemical conditioners to their bread doughs to strengthen gluten and make the dough easier to work with. Some home baking experts, and many baking retailers, recommend that amateurs follow suit. In my opinion, properly handled dough, even if it is made with lower-gluten flour such as whole wheat or rye, doesn't usually need any help. But if you are not satisfied with the way your loaves are rising, you might try one of the following all-natural additives for higher-rising bread.

Ascorbic acid. Another name for vitamin C, ascorbic acid encourages yeast activity and strengthens gluten, allowing it to rise higher than usual without collapsing during proofing. Not only is it routinely added to commercial bread dough, but it is also a common ingredient in traditional French bakeries, where it helps to produce characteristically light baguettes. You can buy ascorbic acid in powdered form from baking supply stores (see Resources, page 273), or you can simply crush a tablet of vitamin C and add no more than ⅛ teaspoon per large loaf.

Dry milk. Some bakers believe that the enzymes present in fresh milk inhibit yeast growth and prefer to use dry milk (which has been heated to destroy these enzymes before being dried) mixed with water in bread dough.

Salt

It is amazing that salt, which exists in such a proportionately small amount in bread dough (most bread dough recipes contain about 2 percent salt), plays such an important role in successful bread baking. Of course, it is a flavor enhancer, bringing out the best flavor of the grain. Without salt, your bread would taste flat and dull rather than rounded and multidimensional.

Salt also plays several chemical roles. It aids in the formation and maintenance of a dough's gluten structure, tightening and strengthening the gluten web so that your dough can rise high. If you were to forget the salt when mixing your dough, it would be slack and sticky instead of bouncy and smooth, and it would spread into a flat mass instead of rising during the fermentation period.

Malt extract. Made from sprouted, mashed barley, malt extract contains enzymes that help break down starches, providing extra nutrition for yeast. Commonly used in bagels (the next time you eat a bagel, concentrate on the flavor and see if you can detect the sweetness of the malt), it can be used in small quantities to encourage yeast production in any bread. Use no more than ¼ teaspoon per cup of flour, or the flavor and sweetness may overwhelm the taste of your bread.

Vital wheat gluten. Vital wheat gluten consists simply of gluten-forming proteins that have been extracted from wheat. If you are dissatisfied with the rise you are able to get from your 100 percent whole-wheat dough or any other dough you make with lower-gluten flour, you might try adding a tablespoon of vital wheat gluten to see what happens.

Loaf improver blends. King Arthur Flour sells custom-blended mixes designed to improve particular types of dough. Their Whole Grain Bread Improver contains vital wheat gluten and ascorbic acid. Their Rye Bread Improver contains vital wheat gluten and malt powder. Their Easy-Roll Dough Improver contains malt extract and dried milk and helps to improve extensibility of doughs that often refuse to be rolled out without shrinking.

Specialty Salts

In recent years, sea salts and other specialty salts have become something of a fetish item among home cooks. In the gourmet grocery store closest to my house, I can buy pink Hawaiian sea salt, French fleur de sel, Maldon sea salt flakes, Nazuna sea salt from Japan, and half a dozen others. Professional artisan bakers often argue that sea salt tastes better than kosher salt, going so far as to claim that a particular type of sea salt from a particular sea tastes better than any other. Although any kind of salt will perform the necessary functions of controlling fermentation and enhancing bread's flavor, you may want to experiment with different salts to see if you have a favorite salt for baking bread. Here are a few you might try (see Resources, page 273, to order in bulk bags convenient for baking).

Bay of Fundy sea salt. This reasonably priced domestic sea salt is harvested in Maine.

Bolivian Rose salt. Hand-harvested from the Andes Mountains in Bolivia, this salt is advertised as ultrapure (because of the unpolluted environment from which it comes) and full of healthy minerals because of its contact with volcanic rock.

Dark pink Himalayan salt. Mined in the Himalayas, it has a striking color.

Fleur de Sel de Guérande. Hand-raked from salt ponds in Brittany, this salt is preferred by many bakers trained in French methods.

Maldon sea salt. My own favorite, this flaky sea salt has been a product of this area of England since the Middle Ages.

Sel gris. Also harvested in Brittany, this salt has a distinctive gray color.

Sicilian sea salt. This salt hails from Trapani, once Europe's largest salt source, where the government has created a nature preserve to protect the salt marshes and saltworks that have been supplying salt to the world for almost 500 years.

Sonoma sea salt. This affordable domestic salt is harvested from the Pacific Ocean off of California.

Salt slows down yeast activity so that the bread dough doesn't become too acidic (acids are a yeast by-product) before it has a chance to reach its maximum volume. Too much acid in a dough will break down the gluten web, resulting in a less voluminous loaf. Relatedly, salt contributes to a bread's well-browned crust. The longer a dough ferments, the more time there is for starches to break down into sugars, which caramelize on the dough's surface as it bakes, forming a beautiful and delicious crust. Breads baked without salt (there are a few examples, most notably the saltless bread traditional in Tuscany) have pale, anemic crusts in comparison to breads containing salt. Finally, salt is a preservative, holding onto the water molecules in bread, keeping it fresher longer.

Noniodized table salt, kosher salt, and fine sea salt will all work in bread recipes. (Avoid coarse sea salt, which won't dissolve as quickly and easily as these other three.) Some artisan bakers prefer sea salt for its flavor, but many believe there is no difference in the taste of bread baked with inexpensive table salt and bread baked with imported fleur de sel.

There is a difference in the way each of these salts is measured, however, since their granular structures vary greatly. Measuring it by the teaspoon isn't the most accurate way to add the proper amount to a bread recipe, since 10 grams of sea salt can physically take up 1½ times the volume of 10 grams of table salt. I use a sensitive electronic scale to weigh out all of my ingredients, including salt, and I urge you to do the same. But if you'd like to measure instead of weigh salt, keep these general equivalencies in mind, with the caveat that different brands of kosher salt and sea salt will vary slightly in volume:

0.25 ounce table salt = 1 teaspoon
0.25 ounce kosher salt = 1½ teaspoons
0.25 ounce sea salt = 1½ teaspoons

Store salt in an airtight container in your pantry so that it doesn't absorb water from the air, which will increase its weight in relation to its saltiness and thus throw you off when you measure it!

Additional Ingredients

Aside from flour, water, yeast, and salt, some recipes do contain additional ingredients that enhance flavor and texture. The following are the most common. As with essential ingredients, choosing the best additional ingredients and handling them properly will go a long way toward ensuring that your bread is the best it can be.

Fats

In general, artisan breads in the European style are fat-free. Even in small quantities, fat added to bread dough coats the protein molecules in flour, inhibiting the formation of the gluten that is so important to the high rise and open crumb that are the hallmarks of country loaves. If you are planning on baking a baguette or a crusty boule, there's no need to run to the store for olive oil or butter, except, of course, to have some on hand for dipping or spreading when your bread is ready to eat!

This is not to say that fats are of no use to bread bakers. There are certain Italian breads — *schiacciata* and breadsticks come to mind — that are enriched and tenderized with olive oil. If you are baking a bread that calls for olive oil, there's no need to use your most expensive bottle of boutique, cold-pressed oil, since the subtlety of its flavor will be lost during baking. But do use a good quality extra-virgin oil from the supermarket, the fruitier the better, so some olive flavor shines through. If you are making something like No-Knead Roman Pizza (page 193), which is drizzled with olive oil when the baking is done, by all means use the best-quality oil you have. It will make a difference.

Exposure to air will cause oxidation in olive oil, leading to rancidity. Heat and light will speed the process of oxidation. So store your oil in a tightly capped bottle in a cool, dark place to extend its shelf life. The shelf life of an unopened bottle of olive oil varies, depending on the olive variety, the time of year the olives were harvested, and how they were processed. In general, olive oil is at its flavor peak two to three months after it is pressed, will keep for one to three years in an unopened container, and should be used or discarded a year after its container has been opened.

Yeast-risen sweet breads and pastries such as brioche and *babka* contain an abundance of butter (generally added to the dough after the flour and water are thoroughly combined and gluten has had a chance to develop), which gives them flavor and richness. If a recipe calls for butter, always use unsalted. There are two reasons for this. First, salted butter may throw off the chemistry of your dough. As discussed earlier, too much salt can weaken a dough's gluten structure and inhibit the activity of the yeast. It can also, of course, make the bread unpleasantly salty. Second, salt is added to butter as a preservative, and salted butter can be held on supermarket shelves much longer than unsalted butter. As a result of its long holding time, it is often not as fresh-tasting as unsalted butter, and it may impart off flavors to your bread. Keep your butter, well wrapped, in the refrigerator for up to 3 months, or freeze it for up to 1 year.

All doughs, including the fat-free variety, will stick to the bowl or container as they rise. So keep on hand some vegetable oil or vegetable oil spray for greasing your bowl, so that your dough releases easily when it's time to divide and shape it after its first rise.

Sweeteners

In limited quantities, sweeteners such as sugar and honey can enhance the natural wheaty flavor of flour and coax a darker crust from the bread as it bakes. A little extra sugar is especially welcome in breads made with flours such as whole wheat, rye, and buckwheat, which have a slightly bitter flavor profile.

But too much sweetener can inhibit a bread's rise. Because it competes with flour in combining with water molecules, a sweetener robs flour of some of its ability to form gluten. It can also rob yeast of the moisture necessary to produce the gases that inflate the cells formed as gluten develops. In general, breads with a relatively high proportion of sugar call for extra yeast as a hedge against this effect. Even so, they'll have a softer, less sturdy crumb than sugar-free breads.

Barley malt syrup is often mentioned in bread-baking books for its supposed ability to sweeten bread dough without inhibiting gluten formation. If this is your goal, make sure to buy diastatic (rather than nondiastatic) barley malt syrup, which contains enzymes that help break down carbohydrates in flour to release flour's natural sugars, thus encouraging gluten formation. Nondiastatic barley malt syrup (which is often called for in bagel recipes) has been heated to the point of neutralizing these enzymes, and it functions the same way sugar or honey does, simply lending its particular flavor and sweetness to the bread. Both types are available by mail and online (see Resources, page 273). Take care that you are ordering the one you really want!

If you have a canister of sugar and a jar of honey in your pantry, you'll be prepared to make a honey and whole-wheat loaf. Store sugar in an airtight container at room temperature and it will keep indefinitely. Honey tends to crystallize over time, but can be reliquefied by gently heating it in the top of a double boiler to dissolve the crystals. An unopened container of barley malt syrup will keep in a cool, dark pantry for up to two years. Once opened, it will decay or even grow mold very quickly. Store opened barley malt syrup in the refrigerator and use it within three months of opening.

Milk, Eggs, and Cheese

When milk is used in bread recipes (replacing some or all of the water), the result is a bread with a richer flavor and a softer texture than bread made with water alone. If whole milk is used, the fat in the milk will keep your bread fresher longer. For recipes in this book and elsewhere, use whole milk unless otherwise directed to reap the benefits of milk's preservative effect.

Eggs give breads a beautiful, yellow crumb and a burnished crust. Think about the deep, rich colors of a well-baked challah or brioche. This is thanks to eggs. They also add great flavor. Eggs are measured by weight. The recipes in this book, as in most books, call for large eggs. If you know the weights of different size eggs, you can make substitutions. A medium egg weighs 1.75 ounces, a large egg weighs 2 ounces, an extra-large egg weighs 2.25 ounces, and a jumbo egg weighs 2.5 ounces. So you can substitute 4 jumbo eggs for 5 large eggs and so forth.

Some of the world's most delicious breads contain cheese. Moist cheese like ricotta can take the place of some of the water in dough, adding fat and flavor. Harder cheeses can be grated, shredded, or cut into small pieces and stirred into dough the way you'd stir in chopped herbs.

On the next page is a simple recipe that lets you experiment with adding a moist cheese to a basic straight dough.

Ricotta Loaves

Makes 2 (8-inch) loaves

7	ounces (¾ cup plus 1 tablespoon) warm room temperature water (78°F)
0.35	ounce/10 grams (1 tablespoon) instant yeast
17.6	ounces/499 grams (3¼ cups) unbleached all-purpose flour
0.75	ounce/21 grams (2 tablespoons) sugar
0.25	ounce/7 grams (1½ teaspoons) salt
¾	cup whole-milk ricotta cheese
2	tablespoons unsalted butter, melted and cooled

1. Combine the water, yeast, flour, sugar, salt, ricotta, and butter in the bowl of a stand mixer or in a large mixing bowl. Stir with a rubber spatula until a rough dough forms.

2. Knead the dough. By machine: With a dough hook, knead the dough on medium speed until it is smooth and shiny and just clears the sides of the bowl, 10 to 12 minutes. By hand: Scrape the dough onto a lightly floured countertop. With floured hands, knead the dough with steady strokes until it is smooth and shiny, about 15 minutes. Take a break midway through kneading if you need to. Resting the dough will only improve its gluten structure. Resist adding extra flour, using a bench scraper to lift the dough from the countertop if it sticks and flouring your hands instead of the dough if possible.

3. Spray the inside of a dough-rising container or large mixing bowl with nonstick cooking spray and place the dough inside. Cover with plastic wrap and let rise until the dough has doubled in size, about 1½ hours.

4. Spray two 4- by 8-inch loaf pans with nonstick cooking spray. Turn the dough onto a lightly floured countertop, divide into two equal pieces, and shape each piece into a loaf (see page 89 for instructions). Place them in the prepared loaf pans, seam sides down. Sprinkle with flour and drape loosely with plastic wrap. Let stand until almost doubled, 1 to 1½ hours.

5. While the loaves are proofing, place a baking stone on the middle oven rack and preheat the oven to 375°F.

6. Place the pans on top of the baking stone. Bake until the breads are golden and an instant-read thermometer inserted into the center reads 200°F, 40 to 50 minutes.

7. Remove the breads from the oven, unmold them onto wire racks, and set them right side up to cool to warm room temperature, about 1½ hours.

Dried Fruit, Olives, Seeds, and Nuts

Many bread recipes can be varied by adding dried fruits, chopped olives, seeds, or nuts. It is important to think about how these additions will affect the hydration of the dough. Certain add-ins can absorb a lot of water, leaving insufficient water for the flour. It may be necessary to add more water to the dough, one way or another.

If you are adding dried fruit, such as raisins, cranberries, cherries, prunes, or apricots, buy the freshest and softest dried fruit you can find. Store it in a resealable plastic bag, squeezing out the air, to keep it fresh. Even then, it's a good idea to soak the fruit in warm water and pat it dry before kneading it in, so that it is plumped and unable to absorb any additional moisture. Likewise, plump and juicy olives are better for bread than leathery dry ones. Keep them refrigerated in their briny liquid, patting them dry before pitting and chopping. Certain seeds — sunflower, sesame, and especially flax — should be soaked in water and then drained before they are added to dough. A good recipe will take into account how much water these rehydrated seeds are bringing to the dough and calculate the percentages accordingly. Keep seeds in resealable plastic bags or airtight containers in the freezer to prevent spoiling.

Chopped nuts require a different type of handling. They, too, should be frozen in airtight bags until ready to use. For the most intense flavor, toast them and cool them completely before chopping and adding them to the dough.

Ingredients
Questions and Answers

Q **There are so many choices in the supermarket. Without knowing how much protein each type of flour contains, how can I read a bag's label for clues that I'm buying the best flour for bread?**

A First, where are you shopping? If you are considering buying a regional brand such as Hecker's (sold in the North and Midwest) or Martha White (sold in the South), it makes a difference. Northern all-purpose flour will generally have enough gluten to make good bread, but it's best to save Southern all-purpose flour, which is lower in protein, for cakes and biscuits.

Next, look for the words *unbleached* and *unbromated,* because this will indicate that the flour hasn't been chemically aged, but rather has been allowed to age naturally.

If buying organic ingredients is important to you, read the label carefully. Make sure you see the word *certified* along with the United States Department of Agriculture seal, which tells you that both farmer and miller have met USDA standards. Beware bags with vague claims such as "all natural," which could mean anything or nothing at all. Certified organic brands such as Hodgson Mill and Bob's Red Mill are widely distributed but often shelved with natural foods rather than with baking ingredients.

The term *stone-ground* should indicate that the wheat has been ground between heavy millstones rather than put through rollers, leaving the starches in the wheat berries minimally damaged and thus making the flour better for bread. But be aware that if flour has been put through millstones prior to roller milling, there is no government restriction against labeling it as stone-ground. Unless the package explains the milling process in detail, there's no way of knowing how much, or how little, the flour has benefited from stone grinding.

If you are dissatisfied with the choices at your local grocery store or would like to make purchases informed by more than what is printed on these flour bags, you could shop online. I have been very happy with my purchases from places like Giusto's or King Arthur Flour. Go to their websites (see Resources, page 273), and if you don't see the information that you need, you can talk to a knowledgeable person in customer service who will likely help you find exactly what you are looking for.

Q **I buy large bags of flour at a warehouse club and then store the flour in the freezer to keep it fresh. Can I use it straight from the freezer?**

A Most people consider water temperature in relation to activating their yeast and encouraging fermentation, but it's important to consider the temperature of your other ingredients as well. Flour that you use straight from the freezer will definitely bring down the temperature of your dough. This might be bad (freezing-cold flour might inhibit yeast activity), or it might be good (if it is a hot summer day and your kitchen is already above 80°F, this is one way to slow fermentation). But your recipe was probably tested with room temperature flour, and especially if this is the first time you are baking a particular bread, it's best to bring the flour to room temperature before starting, to replicate the author's results as closely as possible.

Q **I opened my canister of flour today and was horrified to see small bugs moving around. I threw it all into the trash. Where did they come from and what can I do to avoid them in the future?**

A You likely saw flour beetles, and you did the right thing by immediately discarding your flour. These bugs don't carry disease, but they are impossible to remove from flour once they begin to hatch. If beetles are in your flour, chances are that they are also infesting other foods in open containers in your pantry — pasta, rice, cereal, crackers, pet food. Go through everything and discard anything that contains bugs. Then, empty out the pantry or cabinet and thoroughly clean it, vacuuming up any crumbs and food particles that may be lurking in the cracks and crevices. Thoroughly wash the surfaces of the shelves and the walls with soap. Before returning uninfested food to the pantry, package each item in an airtight container or bag.

Where did the bugs come from? The beetle eggs originated either in the flour sack you brought home from the market (flour beetles are a persistent problem at flour mills) or in another package, and they then migrated to your flour to feed once they hatched. These eggs can lay dormant indefinitely in a cool, dry place, but they will begin to hatch once the weather becomes warm. To prevent future infestation, you can do a couple of things. At temperatures below freezing, flour beetle eggs will die, so if you live in a warm climate or it is summertime you might consider freezing your flour for a day or two before putting it in the pantry; or you could store it in the freezer indefinitely.

Q **Is it true that cinnamon kills yeast? Or is this just an old wives' tale?**

A Cinnamon does contain a chemical compound, *cinnamic aldehyde,* that inhibits yeast activity. If you are adding a teaspoon or more of cinnamon directly to a bread dough, you will want to add about 50 percent more yeast to the dough as well, to counteract this effect. But if you are making something like a yeasted coffee cake or cinnamon buns, for which the cinnamon is sprinkled onto already fermented dough, then the cinnamon will not come in contact with a large enough percentage of the dough to be able to inhibit the yeast activity.

Q **My natural foods store was out of the regular stone-ground wheat flour that I usually buy, but it had graham flour. Is this the same as whole-wheat flour?**

A Graham flour was popularized by Dr. Sylvester Graham, a nineteenth-century advocate of vegetarianism and health foods. Graham believed, among other more eccentric things, that people should eat only home-baked bread made from whole-wheat flour. Graham flour that is sold today is more coarsely ground than regular whole-wheat flour, producing rustic, hearty whole-wheat loaves. It can be substituted for regular whole-wheat flour, but be sure to weigh it rather than measure it by volume when making the substitution, because its coarse grind means that its weight-to-volume ratio differs from that of regular whole-wheat flour.

Q **What is corn flour? Is this the same as cornmeal?**

A Corn flour and cornmeal are both made from ground whole corn kernels, but corn flour is more finely ground. Corn flour is suitable for yeast bread baking when used in conjunction with wheat flour (it doesn't have any gluten, so don't try to use more than 20 to 25 percent corn flour in your dough), while cornmeal is more often used in quick breads and muffins, although a small quantity can add nice crunch to a wheat bread. Masa harina is corn that has been processed with lye, like hominy, to remove the tough hull before finely grinding it. It is used to make corn tortillas. Cornstarch, which is primarily used as a thickener in gravies and pies, is occasionally used in cookie dough and cake batter, in conjunction with flour, to make those baked goods softer and more tender. It is made by grinding only the starchy endosperm of the corn.

Q I see bright yellow semolina breads in a local bakery. Is semolina a type of corn flour?

A Although semolina has a color similar to cornmeal, it is in fact milled from durum, a type of wheat with a sunny yellow color. Durum wheat is most commonly used in pasta making, which is why pasta, even when made without egg yolks, has a distinctly yellow hue. It is also often ground to make cereal (Cream of Wheat is made from durum). But it can also be milled to make bread, and the flour produces loaves with a beautiful, creamy yellow crumb and burnt orange crust. If you would like to bake bread with semolina flour, first be sure that you are buying the right product. Coarsely milled semolina is used in pasta making, so look for flour milled more finely, especially for bread baking. You can substitute up to 50 percent semolina flour for regular wheat flour in a recipe. Because semolina won't form as strong a gluten structure as regular wheat flour, larger amounts may compromise the rise of your bread. If you do substitute semolina for some of the flour, it's a good idea to use a higher-protein bread flour for the balance, to make sure that your dough has sufficient strength.

Q What is bread machine yeast? Can I use it if I'm not using a bread machine? And can I use instant or active dry yeast if I am using a bread machine?

A The essential difference you need to keep in mind when using a bread machine is between active dry yeast, which needs to be soaked in water before using, and instant yeast, which can be mixed with dry ingredients before it is rehydrated. Active dry yeast is not recommended for many bread machine recipes, since very often those recipes will instruct you to place all of the dry ingredients into the machine before adding water. If you are using a bread machine, you will want instant yeast, sometimes called bread machine yeast. As always, avoid rapid-rise yeast, which will cause your bread machine bread to ferment very quickly, and do little to enhance its flavor.

Q Can I substitute maple syrup for honey in a bread dough recipe?

A Maple syrup is about 50 percent less sweet than honey or sugar, but it can be substituted for either in bread recipes. If you want to use maple syrup instead of honey, decrease the water in your recipe by the same amount that you increase the maple syrup in relation to the honey. For example, if you are using 1½ tablespoons of maple syrup instead of 1 tablespoon of honey, subtract ½ tablespoon of water to ensure that your dough is properly hydrated. If you want to use maple syrup instead of sugar, increase the measure by 50 percent, and decrease the amount of water according to how much syrup you use. So if the recipe calls for 2 tablespoons of sugar, use 3 tablespoons of maple syrup, and subtract 3 tablespoons of water so that your dough isn't too wet.

Q **Can I substitute yogurt or buttermilk for milk in a bread recipe?**

A Either yogurt or buttermilk can be used instead of milk in breads such as *pain de mie,* to give your bread a slight tanginess. Because we are talking about yeast breads and not quick breads, there are no worries about adding baking soda to neutralize the acids in these cultured dairy products. I have even seen recipes for brioche made with yogurt. Be aware that, especially when using yogurt, you may have to add an extra tablespoon of milk or water to achieve the same consistency that would have been achieved with milk alone.

Q **I thought the eggs in challah were supposed to make these breads rich and moist, but my fat-free breads seem more moist than my enriched breads. Why?**

A Egg yolks certainly do contain fat, so you'd think that the addition of eggs to bread dough would contribute to the moist mouthfeel. But egg whites have the opposite effect, drying out bread. Adding a little sugar to the dough can help, since sugar molecules will hold onto moisture, helping to preserve the bread. Extra fat in the form of butter will also prevent your challah from becoming stale too quickly.

Chapter 2
Equipment

FOR MOST OF ITS HISTORY, bread was made with primitive tools — a bowl, a work surface, a wood-fired oven — and in many places around the world, it still is. So it shouldn't be surprising that with high-quality, carefully chosen ingredients and some knowledge and experience of technique, it is possible to produce the most wonderful breads in a minimally equipped kitchen.

There are certainly some pieces of equipment that are necessary for crafting the best Pullman loaf, seeded Jewish-style rye bread, or brioche rolls. It would be difficult to make that Pullman loaf without a Pullman loaf pan, and you'd definitely want a wire rack for cooling it when it came out of the oven. Other items are nice to have but not essential. No need to buy a special dough-slashing tool called a lame if you have a single-edge razor blade, or even a serrated knife. A dough-rising container would make it easy to check on the progress of your dough as it ferments, but dough will rise just as well in a roomy bowl. Here is an alphabetical list of all of the equipment used in recipes in this book (and most other books about bread), with some shopping advice in case you are in the market. Essentials are marked with a check mark ✔.

Baker's peel

This thin, flat wooden or metal sheet with an attached wooden handle is the traditional tool for sliding breads onto a preheated baking stone. I prefer metal to wood because it lasts longer and is easier to clean. If you don't have a baker's peel, you can use a rimless baking sheet to do the same job, although you'll have to get closer to the very hot oven and stone than you would if you were using a handled peel.

Baking sheets ✅

Bread bakers use both rimmed and rimless baking sheets. Rimmed sheets give certain breads, such as focaccia, their shape. It's convenient to bake other kinds of breads and rolls on a rimless sheet lined with parchment. Then, when your bread is baked, you can easily slide it, still on the parchment, right off of the sheet and onto a wire rack. If you're in the market for new baking sheets, look for heavy-duty aluminum sheets that won't warp at high temperatures. Light colors are better than dark, which tend to overbrown the bottom crust before the top crust is done.

Baking stone ✅

A baking stone mimics the even and intense heat of a professional hearth oven, delivering a blast directly to the bottom of the dough on contact to encourage the incredible oven spring that is one of the hallmarks of hearth-baked breads. Without a baking stone, your breads will never reach their potential height, nor will they develop the chewy crust of the best professionally produced breads. If you are buying a new stone, get the largest one that will fit in your oven, to accommodate any bread or pizza that you might want to make. To avoid cracking, be sure to follow the manufacturer's directions for seasoning the stone, which usually involve heating it once or twice in a moderate oven before using it in a very hot one.

Banneton

A banneton is a willow basket used by French bakers to help dough rounds keep their shape as they rise. Bannetons come in various shapes — round, oblong, oval — to support various shapes of bread dough. Lined with canvas or unlined, the baskets are breathable, so dough won't stick to them and deflate when overturned onto a baker's peel. If you don't have a banneton, you can easily improvise one by lining a bowl with a clean kitchen towel.

Rosemary Focaccia
1 (10- by 15-inch) flatbread

Most breads are baked free-form or in loaf pans, but focaccia, the popular Italian-style flatbread, is baked on a rimmed baking sheet and cut into squares, rather than slices, before it is served. This particular recipe is adapted from one my husband developed years ago for his book *The Complete Italian Vegetarian Cookbook*. In addition to water, flour, yeast, salt, and olive oil, he adds a little mashed potato to the dough, which makes it soft, moist, and high rising, perfect for splitting and using for sandwiches. Knead this dough by hand or in a stand mixer. A food processor will make the potatoes gummy.

FOR THE DOUGH

1 (8-ounce) baking potato, peeled and cut into 2-inch chunks

8 ounces (1 cup) warm water (110°F)

0.17 ounce/5 grams (1½ teaspoons) instant yeast

17.85 ounces/506 grams (3½ cups) unbleached all-purpose flour

0.35 ounce/10 grams (2 teaspoons) fine sea salt or kosher salt

1 tablespoon extra-virgin olive oil

FOR THE TOPPING

3 long sprigs fresh rosemary

2 tablespoons extra-virgin olive oil

0.17 ounce/5 grams (1 teaspoon) sea salt

1. Place the potato in a medium saucepan and cover with water. Bring to a boil, turn down the heat, and simmer until tender, about 15 minutes. Drain, mash with a potato masher, and set aside to cool completely.

2. For the dough, combine the water, yeast, flour, salt, olive oil, and mashed potato in the bowl of a stand mixer or in a large mixing bowl. Stir with a rubber spatula until a rough dough forms.

3. Knead the dough. By machine: With a dough hook, knead the dough until it is smooth and soft and passes the windowpane test (see page 71), about 7 minutes on medium speed. By hand: Scrape the dough onto a lightly floured countertop. With floured hands, knead the dough with steady strokes until it is smooth, 10 to 12 minutes.

4. Spray the inside of a dough-rising container or large mixing bowl with nonstick cooking spray and place the dough inside. Cover with plastic wrap and let rise until the dough has doubled in size and doesn't spring back when poked with a fingertip, 1½ to 2 hours.

5. Spray the bottom and sides of a 10½- by 15½-inch metal baking pan that measures at least 1 inch deep with nonstick cooking spray. With moistened hands, flatten the dough and press it into the pan. Lightly sprinkle the top of the dough with flour and loosely drape with plastic wrap. Let stand until puffy and almost doubled, about 1 hour.

6. Preheat the oven to 425°F. Just before baking, use your fingertips to dimple the dough at 2-inch intervals. Tear off 1-inch pieces of rosemary and poke a piece into each of the indentations. Drizzle the dough with the olive oil and sprinkle with the sea salt.

7. Bake until the bottom of the focaccia is golden brown and crisp and the top is golden (you can peek underneath by carefully lifting the bread from the pan with a metal spatula).

8. Use a spatula to remove the focaccia from the pan and slide it onto a wire rack to cool for at least 15 minutes. Serve warm, or cool completely and serve at room temperature.

Specialty Baking Pans

Certain breads are so associated with a particular shape that if you want to make an authentic version you'll need to invest in a specialty pan. See Resources, page 273, to buy any of them online.

1 Brioche pan. Brioche dough can be baked in a regular loaf pan, but it won't be recognizable on sight as brioche unless it is baked in the traditional round, fluted pan. Made of high-quality tin or aluminum, stamped and pressed into a classic fluted shape, these pans come in all sizes, for baking everything from mini to monster brioche.

2 English muffin rings. To make authentic griddle-baked, yeast-risen English muffins, you'll need a set of aluminum rings to give shape to the dough as it bakes. But if you don't have them, you can cut your dough with a biscuit cutter. The resulting muffins will be less uniform in shape but just as tasty.

3 Kaiser roll stamp. This is actually not a pan, but a metal or silicone stamp to press into dough rounds to give them the characteristic swirled cuts of a kaiser roll.

4 Panettone pan. This tall, fluted pan, made of either metal or ceramic and similar in look to a brioche mold, is used to make the traditional sweet yeasted Italian Christmas bread. Often, paper molds (see Resources, page 273) are used instead,

Bench scraper

This rectangular steel blade with a wooden handle is used to slice through dough cleanly, dividing it without destroying too much of its cell structure. It also comes in handy during kneading, for scraping up sticky dough from a countertop. If you don't own a bench scraper, you can use a sharp chef's knife for these tasks.

Bread box or storage bags

Storing your loaves in a resealable plastic bag will keep the interior from drying out but will make the crust soggy over time. For long-keeping sourdough breads, a better choice is a bread box or a special breathable bread storage bag (see Resources, page 273), which allows just enough ventilation to keep your bread's crust crisp without hastening staling.

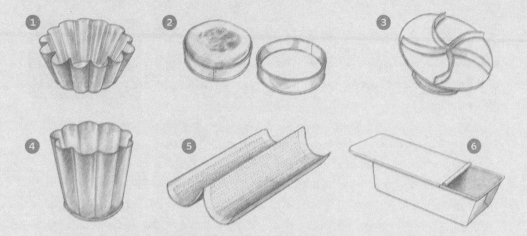

since panettone is usually given as a gift as well as served at home.

⑤ Perforated French bread pan.
An alternative to hand-shaping baguettes and proofing them in a *couche*, this double- or triple-baguette pan made of perforated aluminized steel makes perfectly shaped baguettes every time. The perforations allow for air to circulate all around the loaves as they bake, promoting a crisp crust.

⑥ Pullman loaf pan. This straight-sided pan with a lid bakes *pain de mie*, a traditional French white sandwich bread, with a minimum of crust.

Cast-iron pan

Preheat a cast-iron skillet or other cast-iron pan on the lower rack of your oven as you are preheating your baking stone, and then drop water or ice cubes into it when you put the dough into the oven to safely create a steamy environment for baking.

Couche

A couche is simply a piece of cloth like the one used to line a banneton, folded in a special way to hold baguettes as they proof. It takes some practice to learn the technique and to get the hang of rolling the proofed dough onto the baking stone. Alternatively, you can improvise a couche with parchment paper and some kitchen towels (see page 140 for instructions).

Equipment for Adding Steam to Your Oven

A moist environment during the first 10 to 15 minutes of baking ensures that the crust of the bread remains supple, so that the loaves can rise fully before the yeast is killed off by the heat.

Cast-iron pan. A steam-injected oven is a standard piece of equipment at an artisan bakery. Most of us don't have the option of steam injection, so we need to figure out how to add steam in other ways. I prefer a method I learned from Daniel Leader, since it is the neatest and least risky. He places a cast-iron pan on a rack below the baking stone and preheats it along with the stone. Then he throws a quantity of ice cubes into the pan when he adds the bread, so that they melt and evaporate during the first few minutes of baking.

Ice cubes. Some bakers take a minimalist approach and simply throw ice cubes onto the floor of the oven. This method requires no equipment at all, although the few times I've tried it I've had to mop up some of the water that drips onto my floor before I could get the oven door closed.

Using an atomizer to add steam to your oven

Water. Alternatively, you could add boiling water to the cast-iron pan, which creates an intense amount of steam very quickly but must be done with care. Award-winning baker and author Rose Levy Beranbaum describes this method: Boil 1 cup of water in a kettle and then pour it into a large (at least 2-cup) Pyrex measuring cup. Put your loaves on the baking stone, cover the glass window of your oven with a kitchen towel (you don't want boiling water to splash onto the glass, possibly causing it to crack), and then quickly and carefully pour the water into the preheated pan. Immediately close the door so that the steam doesn't escape.

Atomizer. Many bakers use an atomizer to spritz water onto the bread and around the oven. Joe Ortiz, author of *The Village Baker,* sprays the inside of the oven 5 or 6 times just before placing the bread in the oven, and then, for larger breads, sprays at 5-minute intervals for the first one-third of the baking time. For this method also, you'll need to close the door quickly after spraying the water, or else it will evaporate into your kitchen. And take care not to spritz the oven light, or you'll risk shattering it.

Steam Maker Bread Baker. An intriguing option for the truly committed home baker (see Resources, page 273); I'm not personally familiar with this, but it has

been recommended by many users in online discussion groups on the subject. This device, which isn't cheap at about $200, consists of an electric steam generator, along with a lid that fits over your loaves and on top of your baking stone. After your loaves are in place in the oven, you cover them and insert the nozzle of the generator into a small hole in the lid, injecting steam into this chamber. You remove the lid after 10 or 15 minutes of baking, depending on the size of your loaves, to let them dry out.

Steam table pan. If the above gadget is too much of a commitment, you can mimic this setup more cheaply by using a steam table pan large enough to cover your breads and at least 6 inches deep (available at restaurant supply stores and online), spraying it with water just before placing it on top of the loaves and letting this moisture plus the moisture evaporating from the dough steam the bread.

Covered Dutch oven

When chef and food writer Mark Bittman published Jim Lahey's recipe for a no-knead country bread baked in a Dutch oven, it stirred up a frenzy of interest in this technique. If you'd like to try Lahey's recipe or a similar one included here (page 76), you'll need a 6- to 8-quart Dutch oven with a lid.

Cutting board

Of course you will need a cutting board, for slicing all of your home-baked bread. The choice comes down to plastic or wood. Plastic boards are cheap, lightweight, dishwasher safe, and easy to maintain. Wooden boards won't warp or stain the way plastic ones tend to, but they do need to be oiled. If you are going to use one board solely for bread, sanitation is less of an issue than if you are going to use one of the boards you have in regular rotation, in which case you'll want to make sure it has been thoroughly washed before slicing your freshly baked bread on it, to prevent the possibility of cross-contamination.

Dough-rising container
(1 quart, 2 quart, and 4 quart)

These containers have straight sides, so if you note where your kneaded dough is when you first place it inside, you will be able to tell when it has risen enough to move on to the next step in your recipe. A bowl large enough to accommodate the risen dough will work just as well, but it's a bit more difficult to gauge the rise because of a bowl's sloping sides.

Dough scraper

A soft and flexible plastic tool that bakers use to scrape dough out of bowls, a dough scraper has a rounded, beveled edge that fits any size bowl and cleanly removes even the stickiest dough to a waiting work surface. If you don't have a dough scraper, you can use a rubber spatula, but the job won't be quite as effortless. At less than $5, this is a fun and useful tool for the home baker.

Electronic digital scale

All professional bakers weigh, rather than measure, their ingredients, for the sake of consistency. A cup of flour can vary in weight by quite a bit, depending on how you measure it. A good-quality digital scale will allow you to weigh flour with amazing accuracy, allowing you to turn out breads that don't vary in quality from batch to batch. Make sure to buy one that displays in decimal (rather than fractional) pounds, gives weights in both ounces and grams (the metric unit is helpful for weighing small quantities of salt and yeast accurately), and that has a tare function, so you can set the scale to zero after the addition of each ingredient if you'd like.

Food processor

A food processor fitted with a metal blade can knead many types of bread dough in seconds rather than minutes. If you are in a hurry or you don't have a stand mixer, a heavy-duty food processor can help you make bread. Most food processors can't accommodate doughs made with more than 3½ to 4 cups of flour, so keep this in mind when thinking about using your machine for this purpose. A machine with a powerful motor is a must. Flimsy, less expensive machines may burn out when they try to knead a large quantity of stiff bread dough.

Heavy-duty stand mixer

While many home bakers find kneading dough by hand a joy, for others the idea of spending so much time and energy transforming a sticky mass of flour and water into a supple, elastic dough is actually a deterrent to baking bread. Luckily, a powerful stand mixer with a dough hook, such as a KitchenAid K5 (5 quart) or a KitchenAid Professional (6 quart), will do the job for you. Some doughs, such as dough for ciabatta, contain such a high proportion of water that they are very difficult to knead by hand without adding so much flour as to compromise their

Kneading Dough: Bread Machine or Stand Mixer?

A 5-quart KitchenAid mixer with a dough hook retails for several hundred dollars (although it is often discounted by big Web retailers such as Amazon and Cooking.com). The Zojirushi Home Bakery Supreme (which retails for about $100 less than a KitchenAid mixer) will not only knead dough, but also will do everything else — ferment, shape, and bake the dough — with the press of a button. So why not buy a good-quality bread machine and let it do all the work for you, instead of investing in a mixer?

You can only answer that question for yourself, but here are a few things to consider before you do so. A bread machine is great for convenience. There's not much to think about. Just add the ingredients, turn the machine on, and take out the bread when it's done. There's no arguing that it's easier than using a mixer, which still requires the baker to watch the dough and judge when it is sufficiently fermented, divide and shape it by hand, get it into the oven, and determine when the bread is fully baked.

But what you get in convenience you lose in creativity and control. If these things are important to you, a mixer will be the better choice. Keep in mind that every bread machine has slightly different specifications, varying from other machines in everything from the size and shape of its interior chamber to its kneading action. Unless you are willing to experiment with recipes and accept some failure along the way, you will be limiting yourself to baking breads developed specifically for your machine.

Manufacturers of bread machines claim that the machines can be used to knead and ferment any dough, giving the baker the option of dividing, shaping, and baking it the old-fashioned way. This may be true, but if you use your machine this way, you'll have less flexibility than if you use a mixer. Some bread doughs, such as those containing a high proportion of rye flour, benefit from a gentle knead at a moderate speed so as not to destroy a delicate gluten structure. Others, like ciabatta or pizza dough, require vigorous kneading at high speed for an extended period of time. Although a bread machine might have a couple of kneading settings, it doesn't have the 10 speeds that a KitchenAid mixer has. Moreover, it is much easier to observe dough as it develops in the bowl of a mixer than it is to judge how it is doing while inside the chamber of a bread machine.

The bread machine has certainly earned a place in the baker's kitchen for its amazing time- and labor-saving capabilities, but precisely because it so effectively takes care of all the little details of home bread baking, it may not be the best choice for someone who wants to learn about the craft by observing, touching, smelling, and tasting the dough.

quality. For very wet doughs such as this, a heavy-duty stand mixer is essential to develop gluten.

Another, more expensive option is a spiral mixer, which mimics the spiraling action of the mixers in a commercial bakery. These mixers, including ones made by Bosch and Electrolux, can handle larger quantities of dough than even the largest KitchenAid model, and they may be worth considering if you plan on doubling or tripling your standard bread recipes.

Instant-read thermometer

A good instant-read thermometer (look for a digital one) will serve you during every step of bread making, from taking the temperature of your water before you mix it with your flour to taking the temperature of your fermented dough to taking the temperature of your loaf to see if it is fully baked. Choose one with a wide range. The Rolls-Royce of thermometers is the battery-operated Thermapen (see Resources, page 273), which can measure temperatures between -50°F and 550°F.

La Cloche clay bread-baking containers

These unglazed stone containers are designed to simulate the baking conditions of a beehive brick oven. Preheated, the dish and cover become an oven within your oven. The dish delivers intense heat to the bottom of your dough just as a baking stone does, while the domed cover steams the crust, allowing the dough to rise to its maximum height. To crisp the crust, you must remove the dome during the last 5 to 10 minutes of baking, allowing moisture to evaporate from the bread's surface. If you want to bake both boules and baguettes in a La Cloche, you'll have to buy both the round and oblong versions. There is also a round La Cloche pan sold without a domed top, for baking deep-dish pizzas. These containers are relatively inexpensive, but they are bulky. If you have the storage space and are curious to see how your dough reacts in this type of baking environment, they might be worth the price.

Bake the Perfect Loaf with the Oven You Have

Unless you are at this moment embarking on a kitchen renovation, it won't really matter to you what kind of oven is recommended by bread-baking experts. Most of us are, for better or worse, married to the oven that resides in our kitchen right now.

There are a few things you can do, no matter what kind of oven you have, to make it good for bread.

Test your oven. Perhaps the most important thing you can do is test your oven to make sure it runs at the temperature you've set it at. If it runs even 25°F hotter or colder than that, it will affect the baking time of the bread. Buy an inexpensive oven thermometer at the hardware store and hang it inside your oven. Then you can adjust the temperature setting to get just the right amount of heat.

Use a baking stone. Absolutely use one if it is called for in the recipe. A baking stone is the best, and indeed the only, way to deliver intense heat to the bottom crust the way a true hearth oven does. If you have a gas oven, you can place your stone directly on the floor of the oven. If your oven is electric, put an oven rack in the lowest position and put the stone on the rack.

Rotate your bread. Chances are, your oven has spots that are warmer and spots that are cooler. To make sure that your loaves bake evenly, rotate them once (or twice for larger, longer-baking loaves) during baking. Just make sure to rotate them only after their crusts have set. During the first third of baking, their structure is still very delicate, and rotating them too soon may cause them to deflate from the motion.

Lame

The slashing of dough serves much more than a decorative purpose. Making strategic cuts in your shaped breads before baking them allows for them to rise in an even way instead of bursting open in random places. French bakers use a special bread-slashing knife called a *lame*, which has a very sharp, curved blade attached to a handle. But you can use a single-edge razor blade or very sharp serrated knife to do the same job.

Loaf pans ✔
(4½ by 8½ inches and 5 by 9 inches)

If you want to bake loaf-shaped breads, you'll need a loaf pan (or two, depending on what size your recipe calls for). Buy metal pans, which conduct heat more effectively than ceramic or glass, for better browning of your crust.

Measuring cups and spoons ✔

If you don't have a scale to weigh all of your ingredients, you'll need measuring cups and spoons. You'll also want measuring spoons for small quantities. Just be sure to use metal or plastic dry measuring cups and spoons for dry ingredients, using the dip and sweep method: Scoop up flour or salt or yeast and then level off the ingredient with the edge of a knife or metal spatula. Use glass liquid measuring cups with pour spouts to measure water and other liquids, judging the accuracy of your measuring by looking at the cup at eye level as it sits on the counter.

Mixing bowls ✔

Use the stainless steel bowls from your stand mixer, or buy a set of inexpensive stainless steel nesting bowls, to mix your dough before you hand-knead it.

Oven mitts ✔

Choose a pair of heavy-duty mitts or pot holders to use for bread baking, since you'll likely be setting your oven to a very high temperature. I like mitts made of Kevlar or silicone, with which I can hold a superheated pizza stone as I transfer it from the oven to my cooktop without feeling any heat at all for almost a minute. Old-fashioned terry cloth is fine, as long as it is a double thickness. Avoid leather and suede mitts, which may be okay for a sheet of cookies but aren't well insulated enough for a baking stone.

Parchment paper ✔

Parchment paper is an indispensable bread-baking tool. Use it to line baking sheets for easy cleanup. Or you can line your baker's peel with parchment, proof your loaf on top of it, and then slide the loaf, still on the parchment, onto the baking stone without fear that the loaf will stick and/or deflate in transit. Buy bleached parchment. Unbleached paper will burn and crumble in the oven at high temperatures. If you bake often, it makes sense to order it in large quantities of precut sheets (see Resources, page 273) rather than to buy it in smaller rolls at the supermarket.

Pastry brush

A pastry brush comes in handy for brushing excess flour from dough rounds, glazing sweet doughs with egg wash, and brushing dough with water before sprinkling with seeds so that the seeds adhere. I like brushes with silicone bristles (see Resources, page 273). They last forever, are dishwasher safe, and won't shed their bristles unappetizingly onto your dough.

Pizza cutter

Buy one with a large heavy-duty wheel for cutting effortlessly through crisp pizza and other thick flatbreads. A pizza wheel is also great in lieu of a bench scraper for dividing dough.

Plastic wrap ✔

The surface of the dough must remain moist during fermentation and proofing to allow for proper rising. Cover your bowl with plastic wrap during fermentation to prevent dough from drying out. Loosely drape a sheet of plastic over shaped breads as they proof so that they won't dry out either.

Rolling pin

Occasionally a bread recipe will require a rolling pin. Either a French-style pin (a wooden dowel without handles) or an American-style pin (a dowel with a steel shaft down the

Clean Slices: How to Buy a Bread Knife

If you bake bread often, you should consider buying a high-quality serrated bread knife. You won't regret the purchase, as there is no better feeling than cleanly slicing through a loaf of homemade bread so that the crumb, no matter how soft, isn't crushed and the crust, no matter how crisp, isn't shattered. Here are some shopping tips if you want to treat yourself to a knife that will give you years of use.

Choose a forged rather than a stamped blade. Begin your shopping by seeking out serrated knives with blades that have been forged from steel heated to a very high temperature and then hammered, tempered, sharpened, and finished to form a sharp blade. This age-old process, which can include up to 50 separate steps, results in a knife that is satisfyingly heavy and well balanced when held. Forged knives always have a *bolster*, which is a support piece between the blade and the handle, and a *tang*, which is a portion of the blade metal enclosed by the handle. Stamped blades, in contrast, are cut from sheets of steel the way cookies are made with a cookie cutter, so the blade is lighter and less substantial than the blade of a forged knife. Stamped knives don't often include a bolster or tang, another reason why they are lighter than their forged counterparts.

Look for pointed serrations. Serrated knives come with either scalloped or pointed serrations. I've got one of each, and while I love my knife with the scalloped serrations for trimming cake layers and cutting through soft breads like brioche, I can always count on the one with pointed serrations to cut through the crustiest loaves, while still handling soft cakes and breads. (As a bonus, a knife with pointed serrations will cut cleanly through a tomato, while one with scalloped serrations will squash the same tomato.) So if I had to pick one all-purpose bread and pastry knife, I'd go with the one with pointed serrations.

Choose a longer blade. You can buy serrated knives with blades from 8 to 14 inches long. If you only make smaller loaves baked in loaf pans, 8 inches will be fine. But if you plan on baking larger, rustic rounds, you'll need at least a 10-inch blade to cut across the entire bread.

Choose a handle with comfort in mind. Good serrated knives come with both straight and offset handles. Both types will slice bread. Some people like the offset style because there is no banging of the knuckles. Others prefer the traditional style for its look. Choose the handle that feels good in your own hand.

center and handles) will do the job, so use what you are comfortable with.

Rubber spatula ✅

It's a good idea to give your ingredients a stir, forming a rough dough, before beginning to knead by hand or machine. Use a large flexible rubber spatula for this purpose.

Serrated knife ✅

A good serrated knife is a true pleasure to use on home-baked bread, slicing cleanly without squashing your beautiful loaves. I have a fantastic bread knife made by Viking (see Resources, page 273) that is one of my prized possessions. Other high-quality knife manufacturers, including Wüsthof and Henckels, make equally sharp and effective knives. A very sharp blade also comes in handy for slashing dough.

Silpat mat (or other silicone pan liner)

A Silpat mat or other brand of silicone pan liner can be used on a nonstick surface or any baking sheet. A Silpain mat (made especially for bread baking) is perforated to allow air to circulate, promoting a crisp bottom crust.

Wire cooling rack ✅

Once your bread is out of the oven, transfer it to a wire rack to cool. A wire rack will enable air to circulate underneath the bread, allowing moisture from the cooling bread to evaporate all around and promoting a crisp bottom crust.

Equipment
Questions and Answers

Q **I bought a baker's peel, thinking it would help me transfer my breads to the oven, but every time I attempt the transfer, my bread sticks to it. Is there a technique I'm not aware of for using this piece of equipment?**

A Recipes will often caution you not to add excess flour to bread dough during kneading and shaping, which leads many bakers to skimp on flouring countertops and baker's peels, surfaces where bread is likely to stick. But liberally sprinkling your peel with flour won't have an effect on the quality of your dough, as it will just coat the bottom surface and will help your dough slide more easily off of the peel. To get the dough from the peel to the baking stone, rest the edge of the peel on the stone and gently but confidently shake it back and forth so the dough slides off without too much jostling. Or you could just line your peel with a piece of parchment, as you'll be directed to do in most of the recipes to come, and simply pull the parchment onto the stone with the loaf still on it.

Q **I hadn't used my wooden baker's peel for a few weeks, and when I took it out of the cabinet it was covered with green mold! What happened?**

A I am guessing that you washed your peel and then put it away when it was slightly damp. The dampness encouraged the mold growth on the wood; any excess flour sticking to the peel helped things along. (Wood's hospitality toward mold is one reason why restaurant kitchens use plastic rather than wooden cutting boards.) If you buy a wooden peel, don't submerge it in water; in addition to growing mold, it might warp. Just wipe it with a damp cloth and let it air-dry before putting it away. Depending on how moldy your peel is, you might try cleaning it rather than tossing it in the trash. For a mild case of mold, scrub it with a mixture of lemon juice and kosher salt. For a more serious case, use a mild bleach solution, rinsing it well after cleaning, of course, and letting it dry completely on a rack in the kitchen for several days before putting it away.

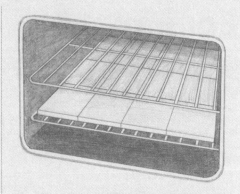

Q Will baking bread on nonstick baking sheets have an impact on the result? What about using an insulated baking sheet?

A If you don't have a baking stone, you can bake your bread on a preheated baking sheet with pretty good results. Choose a rimless sheet, so that you can slide your dough from a baker's peel right onto the sheet as you would slide it onto a baking stone. At temperatures above 500°F, nonstick coatings will deteriorate and/or lose their nonstick quality, so I don't recommend nonstick baking sheets for most breads, which bake near or above this temperature. An insulated sheet is designed to bake delicate cookie dough without burning the bottoms of the cookies, so it isn't the ideal choice for bread, where a dark bottom crust is desirable. Instead, stick with a heavy-gauge aluminum pan for the best results.

Q I've heard I can use quarry tiles from a home improvement store in place of a baking stone. Is this true?

A Yes, you can use quarry tiles, which cost just pennies apiece, with a few caveats. First, make sure they are unglazed. Glazed tiles may contain lead, which will be released into the air and into your bread when heated to high temperatures. Earthenware and ceramic tiles, both made from clay, will work. If you are using a gas oven, place the tiles directly on the oven floor. If your oven is electric, place them on a rack set in the lowest position. Leave at least an inch of space between the tiles and the oven walls, for good air circulation. Tiles that are ½ inch thick are best for baking bread. Thinner tiles may crack when heated to 500°F. Thicker tiles will take more than an hour to heat up.

Q My oven has a convection setting. Is this good for bread?

A A convection oven can be great for bread, especially for developing a well-browned and chewy crust. A few adjustments to your recipe may be necessary, however, to take into account the fact that convection ovens brown foods more quickly than conventional ovens. First, you might have to lower the temperature by 25°F, to prevent the surface of your loaf from browning before the interior has had a chance to rise to its full potential. Relatedly, you might have to add more ice cubes or water to the oven at the beginning of baking, to prevent the crust from drying out and hardening. Be sure to add enough steam to the oven to keep the crust supple.

Q **Why does a Pullman loaf pan have a cover?**

A A Pullman loaf pan, sometimes called a pain de mie pan or a sandwich loaf pan, employs a cover in order to bake a perfectly rectangular loaf with a flat top. As the bread rises in the oven, it completely fills the interior space of the pan but can't form the rounded top that it would if allowed to rise uncovered. Pullman loaf pans are beautiful but expensive, and they require special care to get them into baking shape and keep them that way. Made of aluminized steel, they must be seasoned before use so that the dough doesn't stick to the bottom, sides, or top of the pan. To do this, brush the interior of the pan and the inside of the top with a little vegetable oil and place both parts in a 250°F oven for 15 minutes. Let the pan cool, wipe the brushed surfaces with a clean cloth, and repeat once or twice to complete the seasoning process. Don't wash the pan when you are done baking with it — just wipe it with a damp cloth.

Q **I don't have a cast-iron pan. Can I use another type of baking pan for steaming bread? What about enameled cast iron?**

A Cast-iron pans won't warp or rust when heated to a high temperature and then moistened with water, which is why they are recommended for steaming. You may use an enameled cast-iron pan, as long as its handle is also cast-iron. Wooden or plastic handles might be damaged or catch fire in a very hot oven.

Q **Do you have any specific tips about judging how much dough has risen in a regular bowl?**

A If you are eyeballing it and think your dough has risen sufficiently according to the recipe instructions, you can then gently press a finger into it. In general, dough that is ready will very slowly spring back (a recipe will specify if it is otherwise); dough that needs more time will spring back quickly. Dough that collapses when you perform this test — well, it's risen for too long! See page 96 for tips on what to do if this happens. Or plan ahead and do this: Measure the approximate volume of your just-kneaded dough in a large glass measuring cup (I have an 8-cup Pyrex measure that I have used for this purpose). Then pour double that amount of water into the bowl in which you're going to ferment the dough, and see how high the water comes up. This should give you an idea of where your dough will be when it doubles in volume. Pour out the water, dry and oil the bowl, place your dough inside, and wait for it to reach that height.

Q **All of the digital scales I see are pretty expensive. Is there a cheaper alternative?**

A It is true that an attractive analog scale can be had for around $10, but in my opinion this is no bargain. With analog scales you run into the same problem that you run into when measuring ingredients by volume: human error. Are you shaving off or adding grams by looking at the scale from a slightly different angle every time? With digital measurement there is never this uncertainty. In addition, analog scales need to be recalibrated before each use for accuracy, and eventually they will wear out and won't be able to be adjusted. If you are committed to home baking, spend the extra money. Over the years that this scale will serve you, the cost will be amortized to practically nothing.

Q **When I'm using my stand mixer, should I always mix and knead with the dough hook, or are there times when the paddle is better?**

A Unless your dough is extremely wet, almost like a batter, then the dough hook is the best choice. That said, don't just dump your ingredients into the bowl and start mixing. The dough hook will be unable to grab them up into a cohesive mass by itself. First, give the ingredients a few turns with a rubber spatula, just to form a rough dough. Then turn the mixer on and let the dough hook smooth out the dough as it kneads.

Q **My mixer doesn't have a dough hook. Can I knead my dough in a food processor?**

A Many bread doughs can be kneaded in a food processor, with a few caveats. First, use the metal blade. The plastic blade (even if it is called a "kneading blade" in the packaging material) won't be able to cut through stiff and sticky bread doughs.

Second, make sure your dough recipe can be accommodated by your food processor. A stand mixer's bowl can hold 6 to 8 cups of flour; a food processor work bowl can only knead doughs made with 3½ cups of flour or less.

Third, consider the temperature of your water. You will want to add water that's a little cooler than the water you'd add to a stand mixer, because the food processor motor will warm up the dough considerably.

Fourth, process your dough in two stages, pulsing the ingredients 2 or 3 times until a rough dough forms, and then letting it stand for 10 to 20 minutes. This resting period, or autolyse (see page 68 for more on autolyse), allows the flour to become fully hydrated and allows gluten to develop prior to kneading. Then process the dough until it passes the windowpane test (see page 71), about 45 seconds.

Finally, you might decide to ferment your dough longer than you might if you had mixed it in a mixer or by hand, to further develop its gluten structure, since the quick kneading of the food processor doesn't develop the dough's gluten as effectively as more extended hand or machine kneading.

Q What should I look for when buying a bread machine?

A The features that you should look for will depend on how you intend to use your machine.

What size loaves will you generally bake? Bread pans in these machines vary in size, baking loaves that weigh between 1 and 2½ pounds, so choose a size according to your needs.

When bread machines first debuted, they all baked loaves in a weird, coffee can shape. Now most have been remodeled to bake conventionally shaped loaves, but some retain the early design. If you are going to use the machine just to mix, knead, and proof the dough, the shape of the pan isn't important, but if you are going to bake your bread in the machine, make sure the pan comes in a shape you like.

The length of time and vigor with which you knead a dough depends on the dough's ingredients (rye doughs should be kneaded more gently than 100 percent wheat doughs), its flour-to-water ratio (wet doughs generally take longer to knead), and the result you are going for (brioche takes less kneading than bagel dough). Does the machine you are considering have the variety of settings to cover the variety of breads you'd like to bake? Does it also give you the ability to control the color of your crust, from light to dark?

Some machines have a compartment for dried fruit, nuts, olives, and other additional ingredients that are added at the end of kneading. If you plan on making these types of breads, such a compartment might serve you well. For more information on bread machines, see pages 241–243 in chapter 9.

Q I placed my brand-new Silpat on my baking sheet and realized that it is about 1 inch larger than the baking sheet all around. Will this slight overhang cause problems during baking?

A This might be a concern when you are baking cookies, with some of them close to the rim of the pan, but if your bread dough is sitting flat on the Silpat, the slight overhang around the edges shouldn't cause a problem.

Q Although I used a very sharp serrated knife to score my bread, the blade still got stuck as I was cutting and the dough deflated slightly. How can I cut more cleanly next time?

A Be confident and slash decisively. Hesitating mid-slash may cause your dough to stick to the knife. You might also lightly spray your knife with nonstick cooking spray if you are working with a very sticky dough.

Chapter 3
The Basic Steps

EVERY BREAD RECIPE consists of variations on a few basic techniques used in a unique combination. The small differences in how the bread dough is kneaded, shaped, fermented, and baked will make the difference between a pizza and a baguette, which, after all, are both made with flour, water, yeast, and salt.

This chapter will explain the basic steps every baker must take to transform basic bread ingredients into a loaf. In the chapters that follow, recipes will demonstrate how variations in technique allow a baker to make breads as different as a peasant loaf, pita bread, and English muffins, all while using virtually the same ingredients and equipment.

Measuring

Before you can mix your dough, you must measure your ingredients. The importance of accuracy when you do so cannot be overstated. Baking a loaf of bread is not like making a pot of spaghetti sauce, where "a bit of this and a pinch of that" can lead to sublime results. Indeed, that is a recipe for disaster. An extra eighth of an ounce of salt may inhibit the rise of your dough. A missing half ounce of water might give your dough a tight and dry crumb rather than the bubbly and shiny interior you were hoping for.

Rather than eyeball quantities of flour, water, yeast, and salt, you should take extra care to make sure that you are using the precise amounts specified in your recipe. Using a digital scale to weigh these essential ingredients rather than measuring them by volume is the best way to do this. Not only does accurate measurement ensure that you will get uniform results from a recipe time after time, but knowing precisely how much flour, water, yeast, or salt you used last time will help you if you suspect, for example, that your bread's crumb was too tight because the dough was underhydrated and you would like to add more water next time. Make sure to keep careful notes when you make an adjustment (I lightly pencil in new quantities, along with a baking date, right onto the recipe I'm working from), so that you can evaluate the results of your experiment and make further adjustments if necessary next time.

By all means, weigh your ingredients carefully and with consistency. But at the same time, don't set anything in stone! Every time you bake, conditions out of your control may require you to make slight quantity adjustments. In the middle of the winter, when the air in your kitchen is bone-dry from your forced-air heating system, your flour might be bone-dry also. So this time around, you may have to add a half ounce or so more water to the dough than the last time you made this particular bread, which was in the middle of the humid summer. Flour changes in its ability to absorb water depending on the weather, the soil the grain was grown in, and other conditions. It may be that a new brand of flour, or even a new bag of your favorite brand, is less or more absorbent than the last bag.

Weigh your ingredients carefully, using previous weights as a benchmark. But don't be afraid to make adjustments as you are mixing and kneading your dough, always keeping in mind what the dough should look like and feel like and how it should behave.

Mixing and Kneading

Mixing your ingredients together and then kneading them into a smooth mass of dough are the next steps. Mixing and kneading accomplish several things at once. Mixing distributes salt and yeast evenly throughout the dough, important for a good rise. Mixing also initiates the process of fermentation, which begins when yeast becomes hydrated. Kneading also introduces oxygen into the dough, which will provide food for the yeast as the dough rises. But most important, mixing and kneading develop gluten in the dough.

If you learn nothing else about the science of bread, take a few moments to make sure you understand what gluten is and how it works in bread dough. All wheat flour contains two types of protein, gliadin and glutenin. When these proteins come into contact with water, they

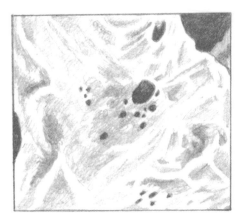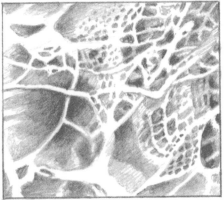

Kneading organizes the proteins in dough and creates a stronger, stretchier gluten web.

bond with each other to form an elastic web called gluten. The more the dough is worked through kneading, the stronger and stretchier this web becomes. When you first mix your ingredients, the dough will feel sticky and lumpy. As you repeatedly flatten and fold it during kneading, you can actually feel the proteins organizing themselves into a coherent design, making the dough feel smooth and supple. In general (and there are exceptions to this rule), the more you knead, the better organized your gluten will be. And the more organized it is, the stronger and stretchier it will be, providing the structure that will allow your bread dough to rise to its full potential in the oven as gases in the dough heat up and expand. At a certain temperature, the gluten web will solidify, and take on the job of the steel supports in a skyscraper, allowing your bread to keep its shape once it has risen, rather than collapsing.

Three Mixing Methods

There are three general methods for mixing dough. The choice of one over the other will determine some important characteristics of the bread you are baking.

The simplest and quickest way to mix dough is the *direct method*. Using this method, the baker will simply stir together all of the ingredients in a large bowl and then knead the resulting dough, either by hand or using a stand mixer, until it is supple and stretchy, passing the windowpane test described a little later. Doughs mixed using this method are sometimes called straight doughs, perhaps because of the straightforward way they come together. In general, breads employing this method also have a simple, straightforward flavor and a relatively short shelf life. They are best enjoyed warm from the oven or cooled to room temperature and eaten on the same day they are baked.

Other doughs are mixed using the *pre-ferment method*. A pre-ferment is a starter used in bread recipes in which the dough is built in two stages. First, a small amount of flour, water, and packaged yeast are stirred together and allowed to stand to encourage the yeast to multiply and fermentation to begin. Then, the pre-ferment is mixed into a larger quantity of flour, water, and salt, supplementing or taking the place of packaged yeast. A pre-ferment extends the total fermentation time of the bread dough without the risk of over-fermentation. This longer, slower

Autolyse: A Resting Period

Every so often you will encounter a bread recipe that will instruct you to mix together your ingredients (leaving out the salt and yeast until later) until a rough dough forms, and then cover the dough and wait anywhere from 10 minutes to 1 hour before adding the yeast and salt and kneading it. What is accomplished by taking this extra step?

During this resting period, called autolyse (pronounced auto-LEEZ), amylase enzymes begin converting starches into sugars, making them immediately available to the yeast when it is added a little later on. At the same time, protease enzymes begin taking apart proteins so that they can link up with other proteins to form gluten. Without any kneading at all, the proteins even begin to organize themselves into the stretchy web so necessary for a high rise. So autolyse gets the dough ready for the yeast, and it also cuts down on kneading time because it does some of the work that kneading would have accomplished.

Autolyse is especially useful when a dough is relatively wet. Many artisan-style breads contain a proportionately large amount of water (which accounts for their beautiful, open crumb but can make them difficult to knead by hand without adding too much flour). If you give your wet dough a rest, the flour will have time to fully absorb the water without mechanical mixing, resulting in a dough that is less sticky and easier to handle than one that hasn't rested.

fermentation allows the lactobacilli in bread dough to produce acids that give the bread a complex flavor. In addition, it extends the shelf life of the bread, because these acids are natural preservatives.

Beyond these two methods is *sourdough baking*. While both straight doughs and doughs employing a pre-ferment call for packaged yeast, sourdough breads contain a culture of wild yeast that allows them to ferment and rise. This method of mixing dough requires the extra step of cultivating some wild yeast before mixing your dough. Although to the uninitiated this may sound mysterious or difficult, it is actually very simple.

Wild yeast lives in flour and in the air in your kitchen, and it thrives on flour moistened with water. The cultivation of a sourdough starter simply involves mixing together some flour and water and letting it stand at room temperature until the yeast in the air are captured by the mixture and begin to multiply. (For a simple sourdough starter recipe, see page 166). Generally, the starter has to be freshened several times over the course of a week or two, with the addition of more flour and water, to provide enough food for the growing population of yeast. Once the starter exhibits signs of vigorous yeast growth (including interior or surface bubbling, an increase in volume, and/or a faintly sour aroma), it is ready to add to flour, water, and salt to form a viable dough.

Whichever technique your recipe calls for, actually mixing the dough takes just seconds. Add your ingredients to your bowl as directed and give them a few vigorous turns with a large rubber spatula until a rough mass forms. This action alone will begin to evenly distribute your ingredients and begin the process of gluten development. If you are using active dry yeast, sprinkle it over your water and let it dissolve before stirring in the flour and salt. If you are using instant yeast, there is no need to dissolve it in water before mixing it with flour. Because a concentration of salt can kill yeast if the two ingredients come into direct contact before the yeast is fully hydrated, it's best to place the salt and yeast on opposite sides of the bowl before stirring. With this rough dough formed, you are ready to begin kneading.

Mixing a rough dough with a rubber spatula

Why Dough Is Kneaded

Mixing your ingredients so they are all moistened will immediately lead to some gluten development. But to develop a dough's gluten to its potential, a baker must knead the dough until the proteins can fully organize themselves into the strongest web possible.

Adding Flavor and Character with Pre-ferments

Different baking cultures employ different pre-ferments to bake simple breads with great character. To clarify their similarities and differences, here are descriptions of the four most common pre-ferments.

Sponge. A sponge is a wet mixture of flour, water, and packaged yeast that is allowed to stand for a short period of time (sometimes as little as an hour) before being mixed into bread dough. Sponges usually contain a relatively large quantity of yeast, making it unnecessary to add yeast to the dough later. By mixing the sponge an hour or so before mixing the bread dough proper, you give the yeast some extra time to ferment, which will add flavor to the bread.

Poolish. A French-style pre-ferment whose name indicates its heritage as a method brought to France by Polish bakers, *poolish* is also a wet pre-ferment, but it generally contains less yeast than a sponge and is allowed to ferment longer, at least several hours and sometimes overnight.

Pâte fermentée. This pre-ferment originated as an economical way for bakers to raise bread — they'd save the leftover dough from the day before and use it (and its yeast) to raise the next day's bread. *Pâte fermentée* translates as "old dough." Its name is apt, since it immediately has an "aging" effect on newly mixed dough, lending its developed flavor and active yeast to a new batch.

Biga. An Italian pre-ferment with a dry, claylike consistency, a *biga* contains proportionately less water than a sponge or poolish. The relatively small amount of water causes the yeast to ferment more slowly, and with less acid buildup, than it does in a sponge or poolish, resulting in a particularly fresh-tasting bread similar in flavor profile to breads employing the direct method but with the extended shelf life of pre-fermented bread.

(For a more complete discussion of these types of pre-ferments, see page 131.)

During kneading, the dough will go through several recognizable stages. In the early minutes, it will still be raggedy and sticky, signaling the inconsistent and incomplete organization of the gluten. As you continue to push and fold the dough, the gluten strands will become less fragile and more extensible. Your dough will develop a bounce, sometimes becoming so bouncy that it is difficult to knead. If this happens, take a 5-minute break to allow the gluten to relax enough to work with. Get back to kneading, and eventually you will be able to see (and feel, if you are kneading by hand) the dough getting smoother. This is evidence of the developing gluten structure so crucial for bread's rise. In addition to creating this structure, kneading aerates the dough, introducing oxygen to the yeast, which becomes active and creates cells throughout the dough that will fill with gases during fermentation and expand during baking. The more air cells that are created, the higher your dough will rise during baking.

To judge whether or not you've kneaded your dough sufficiently, follow the cues given in your recipe, and use your senses. Look at your dough and run your hands over it. If it is smooth and shiny, it has developed the coherent gluten web that will give it structure. Perform the windowpane test: Take a golf ball–size piece of dough and press it into a disk. Then gently pull it with your fingers until it is thin and translucent. Can you do this without tearing it? If so, then it is sufficiently elastic to stretch to great heights in the oven. If it can't stretch without tearing, knead it for a few minutes longer and test it again before proceeding to the next step.

The stages of dough during kneading

Raggedy and sticky

Bouncy and firm

Firm

The windowpane test for judging your kneading

Ways of Kneading

Beginning bakers often wonder whether there is a "best" way to knead bread. The answer is that there are several ways to knead, and choosing the best one will depend on a few things, including your experience, the recipe, how much time you have, and your kitchen equipment. Here are the options:

HAND KNEADING

Hand kneading has its advantages. It requires nothing in the way of special equipment. You'll need a mixing bowl to mix together your wet and dry ingredients and a countertop on which to knead your dough. It is a great way to learn about how gluten develops. With hand kneading you will actually be able to feel the dough shift under your fingers from a sticky mass to a smooth and workable round. If you've kneaded dough by hand to this stage, you will never again wonder whether or not you've kneaded sufficiently. Even when mixing dough in a machine, you will be able to use your experience to judge whether or not the machine has sufficiently kneaded the dough.

There are some downsides to hand kneading. It is difficult to resist adding too much flour to wet doughs during hand kneading, especially if you haven't worked much with these types of doughs. Continually adding flour during kneading will alter the ratio of flour to water in the recipe, defeating the basic purpose of mixing a wet dough. So if you are going to knead by hand, resolve to add as little flour as possible. Periodically using a bench scraper to scrape up sticky dough from the counter will help, until the dough becomes less sticky as you work with it.

If you are using a high-gluten flour (sometimes called for to produce very crusty country loaves or pizzas), you may find that you knead and knead and never achieve the smoothness and elasticity that you are looking for. The more gluten a dough has, the longer it will take you to develop it, and you may run out of endurance and patience before you are done. If you don't have the time or muscle, you might think about kneading these particular doughs by machine.

Hand-Kneading Techniques

Never kneaded before? Here's how:

Most American baking manuals will instruct you to use a two-handed technique to knead bread. Sprinkle a countertop lightly with flour, place the dough on the counter, sprinkle it with a little more flour, and then push downward and outward on the dough with the heels of both hands. Pull the far edge of the dough back over the top, rotate the dough, and then repeat, lightly sprinkling the countertop with flour and flouring your hands as necessary.

There are many variations on this technique. Some people prefer to use just one hand to knead. Kneading the dough inside a lightly oiled mixing bowl is a good way to avoid adding excess flour while you develop the gluten.

A few years ago, Richard Bertinet wrote a popular book on bread, describing his method of slapping the dough (sometimes called "the French fold") to build gluten. He turns the sticky mass of dough out onto an unfloured countertop, scrapes it up, and then slaps it back down onto the counter. With part of the dough still sticking to the counter, he pulls it up and away, folds it over on itself, and repeats the slapping and pulling motions until the dough becomes smooth.

Choosing a hand-kneading method is a matter of trying them all out and going with one that is comfortable for you when working with a particular dough. Some people find that the stretch-and-fold method is good for moderately hydrated doughs, while the knead-in-the-bowl method or Bertinet's method work better for very wet doughs. Then again, some people prefer to hand-knead only doughs with a relatively small amount of water and save the wet doughs for the mixer. With a little experience, you will know what works for you.

Traditional two-handed kneading technique

KNEADING WITH A STAND MIXER

When American home cooks rediscovered bread baking in the late 1960s and '70s, hand kneading was considered the most authentic, and therefore the only, way to knead dough. But as bakers became more sophisticated and professional-style mixers became standard in home kitchens, many of us have realized that using a heavy-duty stand mixer has many advantages.

While some people find the repetitive motion of hand kneading relaxing and even meditative, to use artisan bread baker Peter Reinhart's word, others, like cookbook author Rose Levy Beranbaum, find hand kneading laborious, time-consuming, and in extreme cases even dangerous (Beranbaum was kneading so many loaves by hand that she suffered repetitive stress injuries to her wrists). Wherever you stand on this spectrum, you will undoubtedly find that machine kneading is quicker than hand kneading. That's why recipes that give instructions for both hand and machine kneading will shave minutes off of kneading time if machine kneading is chosen.

Even if you are a die-hard proponent of hand kneading, you may want to give machine kneading a try with certain very sticky doughs. Not only does the mixer make quick work of very wet Ciabatta (page 145) dough, but it also has the perfect touch with multigrain doughs such as the Rye Loaf with Rye Berries (page 233). Doughs containing low- or no-gluten flours such as rye will never become as smooth and workable as 100 percent wheat doughs, no matter how long you knead them by hand.

Only a heavy-duty stand mixer fitted with a dough hook (see Resources, page 273) has the power and the solid construction to knead bread dough for any length of time. If you attempt kneading with a lighter machine, you will quickly burn out its motor. Never leave the mixer unattended, since at higher speeds or with larger quantities of dough it may "walk" across the counter and right onto the floor. And take care that your dough doesn't overheat in the mixer, especially if it has an extended mixing time. If you plan on mixing your dough for more than 10 minutes, you might adjust the temperature of your water downward, in order to wind up with a dough that will rise as expected rather than over-fermenting.

The dough hook is great for kneading, but it may spin around uselessly, failing to bind the ingredients, if the flour hasn't been moistened already. Make a rough dough by mixing your ingredients together with a rubber spatula before placing the bowl in the mixer and kneading with the dough hook.

For most doughs, 7 to 10 minutes on medium-low speed will do the trick, although very wet doughs and doughs made with high-gluten flour may require a higher speed and/or longer kneading time for proper gluten development. To save your motor, very stiff doughs may need to be mixed on a lower speed.

KNEADING WITH A FOOD PROCESSOR

A food processor can do a great job of kneading dough in seconds rather than minutes. Keep a few things in mind before using your processor to knead. A standard food processor won't hold doughs that contain more than 18 ounces/510 grams or so of flour. So either choose a recipe that uses this quantity or less, or adjust your recipe to fit the machine.

Use the metal blade, which not only is strong enough to handle bread dough but will also cut through the dough rather than tear it. Tearing will damage the gluten strands, while cutting will slice through them cleanly, allowing them to link up with each other after processing is complete.

The food processor motor can really heat up the contents of the work bowl, so definitely adjust the temperature of your water with this in mind. It should be no warmer than cool room temperature, about 70°F. But don't add ice-cold water, which may kill the yeast.

Autolyse can really boost the gluten quality in dough kneaded by the food processor, as well as allow the yeast to hydrate and thus give fermentation a boost. Mix the dough in two stages to take advantage of these effects. First, pulse your ingredients two or three times until a rough dough forms. Then let the dough sit in the bowl for 5 to 10 minutes to allow the flour and yeast to absorb the water. To finish kneading, process the dough until it is smooth and elastic and passes the windowpane test (see page 71), no longer than 45 seconds.

If the dough gets caught under the blade, remove the blade, scrape the dough out of the bowl and onto a lightly floured countertop, replace the blade, and try again. Or finish kneading on the countertop by hand. Rose Levy Beranbaum recommends a few seconds of hand kneading after processing to give the dough an even temperature throughout, since the

Fermentation without Kneading

After all this discussion of how kneading is essential for developing gluten in bread dough, you might wonder about so-called no-knead bread.

Unless you are a baker living under a rock, you've no doubt heard about this technique for artisan-style no-knead bread, popularized by Jim Leahy in his now-legendary *New York Times* recipe and then expanded upon by Nancy Baggett in her book *Kneadlessly Simple* and by Leahy in his own book, *My Bread*.

It is indeed possible to produce a crusty, well-risen loaf with absolutely no kneading by relying solely on autolyse to develop the gluten in the dough. It stands to reason that if you let your dough rest for 30 minutes and it develops a moderate amount of gluten, if you let it rest for 12 hours it will develop a whole

No-Knead Raisin-Walnut Bread

Makes 1 large round

This bread benefits from coming into direct contact with the preheated cast-iron pot, which gives it an incredibly chewy crust. Baking it covered for the first 30 minutes has the effect of steaming, since the water escaping from the dough keeps the surface moist while the loaf rises.

1¼	cups walnut pieces
10.6	ounces/300 grams (2 cups) unbleached all-purpose flour
5.3	ounces/150 grams (1 cup) whole-wheat flour
0.025	ounce/1 gram (¼ teaspoon) instant yeast
0.25	ounce/7 grams (1½ teaspoons) fine sea salt or kosher salt
13	ounces (1½ cups plus 2 tablespoons) room temperature water
¾	cup raisins

1. Preheat the oven to 350°F. Spread the walnut pieces on a baking sheet and toast until fragrant, 5 to 8 minutes. Cool completely, and then coarsely chop.

2. Combine the all-purpose flour, whole-wheat flour, yeast, salt, water, raisins, and nuts in a large mixing bowl. Stir the mixture with a rubber spatula until it comes together to

lot of gluten. But some modifications to the conventional recipe must be made for this method to work. During traditional autolyse, the flour and water are mixed together without salt or yeast simply to enhance the flour's absorption of water prior to fermentation. No-knead recipes not only aim for gluten development during autolyse, but also want to accomplish proper fermentation at the same time. There is a danger with such a long fermentation period at room temperature that the yeast will exhaust their food supply and become weak. To guard against this, no-knead recipes contain a proportionately tiny amount of yeast, ensuring that there will be plenty of food for them to feast on while the proteins in the flour organize themselves. Here is a recipe for a deliciously moist and flavorful no-knead raisin-walnut bread. The timing works well whether you want to mix the dough before bed in order to serve the bread midmorning or mix it in the morning so that it's ready for dinner.

form a rough dough. Cover the bowl with plastic wrap and let the dough stand at room temperature overnight, or for up to 18 hours.

3. Place a piece of parchment paper inside another large mixing bowl, with its corners overhanging the edges of the bowl, and spray the parchment with nonstick cooking spray. Lightly flour a work surface and turn the dough out onto it. Sprinkle the dough with a little more flour and knead it 2 or 3 times, folding it over itself, flattening it, and folding over again. Form a ball by gathering the edges of the dough together and twisting them into a topknot. Place the ball of dough, topknot side down, into the parchment-lined bowl. Cover the bowl with plastic wrap and let the dough rise at room temperature until it has doubled in size, 2 to 2½ hours. It will be very soft but not springy.

4. About 1½ hours into the rise, position an oven rack in the bottom third of the oven and place an 8-quart covered cast-iron or enameled Dutch oven on the rack. Preheat the oven to 425°F.

5. Sprinkle the dough in the bowl with flour. Use a sharp serrated knife or a razor blade to slash two ½-inch-deep intersecting lines into the loaf to create an X. Carefully remove the pot from the oven and remove the lid. Use both hands to carefully place the parchment, with the dough still on it, in the pot. Cover the pot with the lid and bake for 30 minutes.

6. Uncover and bake until the loaf is well browned, 20 to 30 minutes longer. Lift the bread, still on the parchment, from the pot and place it on a wire rack. Cool to room temperature, about 2 hours, before serving.

portions closer to the blade will be much warmer than the portions cling-ing to the outer edges of the bowl.

KNEADING WITH A BREAD MACHINE

Any bread dough can be kneaded in a bread machine following the man-ufacturer's instructions, fermented in the machine or in a bowl on the countertop, and then shaped by hand and baked as you would any hand-kneaded or stand mixer–kneaded bread. Just be sure that you know the capacity of your bread machine and that your recipe doesn't exceed this capacity. When you knead dough in a bread machine, you cede some con-trol over the kneading process to the machine, and your bread may suf-fer as a consequence. Most machines have several kneading programs to choose from, depending upon what type of bread you are baking. But these programs don't allow for the kind of custom kneading — varying the kneading time and intensity, taking rests for the dough to relax between periods of kneading — that some bread doughs require. It takes the most expensive machine, programmed by a very meticulous and experienced home baker, to knead with this specificity.

Fermentation

Once you have kneaded your dough, you will transfer it to a dough-rising container or a large bowl and let it rise at room temperature. This step is called bulk or primary fermentation. During the first few minutes of fer-mentation, the yeast will consume the oxygen that's been incorporated into the dough during kneading. Once this oxygen is gone, it will begin to feed on the glucose and fructose in the flour, producing carbon dioxide and alcohol.

The carbon dioxide produced by the yeast is trapped in the gluten web of the dough, pressing on the cell walls so it expands and rises. No mat-ter what kind of yeast you are using, packaged or natural, and no matter whether you are using a pre-ferment or a sourdough starter or you have made a straight dough, once the yeast begins to feed, rising will occur. At the end of the fermentation period, you will be able to smell the alcohol in the dough. (This alcohol will burn off during baking, so your bread will be nonalcoholic!)

At the same time that yeast are feeding on glucose and fructose, friendly bacteria called lactobacilli will begin to feed on maltose, a sugar in the flour that yeast can't digest. Bacterial fermentation takes longer to occur than yeast fermentation, so the yeast will produce abundant carbon dioxide and alcohol in an hour or two, while lactobacilli don't begin to produce acids until 8 to 12 hours after you've mixed your dough. This lag is meaningful for two reasons.

The acids produced by lactobacilli help slow down yeast fermentation, which prevents the yeast from proliferating too quickly, exhausting their food supply, and becoming too weak to raise dough during the long fermentation required in some recipes. If your dough is going to ferment for only a couple of hours, there is little risk that the yeast will exhaust their food supply, so these acids are unnecessary. But if your dough is going to ferment for many hours

Gas bubbles cause bread dough to rise. The carbon dioxide produced by the yeast is trapped in the gluten web of the dough, pressing on the cell walls so it expands and rises.

(which is the case when you add up total fermentation times for many doughs employing pre-ferments and sourdough starters), it will need these acids in order to keep its yeast supply healthy.

Straight doughs neither require acids produced by lactobacilli to check yeast growth nor reap the flavor benefits that these acids bestow upon long-fermented breads. Long-fermented doughs can taste milky, tangy, or flat-out sour depending upon how much acid you've allowed your dough to develop. One of the most fascinating and fun things about baking your own bread is the ability you will have to alter its flavor by tinkering with its fermentation.

Fermentation can take place in temperatures ranging from 30°F to 130°F, but it just so happens that the optimum range for fermentation is room temperature — anywhere from 68 to 81°F. Professional bakers ferment their doughs in special temperature-controlled chambers where they know the temperature will never vary more than a tenth of a degree,

Temperature and Bread

When I baked my first breads as a teenager, I was utterly terrified that bringing my dough to the wrong temperature during any step in the process would kill my yeast and result in a flat-as-a-pancake round or heavy-as-a-brick loaf rather than a lofty boule or airy brioche. I've since learned that yeast can be active enough to raise bread at temperatures as low as 50°F and as high as 138°F. Because the temperature in my kitchen is well within this range, I no longer worry too much about the premature death of my yeast.

It is true, however, that some temperatures are better for mixing, fermenting, and baking bread dough. For optimum results, recipes will often give you guidelines not only about oven temperature, but also about the temperature of your water before you mix, the temperature of your dough once it is kneaded, and the temperature of the spot in your kitchen where you plan to let it ferment. These recommendations vary from cookbook to cookbook and even from recipe to recipe, but in general bakers agree that the following temperatures are desirable for bread.

Water temperature. The thinking on water temperature has changed in this country over the past 20 years. While older books such as Bernard Clayton's *New Complete Book of Breads* (1973; updated 1987) most often call for warm (105 to 115°F) or even hot (120 to 130°F) water or other liquid in order to hasten fermentation, newer books like *Local Breads*, *My Bread*, and *Crust and Crumb* follow a European model and call for room temperature liquid to encourage flavor development over a long fermentation period.

Dough temperature. While yeast is most active between 85 and 95°F, most professional bakers agree that kneaded dough should register about 75°F to ensure a good rise while giving the dough enough time to develop good flavor.

Fermentation and proofing temperatures. Many recipes will give approximate fermentation and proofing times along with a suggested room temperature (for example, "2 to 2½ hours at 76°F"). If no fermentation temperature is given, then warm room temperature, between 75 and 78°F, is assumed. If your kitchen is a chilly 68°F in the winter or a sweltering 81°F in the summer, keep an eye on your dough as it ferments and adjust the time accordingly.

Baking temperature. There is no single correct baking temperature for breads. In general, hearth breads will rise better and develop a chewier, more flavorful crust at higher temperatures, between 450 and 525°F. Sometimes you'll be directed to start a bread at a higher temperature, to get maximum oven spring, and then to turn down the heat in order to cook the interior properly before the crust burns. Enriched breads, and breads meant to have a more yielding crust, will often be baked at lower temperatures, between 350 and 400°F. Use an oven thermometer to make sure your oven settings match the actual oven temperature, and your breads will be fine.

Internal temperature of bread. Bread has to reach an internal temperature of between 190 (for softer breads) and 210°F (for artisan-style loaves) before it is done in the oven.

Eating temperature. Although it is difficult to resist eating bread that's still warm from the oven, try to wait until it reaches a temperature of about 80°F before slicing into it. Bread that is warmer can be difficult to slice, but more important, when you eat warm bread you are more likely to experience its warmth than the flavor you've worked so hard to coax from it as you've kneaded, fermented, proofed, and baked it.

Professional bakers are fanatical about controlling temperature during every step of baking: Ensuring that your water is always at 80°F, or that your fermentation chamber maintains a steady 76°F, is important in producing hundreds of loaves of consistently good bread. You may cultivate the same fanaticism, but it's doubtful that you'll be able to exercise the same amount of control.

The temperature in your kitchen probably varies from season to season, if not from day to day. Do your best to follow temperature guidelines in recipes, compensating by using cooler water on very warm days or warmer water if you've just taken a bag of flour out of the freezer. Don't try to rush things along by using water that is 10°F hotter than what your recipe calls for. But don't worry if your dough is a few degrees off. Using a thermometer, a clock, your senses, and your experience, you will be able to tell by look and feel how fermentation is progressing, producing loaves that are increasingly consistent and high in quality.

ensuring uniform rising times for every batch. At home, we can't be so precise. Most baking books assume a room temperature of between 70 and 78°F and provide rising times to reflect this assumption. If your kitchen is cooler or hotter than this, you can use those rising times as a guide, but in order to decide when it has fermented long enough you'll have to judge your dough by how it looks and feels as much as by how long it has been sitting in its dough-rising container.

Turning the Dough

Some recipes will recommend that you give the dough a "turn" halfway through bulk fermentation. To do so, slide your hands underneath the dough and pick it up from underneath, so it droops over your hands. Then set it down again, on one of its drooping sides, back in the bowl, so that much of the gas is expelled but the cells holding it aren't destroyed. If you are working with an older recipe that instructs you to "punch down the dough" partway through fermentation, ignore this command and fold instead!

What is the difference between punching down dough and folding it, and why is punching recommended for some doughs? In the past, punching down was often recommended to degas the dough, the idea being that too much accumulated gas too early on can inhibit fermentation. But excessive handling of the dough can do more harm than good, expelling gas but also tearing and damaging the gluten that's been developing up until that point. Folding the dough will expel gas without doing damage. It has the added benefit of developing gluten in a gentle way, stretching and strengthening the strands. This can result in a dramatic improvement in the rise of wet doughs, helping them puff up instead of spread out flat in the oven.

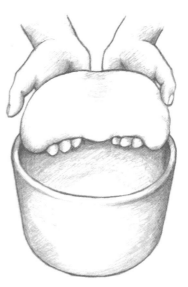

Turning the dough

Dividing the Dough

If your recipe makes more than one loaf, you'll need to divide it when fermentation is complete. To do so, turn the dough onto a lightly floured countertop and cut through it with a bench scraper or sharp chef's knife. Use a decisive motion and avoid sawing through it or tearing it in any other way. The idea is to preserve as many air cells and as much gluten as possible during the process. It's important to cut the dough into pieces of equal weight, since baking times will be different for loaves of substantially different sizes. A half an ounce here or there isn't a big deal, but if you realize that you've cut your dough very unevenly, with one piece weighing substantially more than the others, weigh the pieces and cut a piece off of a larger one to add to a smaller one. But avoid combining a lot of little pieces to make one larger piece. The resulting bread won't have the integrity of a loaf made of a single piece of well-fermented dough.

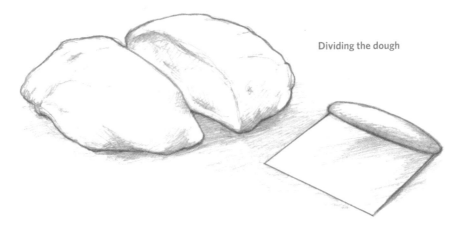

Dividing the dough

Pre-shaping

Before shaping your dough pieces into rounds, pan loaves, or baguettes, you'll need to pre-shape it into more or less uniform pieces, getting them ready for final shaping. Depending on the bread you are baking, you'll shape your pieces into rough rectangles or rounds.

Pre-shaping the dough

Bench Rest

After pre-shaping your dough pieces, lightly drape them with plastic wrap and let them sit on the countertop to allow the gluten to relax before attempting final shaping. The duration of the bench rest depends on how tightly you've pre-shaped your loaves. If you have just gently divided your dough and folded the pieces into rough rectangles, they might require only 10 minutes to rest. If you have formed them into tighter, more cohesive rounds, they might need 20 to 30 minutes to relax sufficiently before they'll be easy to work with.

Shaping

There are dozens, if not hundreds, of ways to shape dough to help it realize its full flavor and texture potential and to give it a beautiful appearance (for shaping dough into baguettes, rounds, loaves, and other common shapes, see page 88). The important thing to remember, no matter what shape you are heading toward, is not to overhandle the dough during this step. Experienced bakers will be able to take a piece of dough and round it into a perfect boule in seconds. Such quickness and lightness of touch will leave the dough's air cells and gluten structure intact, and the result will be a tall bread with an open crumb. For beginners, achieving such perfection will take much longer. Extended shaping time may translate into a lower-rising, denser bread. So it's better to have an imperfectly shaped but well-risen round than a perfectly shaped but underrisen one. Practice makes perfect. The more you bake, the easier it will become to shape dough beautifully without damaging its structure and decreasing its rising potential.

Depending on what kind of bread you are baking, you may have to transfer your shaped dough to loaf pans, bannetons, or a couche to help it maintain its shape. Or you might simply place it on a piece of parchment paper set atop a baker's peel or rimless baking sheet. Sprinkle your shaped dough with a little flour and lightly drape it with plastic wrap to prevent the surface from drying out.

Proofing

Before they can be baked, most loaves (with some notable exceptions, including pizza and other flatbreads) must ferment a second time, allowing them to rise to almost (but not quite) their full height. This second fermentation period is called proofing. Proofing time is determined by variables including the size of your breads, the liveliness of your yeast, and the temperature in your kitchen. Properly proofed loaves will increase in size anywhere from 50 percent to 100 percent. When you press a fingertip into the dough, it will spring back slowly. Judging whether a loaf has proofed sufficiently is tricky, but it gets easier through experience. Under-proofed loaves won't reach their rising potential in the oven. Overproofed loaves will have risen too much on the countertop and will be so delicate that they will collapse in the oven before solidifying.

Retarding the Loaves

Certain recipes will direct you to refrigerate your shaped loaves for up to 12 hours after shaping instead of proofing them. Not only does retarding give you some flexibility in determining when to bake, but it also can considerably improve your bread by giving the lactobacilli in the dough enough time to produce flavorful acids. (Beyond 12 hours, these acids will begin to break down the dough's gluten and compromise its rise.)

Any dough made with white flour can be retarded, for either or both of these reasons. Simply shape the dough, drape it with plastic wrap, and refrigerate it, bringing it back to room temperature on the countertop before baking (this can take as little as 30 minutes or up to several hours depending on the shape and size of your loaf, so plan accordingly). Doughs made with whole-wheat, rye, and other low- or no-gluten flours shouldn't be retarded. They have a weaker gluten structure than white breads, which may be more quickly compromised by the buildup of acids during a long, slow fermentation.

Scoring

Some loaves, such as ciabatta and challah, are not scored before baking. But many, if not most, loaves are slashed with a razor, lame, or sharp serrated knife just before baking. Some breads, such as the wheat sheaf–shaped *epi* or the *fougasse*, are scored to give them their distinctive shape. But scoring is not simply decorative. Scoring allows the baker to control the expansion of the dough as it rises in the oven. Unscored, your loaves will either burst open at weak spots in the dough or not expand to their full potential. Strategic slashing weakens the surface of the dough in spots where you want it to split open, giving the loaves an artful appearance and at the same time allowing them to rise fully.

Don't be timid when scoring sticky bread dough. If you hesitate mid-slash you may tear and/or deflate the dough. Use a very sharp blade and make quick and decisive cuts. How deeply you should cut will depend

Decorative Scissor Scoring

Most breads are scored with a sharp knife or razor blade, but you can get some eye-catching effects using a pair of kitchen shears instead.

Epi. Instead of scoring your baguette with several long horizontal cuts, you can use scissors to make this wheat sheaf shape. Place the scissors at a slight angle on the top of the rolled baguette, near one end, and make a shallow cut. With your fingers, gently pull the cut piece to one side. Repeat the cutting a little further down the baguette, pulling the next piece to the other side. Cut the dough this way from end to end, alternating the direction of the cut pieces.

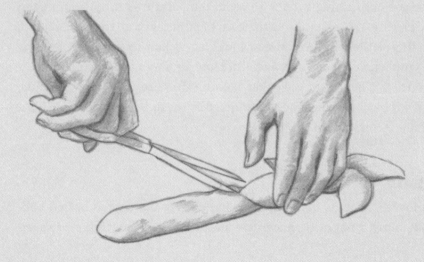

on the strength of the dough. Soft doughs should be given shallow cuts. Cut too deeply and you will cause your dough to spread rather than rise. Resilient, bouncy doughs can and should be cut more deeply. These cuts will bloom into beautiful decorations in the oven.

Scoring with a razor: before and after

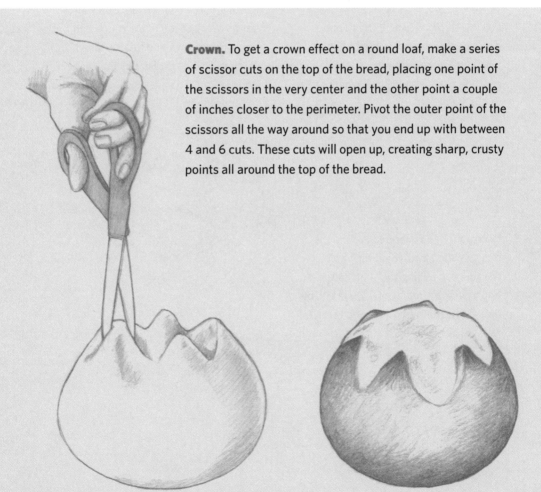

Crown. To get a crown effect on a round loaf, make a series of scissor cuts on the top of the bread, placing one point of the scissors in the very center and the other point a couple of inches closer to the perimeter. Pivot the outer point of the scissors all the way around so that you end up with between 4 and 6 cuts. These cuts will open up, creating sharp, crusty points all around the top of the bread.

Four Common Bread Shapes

Most breads come in one of the following shapes or in a variation on one of them. Here are the steps you should follow to make boules, baguettes, *bâtardes*, and loaves.

Boule. A boule is a large round. Use the same steps, rounding with one hand instead of two, to make small round rolls.

1. On a lightly floured countertop, gather the pre-shaped dough together into a ball by cupping your hands around it and rotating it several times.

2. Pull the slack surface of the dough downward toward the countertop and pinch it together underneath the round, creating a tight, smooth skin over the round.

3. With your hands cupped around the dough, rotate it as you drag it across the counter, pulling the skin tighter and tighter by pulling any loose bits of dough toward the bottom and incorporating them into the seams underneath.

Bâtarde. This torpedo-shaped bread is formed by first rounding the dough and then tapering the ends.

1. Form a round as you would when shaping a boule.

2. Place the round seam side down on a lightly floured countertop. Cup your palms over the top of the round and gently roll it back and forth in small motions to elongate it, placing gentle pressure on the ends as you roll in order to taper them.

Baguette. Customize your baguette by making it as long and thin or as short and fat as you'd like. French baguettes typically have tapered ends. Italian breads are of a uniform thickness with rounded ends.

1. Pat the pre-shaped dough into a 4- by 7-inch rectangle. Fold it into thirds, as if folding a letter, pressing the top fold into the other two folds with your fingertips to seal.

2. Use the side of your hand to make a shallow groove across this rectangle. Fold the rectangle in half along the groove and pinch the edges together to seal.

3. Place the dough seam side down on a lightly floured countertop. Place both of your hands in the center of the dough log and gently roll it back and forth in small motions, moving your hands toward the ends of the dough as you roll to stretch it into a longer log. To taper the ends, apply a little more pressure on the tips as you roll.

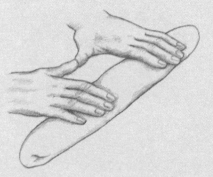

Pan loaf. Even if a loaf is going to be baked in a pan, it still needs to be folded and rolled into shape for an optimum rise.

1. Press the dough into an 8-inch square.

2. Make a groove across the square with the side of your hand and fold the dough over itself, pressing lightly on the edges to seal.

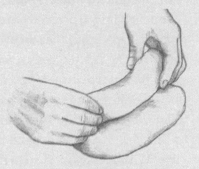

3. With the seam side down, roll the rectangle back and forth on a lightly floured countertop until it is the same length as your loaf pan.

When your dough is shaped, place it on a parchment-lined baker's peel, or in a banneton, couche, or loaf pan for its second rise. Remember to place it seam side down unless otherwise directed, or else its seams will split wide open during baking.

Baking

While your dough is proofing, prepare your oven for baking. If you are making a hearth bread, one that bakes directly on a baking stone, you'll need to preheat your baking stone for about 1 hour before baking to heat it sufficiently for proper oven spring. Loaves baked on a baking sheet will never rise as high as loaves baked directly on a preheated baking stone. If you are making a pan loaf, you may only need to set your oven rack to the suggested position and turn on the oven. Some lower-gluten pan loaves, however, such as those made with rye flour, do well when placed on a preheated baking stone. So read your recipe carefully to see what kind of preparation is suggested.

Oven spring is the final phase of fermentation. When 70°F dough is placed in a 450°F oven, several reactions take place. Yeast becomes more active, gases expand, alcohol begins to boil off, and steam is produced. All of this molecular activity causes the dough's gluten-strengthened cells to inflate quickly and dramatically. To maximize oven spring, make sure your dough is well proofed but not overproofed and your oven is set at the proper temperature (use an oven thermometer if you are concerned that your oven isn't giving you an accurate temperature reading).

If your recipe directs you to do so, prepare to steam your loaves during the first few minutes of baking (see box, page 48). Adding steam to the oven temporarily keeps the surface of the dough soft and stretchy, so that the bread can expand to its full potential while the yeast is still alive. Without steam, the surface of the dough may dry out and harden before the interior air cells have finished expanding, resulting in under-risen bread. There are several ways to steam bread. Some bakers like to place ice cubes directly on the oven floor, while others use a spritzer to mist water over the loaves periodically during the first few minutes of baking. In my opinion, the neatest and most effective method is to place a cast-iron skillet on the rack right underneath your baking

stone while you preheat the oven. When you put your loaves in the oven, dump some ice cubes into the skillet. Your dough will benefit from an initial burst of steam and then continuous moisture as the rest of the ice evaporates.

After 15 to 20 minutes of baking, fermentation ceases and so does rising. When bread dough reaches a temperature of 140°F, yeast dies. At about the same time, the starches in the flour begin to gelatinize and the proteins coagulate, setting the dough's structure. But the bread still has a way to go before it has finished baking.

First, the crust dries out and firms up. At about 325°F, the sugars on the surface begin to caramelize and brown. At 350°F, further browning occurs when amino acids and simple sugars in the crust react in a particularly delicious way (this is called the Maillard reaction, and you may remember it from high school chemistry as the moment when cooked food begins to look and smell very appetizing indeed).

But don't pull your bread out of the oven simply because it's brown and smells great. Before your loaf is ready to come out of the oven, most of the bread's water molecules must migrate from the interior of the loaf to the crust before evaporating into the air of the oven. This process, called *starch retrogradation,* is complete when the interior of the loaf reaches about 200°F. But even if you get this reading on your instant-read thermometer, you might want to keep your loaf in the oven for an extra 5 minutes to ensure that sufficient water has left the crust. If too much remains, the crust will get soggy as your bread cools.

Cooling Your Bread

No matter how irresistible it looks and smells fresh from the oven, it is important to give your loaf some time to cool before tearing into it. Slide it onto a wire rack to allow air to circulate below it as well as all around it, and resist the temptation to sample your handiwork. Although it may look solid and beautifully browned, your bread is not finished baking until it has cooled to about 98°F. During this cooling period, starch retrogradation continues, as more water molecules inside the bread migrate to the crust and evaporate, leaving the interior of the bread moist but not spongy or doughy, as it would be if you had sliced into the loaf while it was still hot. For small rolls and thin baguettes, as little as 15 minutes could be enough time. For large country loaves, it may take 2 hours or longer for enough starch retrogradation to take place, allowing the interior to firm up enough for slicing.

Storage

Starch retrogradation doesn't cease when the bread is cooled. In fact, your bread will continue to lose moisture through this process until it becomes hard and stale. But you can slow down starch retrogradation and even reverse the process, prolonging the shelf life of your bread, by storing it properly. If you don't plan on eating your bread in the 24-hour period after baking it, wrap it tightly in plastic wrap and then in aluminum foil and place it in the freezer. Freezing will halt the process of starch retrogradation. Well-wrapped frozen bread will stay fresh for up to 2 weeks. Defrost it on the countertop and then crisp up the crust in a 350°F oven for 5 minutes. It will taste as good as a freshly baked loaf.

If you plan on eating your bread the next day, you can store it in a resealable plastic bag at room temperature. The crust will become slightly soggy, but this is actually a good thing. When you reheat the bread in a 350°F oven, the water in the crust will be drawn back into the crumb, freshening it if it has begun to stale. Or you can store it in a bread box or bread bag specially designed to allow enough air circulation to preserve the crispness of the crust without allowing the interior of the bread to dry out (see Resources, page 273).

One thing you should definitely not do is refrigerate your bread, since at temperatures just above freezing it will dry out more quickly than it will in the freezer or at room temperature. The exception are breads containing a large proportion of oily nuts or seeds, which require refrigeration to keep them fresh.

However you decide to store your bread, make sure it is fully cooled before you do so. Condensation will form on warm bread that is wrapped in plastic, encouraging the growth of mold.

The Basic Steps
Questions and Answers

Q My recipe just gives a volume measurement for yeast, ½ teaspoon, not a weight measurement. How can I be sure I'm using the right quantity?

A The author of your recipe may be assuming that you won't have a scale that is sensitive enough to weigh out such a small amount in ounces, thus the volume measurement. The most fanatical bread book authors (including Rose Levy Beranbaum, Daniel Leader, and Peter Reinhart) will give weight measurements in grams as well as ounces, so that you can weigh even the tiniest amount of yeast with accuracy. For the record, ½ teaspoon of yeast is about 0.05 ounce or 1.25 grams.

Q I'm a couple of minutes into kneading and I realize I forgot to add the yeast and salt! Can I add these during kneading?

A Yes, with two caveats. Use instant yeast, which will become fully hydrated during kneading without soaking in water first. And when you add the yeast and salt, make sure to place them in two different locations — opposite sides of the mixing bowl or opposite points on the mass of dough that's sitting on the countertop. If they come in contact with each other in such large proportions, the salt might kill the yeast before fermentation gets under way.

Q I tried kneading my dough and adding as little flour as possible by flouring only my hands, but it was a mess. Bits of dough stuck to the flour on my hands, and after a minute or two my fingers were covered with it. Is there a better method for kneading without adding too much flour?

A Next time, try coating your hands with a thin layer of olive oil instead of flour. The oil may do a better job of letting your hands handle sticky dough. Of course, if your dough is so sticky that it's impossible to handle, you might consider kneading it in a stand mixer or food processor next time. Or consider the possibility that it may in fact need a tablespoon or two more flour to become a workable mass.

Q I refrigerated my biga overnight as directed, but when I tried to mix it into my dough the next morning, it was too hard and crumbly to incorporate evenly. Do I need to bring the biga to room temperature before proceeding with mixing? If I have to let it sit on the counter for an hour, using a pre-ferment doesn't seem like much of a time-saver!

A Refrigerating your pre-ferment, whether it is a stiff biga or a more soupy poolish, is not so much a matter of convenience as it is a way to control the fermentation of the starter. At a lower temperature, it can ferment more slowly than at room temperature, without the risk of over-fermenting. But it is true that a stiff pre-ferment will be difficult to incorporate into dough when it is icy cold. Bringing it to room temperature is a good idea. When it has warmed up a bit, break it into clumps before adding it to the bowl. Daniel Leader suggests pouring the water over the biga to soften it, breaking it up as it sits in the water, and then adding the rest of the dough ingredients to the bowl. If you don't want to wait for a biga to come to room temperature, take a look at Jeffrey Hamelman's recipe for ciabatta in *Bread: A Baker's Book of Techniques and Recipes,* which employs a biga fermented at room temperature that can be used as soon as enough fermentation has taken place.

Q Is it cheating to use a packaged sourdough starter instead of cultivating one from scratch?

A Not at all. Packaged sourdough starter consists of dehydrated wild yeast and lactobacilli. When you cultivate a sourdough starter on your own, it has to capture wild yeast from the air, a process that can take days. Adding a teaspoon or so of dehydrated sourdough to your flour and water mixture can give your culture a considerable head start, since the dehydrated yeast will immediately begin to ferment, along with any yeast that the mixture captures on its own. Once your culture is active, you can start baking with it. Every time you feed it, the percentage of packaged sourdough in the mixture will decrease. Over time, your culture will be teeming with the wild yeast native to your kitchen and will be as authentic as one begun from scratch.

Q I weighed out my ingredients to the last gram, but my dough seemed very wet. Should I add more flour to reach the right consistency?

A It may happen that even if you weigh out your ingredients, your dough may be off balance, due to the humidity in your kitchen perhaps, or due to a batch of flour that is less absorbent than normal. But before you add more flour, let your dough stand for 10 or

15 minutes, to give it a chance to fully absorb the water. With a rest, you might find that you don't need the extra flour after all. If your dough is still too sticky and unworkable, add flour 1 tablespoon at a time until you can comfortably knead it, guarding all the time against adding too much.

Q **I began to hand-knead my dough, and it seemed very dry and tough. How can I add more water at that stage?**

A It is a lot easier to add extra flour than it is to add extra water at this stage, but not impossible. Press the dough into a rectangle and then dimple it all over with a fingertip. Then drizzle about 1 tablespoon of water into the indentations, fold the dough in half, shape it into a ball, and continue to knead. Repeat once or twice if necessary until you have incorporated enough water to make kneading comfortable.

Q **I don't have a heavy-duty stand mixer or a bread machine, but I'd like to try some of these very wet dough recipes. Any suggestions about how to hand-knead without adding too much flour?**

A Lightly flour the countertop and dust the dough with flour, but instead of sprinkling more flour onto the dough as you knead, dust your hands with flour instead. This will keep you from adding too much. Or give your hands a light coating of vegetable or olive oil instead of flour (this is good for the skin, too!). Keep a bench scraper handy to scrape the dough up periodically, gathering it together into a mound if it's spread out and stuck to the counter. And give your dough frequent rests. For every few minutes that you knead, let it sit for 5 minutes, to let the flour fully absorb the water and to allow the gluten to weave its web.

Q **My rye bread recipe specifies that I should machine-knead the dough on a very low speed for about 15 minutes. Can I increase the speed and cut down the kneading time?**

A As I'll discuss in greater detail in chapter 7, rye flour has substantially less gluten-forming proteins than wheat flour. The gluten that forms in rye doughs is also more delicate than the gluten in wheat doughs. So don't rush when working with rye. Gentle kneading is required, both to develop its gluten and so that the delicate gluten strands aren't torn.

Q After reading several books by prominent bread experts, I'm more confused than ever about kneading. Some bakers say that for optimum gluten development it is of the utmost importance to knead the dough fully. But others insist that it's important not to overknead the dough, because too much oxygen will bleach the flour and make it less flavorful. What should I believe?

A The wonderful thing about bread baking is that, although there is a strong scientific component to the process, there is also plenty of room for debate. Bakers will argue about the best way to coax the highest rise from the bread, and those who believe that kneading is the answer will never cede their ground to others, just as qualified and experienced, who rely on autolyse, turning the dough, and other techniques instead. In my opinion, kneading time and intensity should be determined by the ingredients you are using and the particular outcome you seek. My favorite Daniel Leader pizza dough and ciabatta recipes require close to 20 minutes of machine mixing on high, and I'm convinced that this long, intense kneading is what makes these superwet doughs able to bubble up and become crisp. But I've also had incredible success with Jim Leahy's no-knead boule, with its beautifully open crumb and incredibly caramelized crust. My advice is to follow a recipe carefully the first time around, and then tinker with kneading and other gluten-building techniques during subsequent baking sessions. This will allow you to develop your own opinions on the subject.

Q I retarded my baguettes in the refrigerator for 12 hours before bringing them to room temperature and baking them. They came out great, but their crusts are strangely mottled by bubbles. What happened?

A The mottled crust of your bread is evidence of the abundant carbon dioxide that built up in the dough during retarding. During baking, this gas escaped through the crust, leaving behind a pattern of bubbles.

Q I guess I overproofed my loaves, because they collapsed on themselves before I could get them from the peel onto the baking stone. Is the dough ruined?

A Jeffrey Hamelman says that you want to proof your loaves so that they rise to 85 to 90 percent of their potential height, but not to 100 percent. "Just as we will fall onto our noses if we lean over 100 percent, so too will the loaves tend to collapse if they receive a full 100 percent proofing before the

An overproofed, collapsed loaf

bake." If your loaves have collapsed, reshape them and let them proof again, this time for a shorter period. They probably won't rise as high in the oven as they would have if you had gotten it right the first time, but your yeast is still alive, and the breads will turn out fine.

Q **I've been scoring my rounds with three parallel cuts, but I'd like to do something more creative next time. Any suggestions?**

A If you've mastered parallel cuts, you can move on to the number (#) symbol. Next, try an asterisk. A little trickier is a spiral: Use the tip of the blade to make one continuous and spiraling cut from the center of the round outward.

Q **Are there other ways to control a dough's rise in the oven without using a razor or scissors?**

A Most French breads are elegantly scored, but scoring is not universal.

In Italy, breads are often baked unscored, resulting in pleasingly uneven shapes. You can take your chances, skip scoring, and see what you come up with. Other Italian breads, such as focaccia and ciabatta, are dimpled with the fingertips for a more even and controlled rise. In Germany and parts of Russia, loaves are pierced all over with the tip of a skewer.

Traditional unscored breads

Q **Can I shape baguette dough into a round?**

A Once you've baked a bread, shaping it as recommended in the recipe, feel free to try new shapes the next time. In some cases, you'll be very surprised at how different the same dough seems when it is baked in a baguette shape and then in a round. Basically, different shapes will get you different crust-to-crumb ratios and different crust characteristics. Baguettes will have more crust than crumb; rounds will have more crumb than crust. Shaping a dough one way or another will significantly change the character of the finished bread.

Q **Can I shape bread dough into rolls?**

A Most doughs can be shaped into small rounds or mini-baguettes or simply cut into free-form pieces to make rustic rolls. Doughs made with a large quantity of high-gluten bread flour or those that are shaped and then retarded overnight may develop crusts that are too thick and chewy for smaller rolls, so choose a dough that's got a high proportion of all-purpose flour, and proof the shaped rolls at room temperature for an hour or two rather than for an extended period in the refrigerator.

Q **Is it possible to add too much steam to the oven when baking bread?**

A Once the crust has begun to harden and color, steam will no longer keep it soft enough to prevent the surface from setting, no matter how much you add. In general, adding more steam than recommended won't hurt a bread, but it won't help it either. There is one exception. If you suspect that your loaves are overproofed, too much steam can hasten their collapse in the oven. Overproofed breads have risen to close to 100 percent of their potential height before they hit the oven. In these cases, you want the crust to harden as soon as possible, before the breads, with their weakened internal structure, spread out or collapse entirely.

Q **I understand that underbaking bread is bad. But is it possible to bake it too long?**

A If the crumb of your bread is tough and dry and the crust is unpleasantly thick, then it is possible that you have overbaked your dough. This is difficult to do with crusty artisan-style loaves, which can reach an internal temperature of 210°F without drying out. Indeed, some of the best artisan breads call for so much water in their formulas that they can become practically charred on the outside without overbaking on the inside, and a long baking time is necessary to allow excess moisture to evaporate from the crust. But softer breads such as brioche and Parker House rolls can indeed overbake. The internal temperature of these breads should reach just 190°F before you pull them from the oven. Still, these breads should have golden, not pale, crusts, and the crusts should feel dry and set rather than damp and soft.

Q How do I use my instant-read thermometer to take the internal temperature of my bread?

A It's important to insert your thermometer into the very center of the bread, so that it can read the temperature of the coolest part of the dough. Push it into the bread through the top of the loaf at the center, and only push it in so that its point will hit the center of the bread. If you push it too far, or not far enough, the thermometer may give you a high reading (the outer portions of the loaf will heat up before the innermost portion), causing you to remove your bread from the oven too soon.

Part Two

TECHNIQUES AND RECIPES

T HE FOLLOWING CHAPTERS contain information and recipes for making all types of breads. Chapters 4, 5, and 6 deal with the three different ways you can build a dough: directly (straight doughs), with a yeasted pre-ferment, and with a wild yeast sourdough starter. Later chapters deal with special ingredients (whole grains), unusual shaping techniques (flatbreads), and the unique category of bread machine baking.

The recipes included in each chapter were designed to illustrate the information in the chapter introductions. Think of them as hands-on lessons in a particular type of bread baking. But they were also developed to delight. I've tried to use my imagination and the knowledge I've gleaned from reading a lot of books, talking with some of the country's best artisan bakers, and spending many hours elbow-deep in dough to come up with breads I couldn't live without. Here they are.

Inevitably, some breads cross categories: There are flatbreads mixed with a yeasted pre-ferment and whole-wheat breads made with sourdough. You will find helpful information in various locations.

When I bake, I set up a few general guidelines for myself to ensure consistency. Here are some of the ingredients, equipment, and techniques I use regularly. To get results close to mine, you will want to follow suit.

Ingredients

These breads were baked exclusively with King Arthur flour either purchased at my local supermarket or ordered from the King Arthur catalog. Of all the national brands, I've had the most satisfying results with these flours. The quality is excellent and so is the support that the company provides. If you are having a problem with your dough, you can call their Bakers' Hotline (see Resources, page 273), and chances are a knowledgeable customer service person will be able to talk you through it. If you are using a different brand of flour, look for a relatively high protein content for its classification (see page 20 for a brand-by-brand comparison). Your results may vary slightly from mine, but excellent breads can be made with any brand of supermarket flour.

For these recipes I stuck with kosher salt, an economical choice with a pure taste. Other salts will work in the recipes. Sea salt is an equal substitution, which is why it appears as an option in the ingredients lists. But volume measurements for table salt are different, so if you'd like to make this substitution, see page 31 before proceeding to calculate how much table salt you should use instead of kosher salt or sea salt.

With the exception of the sourdough breads, all these breads were raised with instant yeast. I like the ease of this product. It doesn't have to be dissolved in water before being incorporated into bread dough. There is also less chance that it will fail the way active dry yeast might if not adequately hydrated.

Except for the bottled spring water I use to cultivate my sourdough starter, I use tap water exclusively in these recipes. I like the taste of my water, and it has never caused my yeast any problems. The vast majority of home bakers can use tap water with great results.

Measurements and Yields

I always weigh flour, salt, and yeast when possible, and I urge you to do the same. But I've also listed ingredients by volume for your convenience. For a weight/volume conversion calculator, see page 266. Very small quantities (¼ teaspoon cardamom, for example) and nonessential add-ins such as nuts and seeds are given in volume measurements.

I use a 5-quart KitchenAid stand mixer when kneading my doughs by machine. Most of these recipes yield 1 large or 2 small loaves, which fit very comfortably in the machine. If you have a larger machine, or strong hands and arms, you may double most of the recipes to double the yield.

A Word about Temperature

The recipe directions assume a room temperature of about 75°F. Water should generally be in the 70 to 78°F range. When you finish kneading your dough, it should be between 75 and 80°F. If the temperature in your kitchen, or of your kneaded dough, is considerably cooler or warmer than this, you'll have to adjust fermentation and proofing times accordingly.

Chapter 4
Simple Breads from Straight Doughs

To prepare a straight dough, you simply mix all of your ingredients together at once. There is no pre-ferment or sourdough culture to prepare before mixing, so there's less work and often less time required to bake a bread using this method.

Straight doughs are great for beginning bakers who are looking for streamlined recipes with just a few steps to success. With no call for a sponge, *poolish*, or *biga*, there are no worries about whether or not the starter is ready to raise bread. With no call for a wild yeast starter, you can cross off your list the tasks of cultivating the starter and keeping it healthy. With fewer steps, it is easy to concentrate on the basic process of bread making, and there are fewer opportunities to make mistakes along the way.

But straight doughs aren't simply or necessarily just a way to learn about baking before moving on to "real" bread. The best straight dough recipes have a place in the repertoire of the most skilled and experienced bakers. According to Daniel Leader, who spent many months in Paris's most venerable bakeries studying traditional French technique before opening his own highly acclaimed artisan bakery, straight dough baguettes are a tradition and a staple item at French boulangeries, baked every few hours almost around the clock. It is true that straight dough breads don't have the longer shelf life of sourdough breads, which is why savvy Parisians consume them as quickly as they come out of the oven, timing their shopping so they can buy them when they are fresh and still a little bit warm.

Made and consumed with this in mind, there is a lot of pleasure to be had from the best straight dough breads. These breads are as close to spur-of-the-moment baking as you can get when working with yeast, satisfying a craving for home-baked bread, if not instantly, then often in as little as three or four hours.

Getting the Most out of a Straight Dough

Because straight doughs don't benefit from flavor bestowed by a pre-ferment or a sourdough starter, they can be bland and unexciting to eat. Every care must be taken to bring out the naturally delicious taste of the wheat and to otherwise enhance the bread's flavor. When choosing a straight dough recipe, gathering ingredients, and making the dough, keep the following in mind to produce the best-tasting bread.

Ingredients for Improving Flavor

It goes without saying that every bread should be made with the highest-quality ingredients. But the fact is that pre-ferments and especially sourdough starters add so much depth and complexity to a simple white dough that the resulting bread, even if it is baked with supermarket flour rather than minimally processed organic flour from a specialty mill, will be outstanding because of the wild yeast culture. You won't have such flavor backup when working with a straight dough. Be picky about your ingredients for best results with your straight dough recipe. Here are some guidelines to follow.

Flour. The primary flavor of a white or whole-wheat bread made using the straight dough method will come from flour. The texture and character of the bread will depend on the quantity and quality of the proteins in the flour, so it makes sense to use the best-quality flour you can find.

Minimally processed flour made from the most flavorful grain will give you the best-tasting, highest-rising straight dough. Millers who work closely with farmers have access to grain grown with bakers in mind. When these millers process the grain, they do so gently, so even their white flour contains traces of flavorful and healthy oils and fiber. They are careful to grind the grain so that enough starch is damaged to encourage the enzymatic action necessary for good fermentation, but not so much as to damage gluten-forming proteins. Buy your flour from a specialty company that caters to informed and demanding consumers, such as Giusto's or King Arthur (see Resources, page 273), and your loaves will reflect the quality of the milled grain.

Yeast. It's not so much the quality of the yeast you use (any supermarket brand that hasn't passed its expiration date will work) but the quantity that is important when making a straight dough. Look for recipes that call for just a small amount, which will result in a slower fermentation and, in turn, a better-tasting bread. For every 16 ounces of flour you use, add no more than ¾ teaspoon of yeast, and your resulting dough will take its time rising, allowing the flavor of the wheat to develop.

Nuts and seeds. Adding nuts and seeds to a straight dough is a great way to give your bread delicious flavor. The oils in the nuts add richness. Toasting them in a 350°F oven for a few minutes before adding them to the dough will bring out their flavor. Toast them just until they are fragrant but are not yet colored — too much time in the oven will make them bitter. Remember to let them cool completely before adding them to your dough.

Presoaked sunflower, sesame, pumpkin, and flax seeds hold a lot of moisture and will extend the shelf life of your straight dough beyond the half a day of a typical unseeded white bread dough mixed using this method.

Cheese. Hard cheeses such as cheddar or Parmesan are a welcome addition to many straight dough recipes. Not only do they add flavor, but they also add moisture to the dough. If cut into small pieces rather than shredded or grated, they will still be melty and gooey when the bread is cooled to warm room temperature. Add hard cheeses during the last minute or two of kneading. This way, they will be evenly distributed but won't interfere with gluten formation, which will have already taken place.

Bacon and ham. Like cheese, the fat from bacon, prosciutto, or cooked ham adds flavor to bread dough and moistens the crumb, improving the texture of many straight doughs.

Herbs. Finely chopped fresh herbs give straight doughs an intoxicating aroma. You can tailor your choice to complement other foods you're serving: I like to serve bread baked with basil and parsley alongside my chicken Parmesan. My tarragon-flavored bread pairs well with my classic beef stew. With broiled salmon I might choose bread baked with dill. Knead herbs into dough in the last minute or two; any earlier and your dough might be tinted green.

Olives. Use chopped and pitted olives in straight doughs to bake intensely flavored breads. Be sure to pat olives dry before adding them to the dough because the brine or oil they are packed in can throw off the recipe formula. Even patted dry, their oils will still add incredible moisture to the dough. As with herbs, mix olives into dough during the last minute or two of kneading, or you might wind up with pale purple or green dough.

Eggs and oil. Straight doughs containing eggs and oil, such as challah, will keep longer than doughs that aren't enriched. Egg yolks also add great flavor to straight doughs. Since the fat in eggs and oil will weaken gluten, consider using a higher-gluten flour such as bread flour in these breads, to give your finished bread a tender crumb without compromising its structure.

Techniques for Improving Texture

If your dream is to bake soulful bread brimming with character, you don't necessarily have to turn to the sourdough recipes in chapter 6. But you will have to employ some tricks of the trade if you want to live this dream with straight dough.

Before you begin to bake, recognize the limitations of straight dough baking, so that you understand the challenges you will be facing. Straight doughs given the standard treatment (knead-ferment-shape-proof-bake) are more often than not dry and lifeless, underrisen and with a tight rather than an open crumb. They smell great but fall short in the flavor department. Techniques to help strengthen gluten will improve a straight dough's rise and crumb structure. Tips on extending fermentation will also improve texture while giving the bread some of the mildly acidic flavor that is the mark of artisan bread. Here are some great techniques, none of them the least bit difficult, that can make the difference between a bland bread and an outstanding one.

Go easy on the yeast. As I've already mentioned, you'll get a more flavorful bread from a straight dough that's had some time to ferment as opposed to one that's been hurried along. One way to slow down fermentation is to start slowly, with just a bit of yeast. Using just ½ to ¾ teaspoon per 16 ounces of flour will allow your dough some time to develop flavor without the risk that the yeast will become so numerous that they'll exhaust their food supply.

Just add water. A major complaint about straight dough breads is that they are dry and stale almost as soon as they come out of the oven. To combat this tendency, make sure your dough is on the wet side. This may mean that your dough is difficult to knead by hand and takes a long time to become smooth and pass the windowpane test (see page 71), since your flour may have difficulty absorbing so much water. Be patient and don't worry. Even if your dough never reaches this stage, it will still bake up into a better bread than a dry dough that handles beautifully.

Limit kneading. I was determined when developing straight dough recipes for this book to use wet doughs, so that my breads wouldn't be dry and compact like so many straight dough breads made with more conventional formulas. But I was having difficulty getting my wet doughs to pass the windowpane test, even after 10 or sometimes 15 minutes of machine kneading. The problem with kneading for such a long time is that it adds a lot of oxygen to the dough. This oxygen combines with flavorful carotenoid compounds in the wheat, and in the process their flavor is neutralized (so is their color, which is why well-kneaded dough is whiter in color than just-mixed dough).

So I was delighted when I read in Shirley Corriher's wonderful book *BakeWise* that some baking experts don't apply this test to all breads, and that sometimes it's better to knead just for a few minutes to combine ingredients, and then to let the dough develop gluten on its own as it rises. Corriher explains that as dough moves in rising, more and more proteins link together, forming a strong gluten web regardless of how little it has been kneaded. So when working with an extra-wet dough, it's better to just let this happen than to risk adding too much flour and/or oxygen.

Fold your dough. The simple motion of folding your fermenting dough can do wonders to encourage gluten development without the strain of kneading. If you are working with a very wet straight dough, feel free to fold it once, twice, or even three times during bulk fermentation to increase dough strength and improve its rising ability. The double or triple rise during bulk fermentation will vastly improve the quality of your dough.

Keep it cool. If you aren't in a rush and you really want to slow down fermentation, you can retard your straight dough overnight in the refrigerator, either before or after shaping. The time the dough spends in the refrigerator is time it can take to develop gluten.

To retard before shaping, let it ferment at room temperature for the suggested amount of time, give it a turn, return it to the bowl, cover with plastic wrap, and refrigerate it for up to 12 hours. Shape the dough when it is cold, and then proceed with proofing. This stage will take longer than if your dough had been at room temperature when shaped.

Recognize the difference between work time and total time. You may be dismayed when you see that it can take almost 36 hours from the time you mix your Cheddar Cheese Boule (page 119) dough to the moment it is ready to eat. You thought this was going to be the chapter with the "quick" recipes! While it is true that the absolute quickest breads, start to finish, are straight doughs (see Daniel Leader's 4-Hour Baguette, page 110), it is also true that to bring out the best in a straight dough it is often necessary to start many hours in advance of when you plan on eating. You may feel that you don't have time for home bread baking if it's going to take that long. But what you have to remember is that you will not be working actively on your bread for most of the time between start and finish. As Rick Curry so wisely puts it in *The Secrets of Jesuit Breadmaking*, "like other living things, bread dough can in fact be left alone at times to grow on its own. With a little bit of planning, you can run errands, pick up the kids from school, cook dinner, and even get a good night's sleep, all while your dough is getting closer and closer to becoming a delicious bread."

The Recipes

The recipes that follow showcase some of the ingredients and techniques that produce excellent straight dough breads. As with all bread recipes, it's the little things that sometimes make the biggest difference in quality. Daniel Leader's 4-Hour Baguette (page 110) uses a lot of water and a small amount of yeast for a moist and flavorful bread. The seeds in the Rustic Flax Seed Rolls (page 114) add incredible moisture and luxurious flavor. Cheddar Cheese Boule (page 119) dough is retarded overnight in the refrigerator for flavor; abundant cheddar cheese doesn't hurt either!

The Peggy Tub Method for Slow Fermentation

In *The Bread Book,* author and cooking teacher Betsy Oppenneer describes an old-fashioned way to keep dough cool in order to prolong fermentation time, named after a large washbasin called a "peggy tub." This method instructs the baker to add ½ cup of extra flour to the dough to make it very stiff, and then to wrap the dough loosely in a large, tightly woven kitchen towel. The baker then fills the peggy tub (or a kitchen sink or other large tub) with cool water and submerges the wrapped dough in the water, making sure the edges of the towel are facing up so that the dough doesn't slip out of its wrapping. It will sink to the bottom, but eventually the dough will float to the top as it inflates. Once it floats to the top, it's taken on the extra moisture it needs and is ready to shape. Or you can leave it in the water for up to 12 hours before shaping.

I don't know if I would try this myself, but it just goes to show you how many ways there are to skin a cat.

Daniel Leader's 4-Hour Baguette

Makes 2 (14-inch) loaves

Daniel Leader's version of the classic Parisian bread is about as simple as a bread recipe can be while still delivering a satisfying handmade bread. The secrets: Adding just a small amount of yeast and making sure the dough isn't too warm after kneading (use cool room temperature water, about 70°F) ensures a slow fermentation for good flavor. A relatively high ratio of water to flour keeps the bread moist. Giving the dough a turn midway through fermentation will help develop the gluten in this relatively wet dough.

8 ounces (1 cup) cool room temperature water (about 70°F or even cooler if your room is warm)

0.08 ounce/2 grams (¾ teaspoon) instant yeast

11.7 ounces/332 grams (2 cups plus 2 tablespoons) unbleached all-purpose flour

0.1 ounce/3 grams (¾ teaspoon) kosher salt or fine sea salt

1. Combine the water, yeast, flour, and salt in the bowl of a stand mixer or in a large mixing bowl. Stir with a rubber spatula until a rough dough forms.

2. Knead the dough. By machine: With a dough hook, knead the dough on medium-low speed until it just clears the sides of the bowl and is still a little lumpy, 10 to 12 minutes. By hand: With floured hands, knead until the dough comes together in a coherent but not quite smooth mass, using a bench scraper to scrape it up from the counter if it sticks, about 15 minutes.

3. Spray the inside of a dough-rising container or large mixing bowl with nonstick cooking spray and place the dough inside. Cover with plastic wrap and let rise until the dough is puffy and you can see some bubbles under the surface (it won't double in size because of the small amount of yeast), about 45 minutes.

4. Give the dough a turn: Slide your hands underneath the dough and pick it up from underneath, so that it droops over your hands. Then set it down again, on one of its drooping sides, back in the bowl. Cover the bowl with plastic wrap and let the dough rise until it has increased in volume by about 50 percent, 45 minutes to 1 hour.

5. One hour before baking, place a baking stone in the middle rack of the oven and a cast-iron skillet on the lower rack. Preheat the oven to 450°F.

6. Turn the dough out onto a countertop lightly dusted with flour. Use a bench scraper or sharp chef's knife to divide the dough into 2 equal pieces. Gently shape each piece into a rough rectangle and fold each rectangle in half. Let the dough pieces rest for 10 minutes.

7. Shape each piece into a 14-inch-long baguette (see page 89). Transfer them, seam sides down, to a parchment-covered baker's peel or rimless baking sheet, positioning them so they're about 3 inches apart on the paper. Pleat the paper in between the loaves to draw them together. Place a rolled-up kitchen towel underneath the paper on the outer side of each loaf to support them and help them keep their shape as they proof. Sprinkle the baguettes with flour and drape with plastic wrap. Let stand until puffy and almost doubled in size, 30 minutes to 1 hour.

8. Uncover the loaves, remove the towels, and pull the paper so it lies flat and the loaves are separated. Use a razor blade, lame, or sharp chef's knife to make three 3-inch-long diagonal cuts on each loaf.

9. Slide the loaves, still on the parchment, onto the preheated baking stone. Drop ½ cup ice cubes into the cast-iron skillet. Bake until the baguettes are golden and an instant-read thermometer inserted into the center reads 205°F, 20 to 25 minutes.

10. Slide the loaves, still on the parchment, onto a wire rack. Let cool for 5 minutes, peel from the parchment, and then let cool to warm room temperature, another 10 minutes or so. Serve warm.

Pan Pizza with Tomatoes, Mozzarella, and Sausage

Serves 2 to 3

A few changes in the handling of 4-Hour Baguette dough will give you a moist, chewy, puffy 4-hour pizza crust, perfect for handling heavier toppings (for a superb thin-crust pizza recipe, see page 193). Kneading the dough in the food processor, with a brief autolyse, develops its gluten quickly and efficiently. Letting it rise voluminously allows many large air cells to be created. Baking it shortly after bulk fermentation, with no proofing period, preserves its status as a flatbread, albeit a deliciously bubbly one.

FOR THE DOUGH

8	ounces (1 cup) cool room temperature water (about 70°F or even cooler if your room is warm)
0.08	ounce/2 grams (¾ teaspoon) instant yeast
11.7	ounces/332 grams (2 cups plus 2 tablespoons) unbleached all-purpose flour
0.1	ounce/3 grams (¾ teaspoon) kosher salt or fine sea salt

FOR THE TOPPING

1	(14.5-ounce) can diced tomatoes, drained
½	pound Italian sausage, removed from its casings, broken up, and cooked thoroughly in a skillet
8	ounces fresh mozzarella cheese, shredded and pressed between paper towels to remove excess moisture
2	tablespoons grated Parmesan cheese
2	tablespoons finely chopped fresh basil
1–2	tablespoons extra-virgin olive oil
	Sea salt and freshly ground black pepper

1. Make the dough: Combine the water, yeast, flour, and salt in the work bowl of a food processor and pulse several times to form a rough dough. Let the dough stand for 10 minutes in the bowl, and then process until it is smooth and elastic, 30 to 45 seconds.

2. Spray the inside of a dough-rising container or large mixing bowl with nonstick cooking spray and place the dough inside. Cover with plastic wrap and let rise voluminously (the dough will triple or quadruple in size), 3 to 4 hours.

3. One hour before baking, place a baking stone in the middle rack of the oven. Preheat the oven to 500°F.

4. Spray a 13½-inch round pizza pan with nonstick cooking spray. Press the dough into the pan, all the way to the edges. If it resists or springs back, let it stand for 5 minutes and press again. Scatter the drained tomatoes over the dough, and then sprinkle with the sausage and mozzarella cheese.

5. Put the pan onto the preheated baking stone. Bake until the edges of the dough are deep golden and the cheese is bubbling, 15 to 18 minutes.

6. Slide the pizza onto a cutting board. Sprinkle with the Parmesan and basil. Drizzle with olive oil. Season with salt and pepper. Let stand for 5 minutes, slice into wedges with a pizza cutter, and serve.

Rustic Flax Seed Rolls

Makes 12 rolls

Flax seeds, soaked for a few hours, absorb a tremendous amount of water. Kneaded into baguette dough, they provide incredible moisture as well as flavor and a little bit of crunch. These rolls are made with a little rye flour, which gives them a wonderful fragrance and flavor. The rye is lower in gluten than wheat flour, so the rolls are very gently divided into rectangles but not really shaped, since too much handling might damage their more fragile gluten structure. Alternatively, you could replace the rye flour with an equal amount of whole-wheat or white flour and shape the rolls into rounds.

⅓ cup flax seeds
10 ounces (1¼ cups) cool room temperature water (about 70°F or even cooler if your room is warm)
0.08 ounce/2 grams (¾ teaspoon) instant yeast
8 ounces/227 grams (1¾ cups) unbleached all-purpose flour
3 ounces/85 grams (½ cup plus 2 tablespoons) whole-wheat flour
1 ounce/28 grams (3½ tablespoons) rye flour
0.1 ounce/3 grams (¾ teaspoon) kosher salt or fine sea salt

1. Combine the flax seeds and 4 ounces of the water in a small bowl. Cover with plastic wrap and let stand overnight. The seeds will have absorbed all of the water and formed a jellylike mass.

2. Combine the remaining 6 ounces water, the yeast, all-purpose flour, whole-wheat flour, rye flour, salt, and flax seed mixture in the bowl of a stand mixer or in a large mixing bowl. Stir with a rubber spatula until a rough dough forms.

3. Knead the dough. By machine: With a dough hook, knead the dough on medium-low speed until it just clears the sides of the bowl and is still a little lumpy, 7 to 10 minutes. By hand: Turn the dough out onto a lightly floured countertop and, with floured hands, use gentle but firm strokes to knead it until it is a lumpy but coherent mass, 12 to 14 minutes.

4. Spray the inside of a dough-rising container or large mixing bowl with nonstick cooking spray and place the dough inside. Cover with plastic wrap and let rise until the dough is puffy and you can see some bubbles under the surface (it won't double in size because of the small amount of yeast), 45 minutes to 1 hour.

5. Give the dough a turn: Slide your hands underneath the dough and pick it up from underneath, so that it droops over your hands. Then set it down again, on one of its drooping sides, back in the bowl. Cover the bowl with plastic wrap and let it rise until it has increased in volume by about 50 percent, 45 minutes to 1 hour.

6. One hour before baking, place a baking stone in the middle rack of the oven and a cast-iron skillet on the lower rack. Preheat the oven to 450°F.

7. Turn the dough onto a countertop lightly dusted with flour. Gently shape it into an 8-inch square. Cut the square into two 4- by 8-inch rectangles. Cut each rectangle into 4 smaller rectangles.

8. Transfer the rolls to a parchment-covered baker's peel or rimless baking sheet, positioning them so they're at about 3 inches apart on the paper. Sprinkle the rolls with flour and drape with plastic wrap. Let stand until puffy and almost doubled in size, 30 minutes to 1 hour.

9. Uncover the rolls. Use a razor blade, lame, or sharp serrated knife to slash each roll diagonally across the top. Slide them, still on the parchment, onto the preheated baking stone. Drop ½ cup ice cubes into the cast-iron skillet. Bake until the rolls are golden and an instant-read thermometer inserted into the center reads 205°F, 10 to 15 minutes.

10. Slide the rolls, still on the parchment, onto a wire rack. Let cool for 5 minutes, peel from the parchment, and then let cool to warm room temperature, another 10 minutes or so. Serve warm or at room temperature.

Challah

Makes 1 large braided loaf

It may seem strange to use strong bread flour in a bread as tender as challah, but remember that the eggs and oil have a weakening effect on gluten, so bread flour is needed to give this bread its characteristic height and airiness. Retarding not only helps to strengthen gluten and develop the dough's flavor, but it also makes braiding a breeze, since stiff, chilled dough is much easier to work with than soft, room temperature dough. Shape the bread straight from the refrigerator and then let it come back to room temperature and proof for a nice long time before baking. Some bakers glaze their loaf before it proofs, since the dough is less delicate at that stage. But I prefer to glaze it right before baking, being careful not to deflate it, since the drying glaze can inhibit the dough's rise if applied earlier.

4 large eggs
8 ounces (1 cup) room temperature water (75°F)
0.1 ounce/3 grams (1 teaspoon) instant yeast
16 ounces/454 grams (3½ cups) unbleached bread flour
1 ounce/28 grams (2 tablespoons) sugar
0.17 ounce/5 grams (1 teaspoon) kosher salt or fine sea salt
2 tablespoons vegetable oil

1. Separate 2 of the eggs. Place the whites in a small bowl, cover, and refrigerate. Combine the yolks, the remaining 2 whole eggs, water, yeast, bread flour, sugar, salt, and oil in the bowl of a stand mixer or in a large mixing bowl. Stir with a rubber spatula until a rough dough forms.

2. Knead the dough. By machine: With a dough hook, knead the dough on medium-low speed until it just clears the sides of the bowl and is still a little lumpy, 6 to 8 minutes. By hand: Turn the dough out onto a lightly floured countertop. Lightly flour your hands (or coat them with a thin layer of vegetable oil) and use even strokes to knead the dough into a coherent but still slightly lumpy mass, about 10 minutes.

3. Spray the inside of a dough-rising container or large mixing bowl with nonstick cooking spray and place the dough inside. Cover with plastic wrap and refrigerate overnight, 8 to 12 hours.

4. On a lightly floured countertop, divide the dough into 3 equal pieces. Gently round each piece (see page 88), drape with plastic, and let stand for 10 minutes to relax.

5. Roll each piece of dough into a tapered 10-inch-long strand. Transfer the strands to a parchment-lined baker's peel or rimless baking sheet and then braid them together (see page 118). Drape with plastic wrap. Let stand until doubled in size, 2 to 3 hours.

6. One hour before baking, place a baking stone in the middle rack of the oven. Preheat the oven to 375°F.

7. Uncover the loaf. Whisk the reserved egg whites and brush them over the loaf. Slide it, still on the parchment, onto the preheated baking stone. Bake without steam until it is a deep golden brown and an instant-read thermometer inserted into the center reads 190°F, 30 to 40 minutes.

8. Slide the loaf, still on the parchment, onto a wire rack. Let cool for 5 minutes, peel from the parchment, and then let cool completely before slicing and serving.

Braiding Dough

This simple method for braiding challah bread can be used with other doughs, such as Brioche. Before you begin, here are a few tips:

- It's important to roll your dough pieces into strands that are equal in both width and length, so that your bread bakes evenly. Use a scale to weigh your pieces before beginning.

- Dust your hands lightly with flour before rolling, and also lightly dust the countertop, so that each strand is lightly coated with flour. This will keep the dough strands separate as the bread bakes, resulting in a beautifully defined shape. Without a light flour coating, the strands might bake into each other, producing a lumpy-looking, rather than a braided, loaf. If your strands don't look well dusted, lightly roll them in a little flour before braiding (but don't overdo it — too much flour will stick together in clumps when you apply the egg wash).

- Begin braiding in the middle, rather than at one end. This will result in the most even-looking braid.

HERE'S HOW TO DO IT:

1. Working with one piece of dough at a time, place your hands together, palms down, over a round and roll the round back and forth as you spread your hands apart, to elongate it. Repeat this motion four or five times until the strand is the desired length.

2. Taper the ends of each strand by applying gentle pressure to them as you roll. The tapered strands will produce a beautifully tapered loaf.

3. Place the 3 pieces side by side on a parchment-lined baker's peel or rimless baking sheet. Weave the strands into a tight braid, working from the middle to one end, and then from the middle to the other end. Gently pull and stretch the strands as you go, so that your finished braid will be an inch or two longer than the strands you started with.

4. Moisten the ends of the strands with a little water, pinch them together, and tuck the pinched ends under.

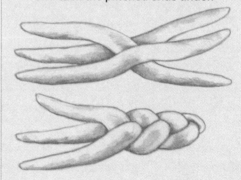

Braiding dough

Cheddar Cheese Boule

Makes 1 (10-inch) round

This rustic round, studded with pieces of melting cheddar cheese, uses several techniques for getting the most out of a straight dough. The mere addition of cheese to the dough boosts the bread's flavor, as does a little bit of whole-wheat flour. I also add some cumin seeds, although they're optional. The dough is retarded in the refrigerator for 18 to 24 hours, giving it plenty of time to develop gluten and flavor. In the summer, when your kitchen may be warm, your refrigerated dough may take as little as 2 hours to begin to rise after you take it out of the fridge, but it may take twice as long in the winter. Budget your time with consideration of room temperature.

12 ounces (1½ cups) room temperature water (75°F)
0.05 ounce/1.5 grams (½ teaspoon) instant yeast
1.1 ounces/31 grams (¼ cup) whole-wheat flour
15.6 ounces/442 grams (3 cups) unbleached all-purpose flour
0.25 ounce/7 grams (1½ teaspoons) kosher salt or fine sea salt
4 ounces cheddar cheese, cut into ¼-inch cubes
1 teaspoon cumin seeds (optional)

1. Combine the water, yeast, whole-wheat flour, all-purpose flour, and salt in the bowl of a stand mixer or in a large mixing bowl. Stir with a rubber spatula until a rough dough forms.

2. Knead the dough. By machine: With a dough hook, knead the dough on medium-low speed until it just clears the sides of the bowl and is still a little lumpy, 10 to 12 minutes. Add the cheese and cumin seeds and knead until well incorporated, 1 to 2 minutes longer. By hand: Turn the dough out onto a lightly floured countertop. Use floured hands and firm strokes to knead it, scraping it from the counter with a bench scraper as necessary, until it is an almost smooth mass. Add the cheese and cumin and continue to knead until they are incorporated, 1 to 2 minutes longer.

3. Spray the inside of a dough-rising container or large mixing bowl with nonstick cooking spray and place the dough inside. Cover with plastic wrap and refrigerate for at least 12 and up to 24 hours.

4. Remove the dough from the refrigerator and let come to room temperature (70°F), 2 to 4 hours.

5. Give the dough a turn: Slide your hands underneath the dough and pick it up from underneath, so that it droops over your hands. Then set it down again, on one of its drooping sides, back in the bowl. Cover the bowl with plastic wrap and let it rise until it has increased in volume by about 50 percent, 45 minutes to 1 hour.

6. One hour before baking, place a baking stone in the middle rack of the oven and a cast-iron skillet on the lower rack. Preheat the oven to 450°F.

7. Turn the dough out onto a countertop lightly dusted with flour. Gently shape it into a rough round (see page 88). Let the dough round rest for 10 minutes.

8. Shape the dough into a tight ball (see shaping rounds, page 88). Line an 8-inch round bowl with a clean kitchen towel and sprinkle the towel with flour or use a banneton if you have one. Place the loaf in the bowl, smooth side down. Lightly drape the bowl with plastic wrap. Let stand until increased in volume by about 1½ times, 45 minutes to 1 hour.

9. Uncover the loaf, place a parchment-lined baker's peel or rimless baking sheet on top of the bowl, and invert the loaf onto the peel. Use a razor blade, lame, or sharp chef's knife to score the loaf, making two 4-inch cuts in an X shape on top.

10. Slide the loaf, still on the parchment, onto the preheated baking stone. Drop ½ cup ice cubes into the cast-iron skillet. Bake until the loaf is deep golden and an instant-read thermometer inserted into the center reads 205°F, 35 to 40 minutes.

11. Slide the loaf, still on the parchment, onto a wire rack. Let cool for 5 minutes, peel from the parchment, and then let cool to warm room temperature, about 2 hours, before slicing and serving.

Cheddar Cheese Boule Variations

It is easy to vary the Cheddar Cheese Boule to create a menu of rustic breads. Just leave out the cheese and cumin seeds, and add flavoring ingredients of your choice during the last 2 minutes of kneading. Here are some suggestions.

Black Olive Boule: 1 cup pitted, chopped black olives and 2 tablespoons finely chopped fresh thyme

Green Olive Boule: 1 cup pitted, chopped green olives and 1 tablespoon finely chopped marjoram

Bacon and Blue Cheese Boule: 10 ounces thick-cut bacon, cut into ½-inch pieces, cooked until not quite crisp, and drained, plus 4 ounces crumbled blue cheese

Fig and Fennel Boule: 1 cup stemmed and chopped dried figs and 1 tablespoon toasted fennel seeds

Apricot and Pecan Boule: 1 cup chopped dried apricots and 1 cup lightly toasted, cooled, and chopped pecans

Cherry and Walnut Boule: 1 cup chopped dried cherries and 1 cup lightly toasted, cooled, and chopped walnuts

Six Flavorful Straight Dough Recipes

If you'd like to explore this mixing method further, consider these other straight dough recipes. They use some of the flavor-enhancing ingredients and texture-enhancing techniques discussed in this chapter to great effect.

Ricotta Loaves (page 35): Full-fat ricotta cheese lends moisture and flavor to these simple loaves.

Rosemary Focaccia (page 44): This bread has a secret ingredient: a mashed potato. The added starch gives the flatbread great tenderness.

No-Knead Raisin-Walnut Bread (page 76): A tiny amount of yeast and an extra-long rise contribute to this crusty loaf's exceptional character.

Overnight English Muffins (page 200): Not only does overnight fermentation in the refrigerator make sense for a breakfast bread, but it also gives homemade English muffins a wonderfully tangy flavor.

Pita Bread (page 195): Brushing the breads with water before baking and taking care not to overbake them are two secrets to making exceptional pita breads.

Spinach and Feta Gözleme (page 207): A very wet dough gives Turkish filled flatbreads a moist and springy texture.

Straight Doughs
Questions and Answers

Q **I thought kneaded dough was supposed to be smooth and bouncy, but in most of these straight dough recipes you say they should look a little lumpy at the end of the kneading period. Why is that?**

A In general, straight doughs have a more delicate gluten structure than doughs that gain initial strength from a pre-ferment or sourdough starter. If these relatively weak doughs are kneaded too vigorously or for too long, the effect can be to destroy the gluten rather than to build it up. For the lightest breads, I'd rather build up a moderate amount of gluten during kneading, and then strengthen the dough through other techniques, such as folding or retarding.

Q **Help! I divided my baguette dough in half, and I can tell just by looking that one of the pieces is at least 30 percent heavier than the other. What should I do?**

A Throw the pieces on the scale to determine the difference. Then cut a piece from the larger one and gently press it into the smaller one. Don't bother to weigh them again. Small differences won't matter too much in baking times, and you don't want one of your baguettes to be made up of more than two pieces, or else there's a risk that the dough won't come together smoothly into the shape you want.

Q **Is it okay to bake my baguettes in perforated French bread pans instead of forming a couche with parchment paper as the recipe directs?**

A Using these perforated pans prevents the inexperienced baker from overhandling the dough during shaping, and the pans help give the breads beautifully rounded edges. So if you tend to damage the dough while attempting to torture it into the perfect shape, you might consider using a perforated French bread pan to protect your breads from their maker. But if you are interested in getting the greatest oven spring and the crispest crust, the parchment paper couche is the way to go. Unlike breads baked in a pan, which won't fully benefit from a superheated baking stone's intense heat, doughs proofed in a couche can be transferred directly to the stone for baking, where they will rise higher and get darker than breads baked in pans.

Q **The crust of my baguettes is chewy and delicious, but it's not shiny and dark golden like the baguettes I see at my bakery. Am I doing something wrong?**

A Steam facilitates the gelatinization of starches on the surface of bread as it bakes, making the crust shiny. If you don't provide sufficient steam, you won't get that shine. Adding ice cubes to a preheated cast-iron skillet should be sufficient to achieve a shiny crust. But it's possible that the steam you create is leaving your oven (some ovens are not as well sealed and insulated as others) before it can do its job. If you suspect that this is the case, try placing an aluminum baking pan (big enough so that it doesn't touch them) over the breads for the first 10 minutes of baking, so that the steam escaping from the dough itself will circulate around the breads. Remove it and continue to bake the breads until they are done.

Q **Can I use my baguette dough to make ficelles?**

A Absolutely. A *ficelle* is generally the same length as a baguette, but half the thickness. This thin bread makes an elegant sandwich when sliced in half and filled with some French cheese, a little ham, and maybe some baby salad greens dressed with a mustard vinaigrette. To make ficelles, divide your dough into 4 equal pieces instead of 2 and shape as directed. Take care to be gentle with the dough, in order not to burst too many of its air cells, since you'll have to roll out your dough pieces so much thinner to reach 14 inches than when shaping baguettes. And, of course, bake them for a shorter period. They should be fully baked after 15 to 18 minutes.

Q **My flax seed rolls didn't rise as high in the oven as my plain white baguettes. What can I do next time to give them a boost?**

A Seeds, including flax, can tear delicate gluten strands and puncture developing air cells. Make sure to knead your dough gently, on medium-low speed. And you can try kneading it a few minutes longer than is recommended in the recipe, to develop extra gluten in compensation for any torn strands.

Q I wanted to substitute sesame seeds for the flax seeds in a recipe, but after soaking they didn't seem to absorb water the same way that the flax seeds did. Do different seeds get a different treatment?

A While sesame, pumpkin, and sunflower seeds will all soften when soaked in water, flax seeds will swell like sponges. Definitely soak your seeds before adding them to your dough (otherwise they will absorb water from the dough during baking, leaving your bread dry). Drain off the excess liquid before using them. And to compensate for the fact that these seeds won't contain the same amount of water as soaked flax seeds, add 8 ounces of water to the dough in step 2 instead of the 6 ounces called for in the recipe.

Q I see that in the Cheddar Cheese Boule recipe the loaf is shaped in a banneton. Why can't you just shape it into a round and proof it on a parchment-lined baking sheet, like some other round breads in this book?

A You could do this, sprinkling the dough with flour and draping it with plastic wrap, but because the dough is rather soft and wet (which is one of the reasons that it will have a beautiful interior when baked), it will tend to spread out, rather than rise, during proofing. Placing it in a banneton, in this case a bowl lined with a floured kitchen towel, will help it keep its shape during proofing.

Q I've noticed that in other recipes for enriched doughs, the dough is fully kneaded before the fat is added. Why isn't this the case with the challah recipe in this book?

A A small amount of fat can increase the volume of your bread by lubricating the gluten, which allows it to stretch further. But in larger quantities, fat molecules coat the proteins in flour before they can bond together into a gluten web. The higher the proportion of fat in the dough, the longer it will take that dough to develop sufficient gluten for a good rise. The recipe here contains a small amount that won't hamper gluten development. But if the recipe you're working with contains as much butter as Brioche (page 250), then it's better to wait until you've developed the dough's gluten before adding the fat.

Q Would it be okay to substitute butter for the vegetable oil in challah, or is there a scientific reason for your choice in fats?

A Either type of fat will work in this dough. It is a matter of taste, or, if you are keeping kosher, a matter of what you will be serving along with your challah. Most kosher bakeries bake challah with vegetable oil so that it can be served with meat, but you can certainly bake a challah with melted and cooled butter for a dairy meal or to suit your preference.

Q **I've seen challah breads shaped in a snail or spiral shape for Rosh Hashanah. How is this done?**

A Challah is most often braided, but in some fancier bakeries you can see special shapes: a fish, a menorah, a dreidel, the Hebrew letter *shin* (which stands for "Almighty"). The spiral, symbolizing the circle of life, is one of the easier shapes to form. To make a spiral-shaped challah, line a baking sheet with parchment paper. Flour a work surface and roll your dough into a long strand. Transfer it to the baking sheet, placing one end in the center. Wind the dough strand around the center, as tightly as you can. Pull on the remaining end as you tuck it under the dough, creating tension that will put pressure on the center of the dough, causing it to rise higher than the perimeter.

Chapter 5
Baking with Yeasted Pre-ferments

BREAD EXPERTS AND ARTISAN BAKERS argue over the details of bread baking, but there is unanimous agreement among them about one thing: The longer a dough is allowed to ferment, the better. The ultimate method for extending fermentation is to cultivate a wild yeast starter and use it to raise your bread. While not difficult, this is a technique that involves a certain level of commitment, not to mention at least a week of feeding and caring for a sourdough culture before attempting to bake.

There are other, easier ways to extend fermentation. The simplest, because it requires the fewest steps, is the "no-knead" method (see page 76 for a recipe and more details). To make no-knead bread, you simply stir together your ingredients and let them sit at room temperature for 12 to 24 hours, allowing the tiny amount of yeast you've added to slowly multiply, producing gases that raise the dough as the proteins in the flour organize themselves into a strong web. A good rise and strong structure are guaranteed. As fermentation slowly proceeds, flavorful acids are produced by friendly bacteria in the dough, giving your bread great flavor and extending its shelf life. A similar result can be had by mixing and kneading a straight dough and letting the dough ferment or proof in the refrigerator long enough (for at least 8 and up to 12 hours) to produce those acids. Retarding your dough this way (see page 85 for more details on this technique) strengthens the gluten that you've already developed during kneading while slowing down yeast activity long enough to allow flavor-enhancing acid buildup without compromising the health of the yeast.

Both of these one-step methods are easy to follow, to be sure, but it is not always convenient to mix an entire batch of dough so many hours or even a full day in advance of shaping, proofing, and baking. To reduce your overall production time as well as coax the most flavor from your flour, try a pre-ferment.

Pre-ferments made with packaged yeast are a great compromise between straight dough and sourdough baking. By taking a portion of your dough ingredients, quickly mixing them together, and letting this small batch of rough dough ferment for a length of time (typically somewhere between 6 and 18 hours), you significantly reduce the production time of the bread itself while ripening the dough deliciously. Adding a ripened pre-ferment to your dough will give it the benefits of a slow rise in several hours rather than a half or whole day.

The Payoffs of a Pre-ferment

Aside from reducing bulk fermentation time, there are numerous benefits to using a pre-ferment. Here are some of them.

Reduced risk of overfermenting your dough. Although no-knead and straight dough recipes include safeguards against this, it is more likely that you will overferment one of these doughs than you will a dough made with a pre-ferment. In the case of no-knead breads, even though a tiny amount of yeast is used, the bread stands at room temperature for such an extended period that yeast can easily multiply out of control rather quickly at the end of the fermentation period. In the case of straight doughs, a relatively large quantity of yeast added to the dough can proliferate out of control if the weather or water is a bit warmer than usual or your yeast is unusually lively. Dough made with a pre-ferment is insurance against any of these things happening before you can shape your loaves and get them into the oven.

Gluten enhancement. The gluten present in a ripened pre-ferment gives bread dough a head start in becoming strong and extensible. Not only that, but the additional acids that a pre-ferment contributes to bread dough have a strengthening effect on the total gluten in the dough. The result is a higher-rising bread than one made without a pre-ferment.

Flavor enhancement. Using a pre-ferment allows the baker to add layers of flavor to a bread. First, there is the enhanced flavor of the wheat itself, nuttiness of which emerges during the course of extended fermentation. The acids that are a by-product of fermentation add their milky-verging-on-tangy taste to the mix. In addition to acids, organic compounds called esters (see box) are produced as a pre-ferment ripens. These compounds, similar to those that give fruits such as pears and apples their aroma, give bread mixed in two stages a complexity that is often lacking in one-stage breads.

Caramelized, crackling crust. Especially during the long fermentation of stiff dough pre-ferments, bacteria and enzymes have plenty of time to

What's That Wonderful Smell?

Although it is undoubtedly a pleasure to eat home-baked bread, it is also a pleasure to inhale its aroma. As when consuming other fermented foods such as wine and cheese, you can enhance your enjoyment by taking a moment before you eat it to enjoy your bread's wonderfully complex smell.

The ingredients themselves contribute wheaty and yeasty notes to this perfume, but a particular chemical reaction during a long fermentation period provides a significant portion of the enticing aroma generated when dough is baked. When the acids produced by lactobacilli come in contact with the alcohol that is a by-product of yeast, they form nonliving organic substances called esters. Just as a wine's fragrance can be described as containing hints of black pepper, apple, or vanilla, a bread's fragrance can be described in similar terms. In fact, food scientists studying pre-ferments have detected at least 45 different esters, each one giving off its own unique aroma and contributing to an extremely complex and delicious end product. So if you find yourself sniffing your baguette and rapturously describing it as milky with notes of honey, walnuts, and herbs, you are only appreciating what your pre-ferment has bestowed upon it in its production of esters.

break down flour's starches into simple sugars. A dough with more sugar will produce a more caramelized crust.

Extension of shelf life. While straight doughs that are mixed, fermented, proofed, and baked all in less than 4 hours are best eaten on the day they are baked, breads employing pre-ferments will stay fresh for at least twice as long. This is because the acids produced while the pre-ferment develops have a preservative effect on bread.

General Tips for Using a Pre-ferment

Yeasted pre-ferments have been around for almost as long as baker's yeast, which became widely available at the turn of the twentieth century. While professional bakers in France appreciated commercial yeast's quickness and reliability, they were unimpressed with the flat and uninteresting bread that resulted from mixing dough directly using it. Because French bakers had traditionally baked two-stage breads using a sourdough starter, it wasn't a great leap for many of them to figure out how to build a starter with commercial yeast before adding it to bread dough. For more than 100 years, baking with a yeasted pre-ferment has been standard practice in traditional French bakeries.

Of course, the French weren't the only ones to catch on to the idea that a two-stage dough raised with commercial yeast produced better bread than a straight dough. Italian, German, and eastern European bakers all developed their own pre-ferment recipes to use with traditional breads, recipes that are still used in bakeries across Europe. Although these recipes vary from region to region, drawing on cultural traditions more than on logic or science, they are in the end very similar in the way they're mixed and fermented. To use one successfully, keep in mind the following guidelines.

Skip the salt. With the notable exception of *pâte fermentée* (see page 133), pre-ferments are salt-free.

Salt is a necessary ingredient in bread dough because it inhibits fermentation. If this seems counterintuitive, remember that the idea when fermenting dough is to control its rise. If yeast is allowed to multiply too quickly, it will exhaust the food supply and ultimately become too weakened to raise bread. With a pre-ferment, in contrast, the idea isn't necessarily to grow the most powerful yeast, but to develop the flour's flavor and encourage the production of acids. A well-fermented starter, one that has sat at room temperature for several hours or more, instantly "ages" the dough, a desirable result with many advantages and none of the risks of letting the dough itself ferment for such a long period.

Most recipes for doughs made with pre-ferments don't rely solely on the starter's yeast, and they call for yeast in the second stage of mixing as well as the first, just in case the yeast in the pre-ferment isn't powerful enough to raise the bread.

Mix, don't knead. One of the beautiful things about using a pre-ferment is how easy it is to make. Just mix together your ingredients, cover, and let stand. Even stiff pre-ferments such as pâte fermentée and biga don't require kneading. Just mix them until a rough dough forms, pressing any loose bits of dough into the larger mass with the side of the spatula. Gluten development through kneading isn't the goal here (although significant gluten development will take place during fermentation). The production of acids is the goal. And to encourage this, all the baker must do is hydrate the flour and yeast with water to get things going.

Ripeness is everything. Just as when you pick a tomato or uncork a bottle of aged wine, you want your dough to be at the peak of ripeness when you add your pre-ferment. A ripe pre-ferment will contain just the right combination of gluten, yeast, and acids to improve bread dough in the second stage of mixing. Different pre-ferments will look and smell different when ripe. In general, "wet" pre-ferments, including sponge and poolish, ripen quickly, while "stiff" pre-ferments such as pâte fermentée and biga will take longer. Learn the signs (see pages 131–135 and your bread will thank you.

Portioning out your pre-ferment. Typically, French bakers use just a small percentage of pre-ferment, 30 percent to no more than 50 percent of the total dough, while Italian bakers sometimes make bread dough that consists of up to 90 percent pre-ferment. How much pre-ferment you add to your dough depends not only on tradition and cultural orientation but also on the pre-ferment's stability and ability to raise bread dough. A smaller portion of a less stable wet pre-ferment is added to dough to grant it the benefits of long fermentation (flavor, enhanced gluten development) without compromising its rise. A larger portion of a longer-keeping and more stable stiff pre-ferment can be added, not only to lend flavor and jump-start gluten development but also because its yeast can still be depended upon to raise dough.

Keep an eye on fermentation. In general, bulk fermentation and proofing will take less time with a pre-ferment than they would without. So keep an eye on your dough and take care that it doesn't overferment during these stages.

A Menu of Pre-ferments

Pre-ferments are often described as either "wet" or "stiff." Loose, even soupy, mixtures that contain relatively more water ferment more quickly and will be ready to use sooner than stiff, claylike starters, which offer resistance to fermentation.

Here are the most common types, along with descriptions of their origins, characteristics, and basic formulas. But keep in mind that pre-ferments are infinitely variable and are often revised to fit a baker's schedule, the type of bread he or she is baking, and his or her personal tastes. They're also more similar to each other than different, so that one baker's sponge may be another's poolish, and another's poolish might resemble his neighbor's biga.

Sponge. If you are an American baker of a certain age, the sponge is the pre-ferment you're probably most familiar with. Before European artisan breads came into vogue, American home bakers in the know turned to recipes in *The Tassajara Bread Book,* Bernard Clayton's *Complete Book of Breads,* and even *The Joy of Cooking* for longer-fermenting white and whole-wheat breads. A sponge consists of abundant water, a bit of yeast, and a portion of the flour required for a whole loaf. A fully ripened sponge will rise voluminously and become very bubbly before collapsing. Use it soon after its collapse, when it is clear that acid production has weakened the sponge's structure but the yeast is still active.

American-style sponges are typically fermented for a relatively short time of just a few hours, possibly reflecting a national interest in getting things done quickly. But a fermented sponge will keep in the refrigerator for up to 24 hours (beyond that it will lose strength and develop an unpleasantly strong flavor), so if you're not ready to bake when it is ready, just cover it with plastic wrap and chill it until you are ready to bake. You can add it to your bread dough when it is cold, because it will be soft enough to incorporate easily even when cold, but do compensate for the drop in dough temperature by using warmer water for the dough.

The sponge used to make Sunflower Seed Bread (page 136 has equal amounts of flour and water, giving it a batterlike consistency. It adds great moisture as well as flavor to the dough. I use whole-wheat flour in the sponge, since I want my bread to have a healthy percentage of bran. But when I'm making a white bread with a sponge, I'll switch to all-purpose flour for the sponge. The nutrients in whole-wheat flour provide a feast for yeast, so your whole-wheat sponge might ferment even more quickly than one made with all-purpose flour.

Poolish. The name of this wet starter signals its origin as a technique that Polish bakers introduced to Austrian bakers, who in turn brought it to France. Like a sponge, a poolish has a much higher proportion of water to flour than does bread dough itself, allowing yeast to multiply quickly. In fact, many recipes for sponges look exactly like poolish recipes. The difference, generally, is in fermentation time. While American-style sponges are often used within several hours of mixing, many European bakers take their time with a poolish, letting it stand at room temperature for 8 to 12 hours and sometimes longer.

The poolish that I use to make the Cornmeal Baguettes recipe in this book (page 139) is slightly less wet than the sponge for the Sunflower Seed Bread. Less water means a little less yeast activity, good for a starter that has to sit overnight at room temperature for full flavor and gluten development. During its long fermentation, the gluten web becomes well organized but also becomes relaxed, making the poolish extremely stretchy.

You can see this extensibility when you scrape the poolish into the mixing bowl. Pull some poolish with a spoon or spatula and you will be amazed at its stretchiness. The poolish lends its extensibility to the baguette bread dough, which has a relatively low protein level because of the gluten-free cornmeal, to create an exceptionally light and airy bread.

Pâte fermentée. Pâte fermentée translates as "old dough." It is a technique derived from the old baker's practice of saving a piece of today's dough to raise tomorrow's bread. So it's not surprising that this stiff pre-ferment contains the same proportions of flour and water as bread dough itself. Unlike other pre-ferments, it contains salt, in the same proportion as regular bread dough.

Because it contains less water than a sponge, and because it contains salt, pâte fermentée ferments more slowly than a sponge. Even so, care should be taken to keep fermentation under control so that the yeast don't exhaust their food supply and become weakened.

A ripe pâte fermentée

Although using a piece of old dough teeming with yeast to raise bread is similar in concept to using a sourdough culture, there is an important difference. While the yeast level in a sourdough culture can be maintained through regular feedings, the yeast in a piece of pâte fermentée will begin to die off within a day of mixing, just as it does in a sponge or poolish. A ripe pâte fermentée will look like fermented bread dough: doubled in volume and bubbly under the surface, but without the fragile struc-

Pâte fermentée cut into pieces

ture of a wet sponge or poolish. To control the rate of fermentation, let your freshly mixed pâte fermentée stand at room temperature for an hour or so and then refrigerate it until it has doubled in volume, at least 8 and up to 24 hours.

The Intriguing Idea of *altes Brot*

During the course of researching pre-ferments, I came upon several mentions of a German technique called altes Brot. Sometimes it was simply another name for the "old dough" method known in France as pâte fermentée. But more often, it referred to the practice of soaking a crustless slice of stale bread in water overnight, squeezing out the extra water, and adding the moistened bread bits to the dough, sometimes along with a starter and sometimes without. According to George Greenstein, author of *Secrets of a Jewish Baker,* altes Brot or "the altus" is the secret to authentic eastern European rye bread, lending the dough extra rye flavor as well as moisture.

Wet (poolish) and dry (biga) pre-ferments

Most of us don't bake every day, so reserving a piece of old dough for the next time we bake isn't an option. But it is easy enough to make a small piece of pâte fermentée the night before you bake. I've read of bakers who freeze pâte fermentée for up to a week before using it, but the risk of a portion or all of the yeast dying when kept at such a low temperature for an extended period is high and one that I don't recommend, especially when mixing a fresh batch is so easy.

Biga. *Biga* is the Italian term for pre-ferment. Although some Italian bakers use a spongelike biga, much more common is a stiff mixture of flour, water, and yeast, drier even than pâte fermentée or bread dough itself.

The stiffness of the starter discourages quick fermentation. Unlike slow-fermenting pâte fermentée, biga has no gluten-weakening salt. So during its slow fermentation period, biga not only develops the incredible flavor of old dough but also becomes wonderfully strong and elastic. Italian bakers add it to their doughs in incredibly high proportions, sometimes up to 90 percent. Often this is done to balance the softness of low-protein Italian flour, but even if you are baking with American all-purpose flour, using a biga will benefit your bread. The resulting bread has layers of flavor and the ability to stay fresh for several days, much like bread baked with sourdough starter.

A ripe biga will double in volume, just like bread dough. Its exterior will be glossy and smooth, and its interior will be bubbly. A mild acidic aroma will tell you that lactobacilli have produced those flavorful acids.

The Recipes

The following recipes demonstrate how the simple technique of building a dough in two stages instead of one results in superior rise, flavor, and crust development. I've tried to match each pre-ferment with a bread that makes sense according to bread traditions and practices. So for a classic American health loaf I employ a quick-rising sponge, for a baguette redux made with cornmeal I use a poolish, for the soft white French sandwich bread called *pain de mie* I prepare pâte fermentée, and for the bubbly Italian ciabatta I mix a big batch of biga. After you have some experience with each style of pre-ferment, you might find yourself gravitating toward one or another for the convenience it offers or for the family of breads to which it belongs. Or you might find yourself going from one to another depending upon your schedule and your mood when you are getting ready to bake.

Sunflower Seed Bread

Makes 1 (9-inch) loaf

Seeded breads made with whole-wheat flour can be dense and structurally under-developed. Using a pre-ferment is one way to get them to rise a little higher. Using some bread flour also helps, adding more protein to the dough than all-purpose flour would. A lengthy kneading time — up to 15 minutes in the electric mixer — is necessary to develop those proteins into gluten. Don't add the seeds until your dough has reached this stage. If you are kneading by machine, you might find that the seeds just spin around at the bottom of the bowl rather than stick to the dough. If this happens, turn the dough onto a lightly floured countertop and knead them in by hand. To help the seeds adhere to the outside of the bread, lightly mist the dough with water before sprinkling them on.

FOR THE SPONGE:

3 ounces (6 tablespoons) room temperature water (75 to 78°F)

0.05 ounce/1.5 grams (½ teaspoon) instant yeast

3 ounces/85 grams (11 tablespoons) whole-wheat flour

FOR THE DOUGH:

¾ cup plus 2 tablespoons raw unsalted sunflower seeds

6 ounces (¾ cup) room temperature water (75 to 78°F)

0.025 ounce/1 gram (¼ teaspoon) instant yeast

8 ounces/227 grams (1½ cups) unbleached bread flour

2 ounces/57 grams (7 tablespoons) whole-wheat flour

1 ounce/28 grams (2 tablespoons) granulated sugar

0.17 ounce/5 grams (1 teaspoon) kosher salt or fine sea salt

1. Make the sponge: Combine the water, yeast, and whole-wheat flour in a medium bowl and stir to combine. Cover with plastic wrap and let stand at room temperature until it is very bubbly and has a mild acidic aroma (it won't rise much, because it is so loose), 3 to 5 hours.

2. Make the dough: Reserve 2 tablespoons of the sunflower seeds and place the remaining ¾ cup in a skillet over low heat, shaking the pan frequently, until they become fragrant and just begin to color. Set aside to cool completely.

3. Combine the water, yeast, bread flour, whole-wheat flour, sugar, salt, and ripe sponge in the bowl of a stand mixer or a large mixing bowl. Stir with a rubber spatula until a rough dough forms.

4. Knead the dough. By machine: With a dough hook, knead the dough on medium-low speed until it just clears the sides of the bowl, 12 to 15 minutes. It will be smooth and supple and will pass the windowpane test (see page 71). Stir in the toasted sunflower seeds and knead for another 1 to 2 minutes. By hand: Turn the dough out onto a lightly floured countertop. With floured hands, knead it with strong strokes, using a bench scraper to pick it up if it sticks to the countertop, until it is smooth and supple, 7 to 10 minutes. Flatten the bread into a disk and knead in the sunflower seeds until well distributed.

5. Spray the inside of a dough-rising container or large mixing bowl with nonstick cooking spray and place the dough inside. Cover with plastic wrap and let rise until the dough has doubled in volume, 1½ to 2 hours.

6. One hour before baking, place a baking stone on the middle rack of the oven and a cast-iron skillet on the lower rack. Preheat the oven to 450°F. Line a baker's peel or rimless baking sheet with parchment paper.

7. Turn the dough out onto a countertop lightly dusted with flour. Gently shape it into a rough round. Let the dough round rest for 10 minutes.

8. Shape the dough into a tight ball (see shaping rounds, page 88). Transfer to the prepared peel, sprinkle with flour, and drape with plastic wrap. Let stand until increased in volume by about 1½ times, 45 minutes to 1 hour.

9. Uncover the loaf. Use a razor blade, lame, or sharp chef's knife to score the loaf, making three 4-inch parallel cuts on top. Lightly mist or brush the dough with a little water and sprinkle with the untoasted sunflower seeds.

CONTINUED →

10. Slide the loaf, still on the parchment, onto the preheated baking stone. Drop ½ cup ice cubes into the cast-iron pan. Bake until the loaf is deep golden and an instant-read thermometer inserted into the center reads 205°F, 35 to 40 minutes.

11. Slide the loaf, still on the parchment, onto a wire rack. Let cool for 5 minutes, peel from the parchment, and then let cool to warm room temperature, about 2 hours, before slicing and serving.

Turn Any Straight Dough into a Two-Stage Dough

The recipes in this chapter are just a taste of what you can accomplish by building a dough in two stages rather than by mixing it directly. To understand the differences in a rather dramatic way, you might try baking a favorite straight dough recipe, one that you have some experience with, using a pre-ferment instead. Using exactly the same ingredients in exactly the same quantities, you will produce a bread with a distinctly different flavor.

In *The Bread Bible*, Rose Levy Beranbaum gives these instructions: Divide the total amount of flour in your recipe by 2.5 and combine it with all of the water in the recipe and half the yeast. Stir the sponge, cover it with plastic, and let it ferment for 1 hour at room temperature or between 5 and 24 hours in the refrigerator. Then combine your ripe sponge with the remaining flour and salt and knead as directed. Remember that bulk fermentation and proofing times will be shorter when proceeding with your recipe.

Cornmeal Baguettes

Makes 2 loaves

In these baguettes, cornmeal takes the place of some of the flour, giving the loaves great flavor and crunch. The poolish helps immensely in strengthening the dough, which needs all of the extra gluten it can get to make up for the lack of gluten in the cornmeal. Your poolish will age your dough, but still take your time while making these loaves. Bulk fermentation should last at least 2 hours, and proofing at least 1 hour, again to let the flour absorb water and encourage gluten formation. And don't skip the 20-minute resting period between bulk fermentation and proofing, which will make your dough easier to work with and also encourage its rise.

FOR THE POOLISH:

4 ounces (½ cup) room temperature water (75 to 78°F)

0.025 ounce/1 gram (¼ teaspoon) instant yeast

5 ounces/142 grams (1 cup) unbleached all-purpose flour

FOR THE DOUGH:

13 ounces (1½ cups plus 2 tablespoons) room temperature water (75 to 78°F)

0.025 ounce/1 gram (¼ teaspoon) instant yeast

8 ounces/227 grams (1½ cups) unbleached bread flour

3 ounces/85 grams (½ cup) stone-ground cornmeal

0.1 ounce/3 grams (¾ teaspoon) kosher salt or fine sea salt

1. Make the poolish: Combine the water, yeast, and all-purpose flour in a medium bowl and stir to combine. Cover with plastic wrap and let stand at room temperature until it is bubbly, almost tripled in volume, and beginning to collapse in the center, 6 to 10 hours.

2. Make the dough: Combine the water, yeast, bread flour, cornmeal, salt, and ripe poolish in the bowl of a stand mixer or a large mixing bowl. Stir with a rubber spatula until a rough dough forms.

CONTINUED $\rightarrow$

3. Knead the dough. By machine: With a dough hook, knead the dough on medium speed until it just clears the sides of the bowl, 12 to 15 minutes. It will be slightly rough, but strands of gluten will be visible if you pull on it with a spatula. By hand: Turn the dough out onto a lightly floured countertop. With floured hands, knead it until it is a cohesive, if slightly rough, mass, about 15 minutes.

4. Spray the inside of a dough-rising container or large mixing bowl with nonstick cooking spray and place the dough inside. Cover with plastic wrap and let rise until the dough has doubled in volume, 2 to 3 hours.

5. Turn the dough out onto a countertop lightly dusted with flour. Use a bench scraper or sharp chef's knife to divide the dough into 2 equal pieces. Gently shape each piece into a rough rectangle and fold each rectangle in half. Lightly drape with plastic wrap and let the dough pieces rest for 20 minutes.

6. One hour before baking, place a baking stone in the middle rack of the oven and a cast-iron skillet on the lower rack. Preheat the oven to 450°F.

7. Shape each dough piece into a 14-inch-long baguette (see page 89). Transfer them, seam sides down, to a parchment-covered baker's peel or rimless baking sheet, positioning them so they're about 3 inches apart on the paper. Pleat the paper in between the loaves to draw them together. Place a rolled-up kitchen towel underneath the paper on the outer side of each loaf to support them and help them keep their shape as they proof. Sprinkle the baguettes with flour and drape with plastic wrap. Let stand until puffy and almost doubled in size, 1 to 1½ hours.

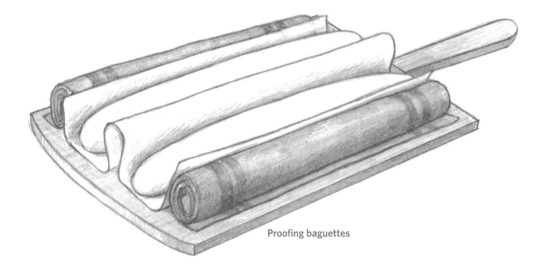

Proofing baguettes

8. Uncover the loaves, remove the towels, and pull the paper so it lies flat and the loaves are separated. Use a razor blade, lame, or sharp chef's knife to make a long diagonal slash down each of the loaves.

9. Slide the loaves, still on the parchment, onto the preheated baking stone. Drop ½ cup ice cubes into the cast-iron pan. Bake until the baguettes are golden and an instant-read thermometer inserted into the center reads 205°F, 20 to 25 minutes.

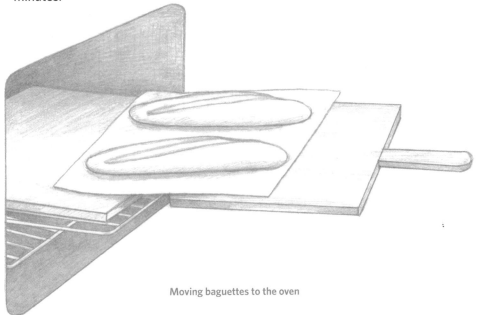

Moving baguettes to the oven

10. Slide the loaves, still on the parchment, onto a wire rack. Let cool for 5 minutes, peel from the parchment, and then let cool to warm room temperature, another 10 minutes or so. Serve warm or let cool to room temperature before serving.

Pain de Mie

Makes 1 (8-inch) loaf

Soft, white sandwich bread made with a traditional French pre-ferment is full of character because it is made with such a large percentage of flavorful "old dough." You might wonder why bread flour is used in both the pre-ferment and the dough, rather than softer all-purpose flour, if the goal is to bake a soft loaf. The full stick of butter in this recipe has a weakening effect on gluten, so to get this bread to rise you need the higher-gluten flour. The pâte fermentée here is more like lean baguette dough (indeed, it has a similar formula) than the enriched pain de mie dough, and it can be used to raise all types of bread, lean and enriched.

FOR THE PÂTE FERMENTÉE:

3 ounces (6 tablespoons) room temperature water (70 to 78°F)

0.05 ounce/1.5 grams (½ teaspoon) instant yeast

4 ounces/113 grams (¾ cup) unbleached all-purpose flour

0.08 ounce/2 grams (½ teaspoon) fine sea salt or kosher salt

FOR THE DOUGH:

10 ounces/283 grams (2 cups) unbleached bread flour

0.25 ounce/7 grams (1½ tablespoons) fine sea salt or kosher salt

0.75 ounce/21 grams (1½ tablespoons) sugar

0.08 ounce/2 grams (¾ teaspoon) instant yeast

½ cup whole milk, at room temperature (75 to 78°F)

½ cup (1 stick) unsalted butter, softened and cut into small pieces

1. Make the pâte fermentée: Combine the water, yeast, all-purpose flour, and salt in a medium bowl and use a rubber spatula to stir until a rough dough forms. Use the spatula to press any loose flour or stray bits of dough into the larger mass. The pâte fermentée won't be smooth. Cover with plastic wrap and let stand at room temperature until it is puffy and increased slightly in volume, about 1 hour. Gently deflate it by pressing down on it with the palm of your hand and then folding it in half. Re-cover and refrigerate until it has doubled in size, 8 to 12 hours.

2. Make the dough: Tear the pâte fermentée into pieces and place in the bowl of a stand mixer or a large mixing bowl. Add the bread flour, salt, sugar, yeast, and milk. Stir with a rubber spatula until a rough dough forms.

3. With the paddle attachment, mix the dough until it just comes together, 2 to 3 minutes. It will be dry and raggedy. With the mixer on low speed, add the butter 1 piece at a time. Continue to mix, scraping down the sides of the bowl as necessary, until it comes together into a ball, another 2 to 3 minutes. Switch to the dough hook, and knead on low speed until it is smooth and supple, 5 to 7 minutes longer.

4. Spray the inside of a dough-rising container or large mixing bowl with nonstick cooking spray and place the dough inside. Cover with plastic wrap and let rise until the dough has increased in volume by about 50 percent, about 1 hour.

5. Give the dough a turn: Slide your hands underneath the dough and pick it up from underneath, so that it droops over your hands. Then set it down again, on one of its drooping sides, back in the bowl. Cover the bowl with plastic wrap and let it rise until it has again increased in volume by about 50 percent, 45 minutes to 1 hour.

6. Turn the dough onto a countertop lightly dusted with flour. Gently shape it into a rough rectangle and fold the rectangle in half. Let the dough rest for 10 minutes.

7. Spray the inside of a 4½- by 8½-inch loaf pan with nonstick cooking spray. Shape the dough into a loaf (see page 89). Transfer it, seam side down, to the prepared pan. Lightly spray the surface with nonstick cooking spray and lightly drape with plastic wrap. Let stand until almost doubled in size, 1 to 1½ hours. The dough should come almost to the top of the pan but not over the top! If this happens, you've waited too long to get it into the oven.

8. One hour before baking, place a baking stone on the middle rack and preheat the oven to 400°F. Uncover the loaf and bake (make sure there's enough room above so that the rising bread doesn't bump into the upper rack) for 10 minutes. Without opening the oven, turn the heat down to 350°F and bake until the top is golden brown and an instant-read thermometer inserted into the center reads 190°F, 25 to 30 minutes longer.

9. Turn the loaf out of the pan onto a wire rack, re-invert the loaf, and let cool completely, at least 2 hours, before slicing and serving.

Ciabatta: The Short History of a Rustic Country Bread

Americans have fallen in love with ciabatta, the rustic, misshapen, airy bread with the chewy crust that can now be found in supermarkets and cafés across the land. But if you think you are enjoying an heirloom artisan bread that hearkens back to the Italian Renaissance, think again.

As an excellent article on the history of this beloved bread in the British newspaper *The Guardian* recently revealed, "the ancestry of at least one form of ciabatta — the long, flat, rustic-looking loaf that takes its name from the Italian word for the slipper it supposedly resembles — reaches back not to the era of the Sistine Chapel, but to the days of Spandau Ballet."

Yes, it's true. Ciabatta is not a traditional Italian bread at all, but was invented in 1982 by an enterprising miller named Arnaldo Cavallari, who was looking for a way to expand his business. Frustrated that a majority of Italian sandwich shops were importing bread from France, he tinkered with some traditional recipes, using his own flour, to come up with a soft, sandwich-friendly bread with Italian character. He even trademarked the name Ciabatta Italiana,

and his company now sells and licenses a variety of ciabatta products across Europe. Although Cavallari owns the name, it hasn't prevented bakers around the world from imitating his instantly popular idea.

Far from feeling scammed, we should celebrate the fact that the Italian miller who set out to make more money had the heart of an artisan. Instead of building his business by trying to cut corners at the mill, he created a bread that showcased his mineral- and gluten-rich product and created a desire for a delicious bread that had not existed before. It just goes to show that great bread doesn't have to come from an ancient recipe, and bakers are learning all the time how to manipulate quality ingredients in new ways for profit *and* pleasure.

Ciabatta

Makes 2 loaves

Ciabatta is made from a very wet dough that gives the finished bread its bubbly texture and free-form shape. A large quantity of superstrong biga makes the dough manageable and prevents it from spreading across the baking stone rather than rising. While most doughs made with a pre-ferment require a relatively short bulk fermentation time, very wet ciabatta dough benefits from a rather long rise, during which the flour in the dough has time to absorb the water. This dough can be cut into 8 free-form rolls after bulk fermentation if you like. Dimple the rolls gently, as you would a larger loaf, and reduce the baking time to about 15 minutes.

FOR THE BIGA:

2 ounces (¼ cup) room temperature water (75 to 78°F)

0.025 ounce/1 gram (¼ teaspoon) instant yeast

2.7 ounces/77 grams (½ cup) unbleached all-purpose flour

FOR THE DOUGH:

7 ounces (¾ cup plus 2 tablespoons) water

0.08 ounce/2 grams (¾ teaspoon) instant yeast

9 ounces/255 grams (1¾ cups plus 2 tablespoons) unbleached all-purpose flour

0.1 ounce/3 grams (¾ teaspoon) fine sea salt or kosher salt

1. Make the biga: Combine the water, yeast, and all-purpose flour in a medium bowl and use a rubber spatula to stir until a rough dough forms. Use the spatula to press any loose flour or stray bits of dough into the larger mass. The biga won't be smooth. Cover with plastic wrap and let stand at room temperature for 1 hour, and then refrigerate until it has doubled in volume, 8 to 16 hours.

2. Make the dough: Tear the biga into pieces and place in the bowl of a stand mixer or a large mixing bowl. Let stand for 15 minutes to warm up. Add the water, yeast, all-purpose flour, and salt. Stir with a rubber spatula until a rough dough forms.

CONTINUED →

3. With the dough hook, knead the dough on medium speed until it just clears the sides of the bowl, 12 to 15 minutes. It will be smooth, shiny, and stretchy.

4. Spray the inside of a dough-rising container or large mixing bowl with nonstick cooking spray and place the dough inside. Cover with plastic wrap and let rise until the dough has risen voluminously, almost tripling in volume, 2 to 3 hours.

5. One hour before baking, place a baking stone on the middle rack of the oven and a cast-iron skillet on the lower rack. Preheat the oven to 475°F.

6. Line a baker's peel with parchment paper and flour the parchment. Turn the dough out onto a countertop heavily dusted with flour (too little flour and your dough will stick like glue). Sprinkle the top of the dough with more flour and use a bench scraper or sharp chef's knife to divide the dough into 2 equal pieces.

7. Transfer the dough to the prepared peel, sliding your hands underneath each piece and stretching it as you place it on the parchment to make a 4- by 15-inch piece. Dimple the surface of each piece with your fingertips to burst some of the dough's larger gas bubbles (do this gently—you don't want to entirely deflate the dough). Drape with plastic wrap and let stand until the dough is bubbly under the surface, 30 to 45 minutes.

Shaping ciabatta

8. Slide the loaves, still on the parchment, onto the preheated baking stone. Drop ½ cup ice cubes into the cast-iron pan. Bake until the ciabatta is well risen and golden, 25 to 30 minutes.

9. Slide the loaves, still on the parchment, onto a wire rack. Let cool for 5 minutes, peel from the parchment, and then let cool to warm room temperature, another 10 minutes or so. Serve warm or let cool to room temperature before serving.

Pre-ferments
Questions and Answers

Q I'm working from an older recipe that says to ferment the sponge to "full drop." What does this mean?

A "Full drop" indicates that the sponge has at least doubled and maybe tripled in volume before collapsing in on itself. If this happened with your dough, you'd be distressed because you'd overfermented it, compromising its ability to achieve a lofty rise in the oven, but with a sponge a bit of overfermentation indicates that the acids are fully developed and ready to flavor the bread.

Q How much time can be saved during bulk fermentation by using a pre-ferment?

A It will depend on the recipe. In general, both bulk fermentation and final proofing will be shorter in a two-stage dough than in a straight dough. Of course, there are ways to hurry a straight dough along. If you add enough yeast to a straight dough recipe and use warm enough water, you can ferment your straight dough in as little time as it takes to ferment a dough made with a pre-ferment, 1 to 1½ hours. But the point isn't simply to save time. The point is to develop the dough's flavor in as little time as possible. A straight dough, like any other dough, will only develop flavor during a fermentation period of at least 6 hours. By developing the acids (and thus the flavor) in a pre-ferment, bulk fermentation time can be cut without adversely affecting the flavor of the bread.

Q I'm interested in experimenting with whole grains. Will pre-ferments made with whole-wheat flour take longer to ripen than pre-ferments made with white flour?

A Yes. Whole-wheat flour, because it contains not just the starchy endosperm but the germ and bran as well, has proportionately less starch to offer yeast than does white flour. So just as whole-wheat bread dough takes longer to ferment and proof than bread dough made with only white flour, whole-wheat pre-ferments require some extra fermentation time to reach the point of ripeness.

But ripening time isn't the only issue when you are thinking of substituting whole-wheat flour for white flour in a pre-ferment. As Peter Reinhart discusses at length in *Whole Grain Breads*, whole-grain breads may require more yeast than pre-fermented white breads. Beyond simply substituting whole-wheat flour for white flour, you might think about adding a little more yeast to your pre-ferment, your final dough, or both.

Q **My recipe calls for whisking the ripened sponge before adding it to the dough. What does this accomplish?**

A Some bakers believe that whisking a loose pre-ferment introduces more air bubbles to the mixture, resulting in a bubblier bread. But I am not convinced that whisking wouldn't do more harm than good by destroying some of the cells created during fermentation even as it adds bubbles. Rather than whisking, I very gently scrape the pre-ferment into the bowl with the other ingredients, hoping to preserve some of the structure developed during fermentation.

Q **I mixed my sponge just 1½ hours ago and it has already risen and collapsed. Is it ready to use?**

A If your sponge shows signs of ripeness after such a short time, it is probably because a higher-than-normal

room temperature or water temperature has accelerated fermentation. Is it a very hot day? Was your water closer to 85 or 90°F than the recommended 75°F? While the yeast may be active, there hasn't been enough time for flavorful acids to develop or for the gluten in the mixture to completely organize. Give your sponge a stir, re-cover it, and place it in the refrigerator for a couple of hours. Cooling it down will allow time for these developments without exhausting the food supply of the yeast.

Q **What is a "soaker"? Is it some kind of pre-ferment?**

A A soaker isn't a pre-ferment per se, although it can improve the texture and rise of a bread dramatically. Certain breads containing whole grains such as cornmeal or cracked wheat call for a soaker step before mixing and kneading. In this step, the grain is soaked in a liquid, usually water or milk. Soaking the grain softens it and helps to release enzymes in the grain that will break down starches into sugars during bulk fermentation, resulting in a bubblier bread with a better crust. This step isn't necessary when making Cornmeal Baguettes (page 139), for instance, because a large quantity of white flour in the dough encourages enough enzymatic action. But in breads that contain a larger proportion of whole grains and non-wheat flours, a soaker step is a big help. Soakers are discussed more fully on page 217.

Q **Once shaped, do loaves made with a pre-ferment proof for a shorter period of time than loaves made without a pre-ferment?**

A Like bulk fermentation times, proofing times for shaped breads may be a bit shorter if using a pre-ferment, depending on how much active yeast was in the pre-ferment. It's best to judge with your senses, rather than by the clock, until you have some experience with a particular recipe.

Q **It took several hours for a whole-wheat sunflower seed bread dough to rise, but my ciabatta dough seemed to double in no time at all. Why the difference in bulk fermentation time?**

A The larger the proportion of pre-ferment in a dough, the shorter the bulk fermentation time. Ciabatta contains a larger proportion of pre-ferment.

Q **Is it my imagination, or do my straight dough baguettes give off a different aroma than the ones I made with a poolish?**

A It is not your imagination. You have a great sense of smell! To get a good rise, straight dough baguettes need proportionately more yeast. So as they bake, they give off a distinctly yeasty aroma. Baguettes made with a poolish, however, smell like toasted wheat, an aroma prized by bread connoisseurs. This is one of the reasons why professional bakers and passionate amateurs prefer breads that employ pre-ferments. The place of yeast in a bread recipe is to serve the grain, not to hog the spotlight with its own distinctive aroma and flavor. With a pre-ferment, bakers are able to raise bread with less yeast, highlighting the grain.

Q **I was disappointed with the pale crust of the bread I baked using a sponge. What can I do next time to improve its color?**

A Breads like Sunflower Seed Bread (page 136) employ a sponge, the quickest fermenting pre-ferment discussed in this chapter. Next time, you might try letting your sponge ferment for a longer period of time (the full 5 hours in the case of the Sunflower Seed Bread), or letting it ferment for the longest suggested time and then refrigerating it overnight, to allow the enzymes in the mixture to break down more of the flour's starches into simple sugars. The more simple sugars your dough contains, the more browning and caramelization (which contributes a wonderful sweetness as well as color) you will get in the oven.

Q I love the taste and texture of ciabatta, but I'm not a fan of its sloppy, free-form shape. Is there a way to shape the dough for a more elegant presentation?

A As is often the case, taste and texture are bound up with particular shaping techniques. So the answer is no. The open and moist crumb of ciabatta is a product not only of a particularly wet dough but also of the hands-off approach that the baker takes to shaping it. Simply draping it on a parchment-lined peel is the best way to preserve the dough's gluten structure and air cells.

Q The crust on my pain de mie got a little soggy after cooling. I don't want it to be chewy, but what can I do to get it to be a little flakier and crisper?

A First, make sure you are baking your bread long enough. Even if an instant-read thermometer registers 190°F when inserted into the center of the bread, starch retrogradation, the process by which water molecules migrate from the center of the bread to the crust, may not have been complete. Next time, let the bread bake for an extra 5 minutes and you may see an improvement.

Something else you might want to consider is whether or not there is too much moisture circulating in the oven itself. Pain de mie has a high moisture content, and not all of the water released from the dough during baking may have escaped your oven. If the baking environment is moist, the surface of your bread will not get as crisp as you'd like. Professional bakery ovens are equipped with vents to allow steam to escape during the last minutes of baking so that breads can dry out sufficiently. To simulate this effect, prop open your oven with the handle of a wooden spoon during the last 10 minutes of baking to allow steam, but not too much heat, to escape.

Q Can I use the pain de mie recipe to make a Pullman loaf?

A A Pullman loaf is a soft, enriched white bread that is very similar to pain de mie but is baked in a special pan with a sliding lid that keeps the dough from rising into a domed top during baking, resulting in perfectly square slices. Go ahead and use the pain de mie dough in a Pullman loaf pan if you'd like, making sure it is equivalent in volume to the 8-inch loaf pan called for in the recipe. But if you don't have a Pullman loaf pan, that needn't stop you from baking a Pullman loaf. Simply grease the bottom of a heavy-duty baking sheet and place it on top of the loaf pan before baking. This will serve the same function as the sliding top. The sides of your bread slices will slope slightly, but the top will be flat and parallel to the bottom, just as with a "real" Pullman loaf.

Q **I find myself baking baguettes almost every day, and I am intrigued by the idea of using pâte fermentée to raise them. Instead of mixing a poolish as the recipe suggests, could I simply reserve a piece of today's dough for tomorrow's bread, as they did in the old days?**

A If you are baking on a daily basis, it would certainly be economical simply to save a piece of dough for the next batch of bread. Why don't you go ahead and try it? Keep in mind that baguettes made with pâte fermentée will have a slightly different character from baguettes made with poolish. Not better or worse, but different. And remember that the starter in the baguette recipe weighs in at about 9 ounces. That means that you'll have to make about 25 percent more dough than what you need for today's bread in order to have enough left for tomorrow. Increase all the ingredients by this percentage, and then weigh out what you'll need for tomorrow. If I were you, I'd increase the yeast by a little more — maybe 35 percent to 40 percent — since a smaller percentage of it will be fermenting more slowly in salted pâte fermentée than what you would have added to a salt-free poolish in the recipe as written.

Chapter 6
Sourdough Baking

COMMERCIAL YEAST BECAME widely available around 1900. But yeast-raised bread was baked for thousands of years before this product came to market, before bakers even knew that yeast existed or what it was. So how did leavened bread rise without those little granules that come in the red and yellow packets? The answer is sourdough, which is nothing more than wild yeast, captured from the environment in a mixture of flour and water and cultivated by the baker until it has multiplied in sufficient numbers to be able to perform the same function as packaged yeast.

You may have heard that wild yeast is difficult to grow outside of San Francisco, that it will die if not fed three times a day, that you can destroy a culture by stirring it with a metal spoon, that tap water will kill it. Myths and misinformation about cultivating, maintaining, and using a wild yeast culture prevent even experienced home bakers from trying sourdough baking. This is a shame, because the process of caring for a from-scratch culture isn't difficult at all (though it does take a week or more of feeding and care). And, as any artisan baker will tell you, sourdough breads are among the most moist, flavorful, complex, and long-lasting breads you can bake.

In this chapter, I'll explain exactly how a sourdough culture is cultivated and used, and then I'll give you a recipe for the very simple sourdough that I have used with fantastic results. Once you have successfully cultivated your own sourdough, I will show you how to use it to bake a sourdough baguette, a sourdough country bread, a semolina sourdough round, and a sourdough rye bread.

Ancient Egyptian Sourdough

In the fall of 1991, Dr. Ed Wood, a forensic pathologist in Idaho with a lifelong interest in sourdough baking, read an article in a local newspaper about a University of Chicago expedition to Egypt, sponsored by the National Geographic Society, to excavate an ancient bakery near the Great Pyramid of Giza. He immediately picked up the phone to track down the expedition's head, Dr. Mark Lehner, and offer his services as a scientist/baker.

Before he knew it, he was on his way to Cairo, where he helped capture wild yeast descended from the microorganisms that the pharaohs' bakers used to raise the first leavened bread, and he used this Egyptian sourdough culture in a replica of the Giza bakery to bake replicas of ancient Egyptian breads.

Dr. Wood later wrote a story about the experience for *National Geographic* magazine, and he expanded the story into a fascinating book, *World Sourdoughs from Antiquity*, which also contains some of the best scientific writing about sourdough for home bakers. Eventually, he turned his passion into a business. You may not have the same energy, funds, or obsessive desire to travel the world in search of sourdough, but you can share some of Dr. Wood's experience by buying some of his dehydrated sourdoughs from around the world, which he sells by mail, along with instructions and recipes (see Resources, page 275).

Re-creating the ancient bakery at Giza

If you are like me, once you have success with sourdough, you will be hooked. By regularly using a portion of your sourdough and refreshing what remains for next time, you will notice how your culture gets stronger and more flavorful as it ages. With proper care and maintenance, your culture will be ready to use whenever you want to bake, and the simple routines involved in baking naturally yeasted breads will become a pleasure and an enhancement to your everyday life and the furthest thing from a household chore.

Commercial vs. Wild Yeast

There are hundreds of strains of yeast that can raise bread. Manufacturers of commercial yeast isolate a single strain that they've identified for the way it will quickly and vigorously ferment. Commercial yeast is extremely reliable, which is one of its great advantages. You can count on it working in a similar way every time you bake.

Sourdough, on the other hand, can contain hundreds of strains of yeast. Its particular yeast profile will depend upon many variables, including what kind of flour you've used, what time of year it is, and where you live.

There are differences in the way commercial yeast and a homegrown sourdough culture are bred. Commercial yeast is cultivated from an isolated strain in sterile vessels and fed with filtered molasses, which contains the sugars and minerals that encourage fermentation. Yeast bred commercially is resistant to the weakening effects of acid buildup, and in any case its environment is carefully monitored to ensure that acids do not inhibit its growth. Once it has reproduced in sufficient numbers, it is dried, alive but dormant until mixed with water. Dried yeast is an incredibly stable product. Although every package has a sell-by date, the reality is that, if it is kept in a cool, dry place in an airtight container, dried yeast will be able to raise bread for months or even years after it has been purchased.

When you decide to grow your own yeast, you can't pick and choose your strains. Your sourdough will grow from the yeast that is available: the yeast that thrives on the tree bark in your yard, the yeast that's arrived in your kitchen on the fruits and vegetables you've toted home from the supermarket, and, predominantly, the yeast that grows on grain and arrived in your house inside your sack of flour. Wild yeast is cultivated in a less pristine environment than commercial yeast: your kitchen. Bacteria, minerals, and chlorine, which may slow down fermentation or even in rare cases kill the yeast entirely, are banished from commercial yeast factories. But these enemies of yeast may very well find their way into your homegrown culture, slowing it down or even stopping it in its tracks. Be prepared, because infrequently a sourdough culture can fail before it is fully established.

Wild yeast is hardy, but unlike packaged yeast it needs some care and feeding if it is to survive indefinitely. A sourdough culture won't last forever on its own because acids produced by the lactobacilli, which are present wherever yeast is, will weaken the yeast and eventually kill it off. So the home baker must keep the acids in the culture under control by refrigerating it to slow down fermentation and by diluting it periodically (once a week at the minimum) with fresh flour and water.

Once your culture *is* fully established, it will certainly be less active and vigorous than packaged yeast. Bread raised with sourdough will take longer to rise. As it changes from week to week, your culture may behave differently in the exact same bread recipe. The home baker must rely on observation instead of the clock and exercise restraint when baking with a sourdough culture. Vigilance and patience have their rewards. Using a sourdough culture is hands down the most effective way to "age" dough, encouraging a marvelously bubbly and moist texture, incredibly caramelized crust, and complexity of flavor comparable to other long-fermented foods such as cheese and wine.

A Word about Lactobacilli and Acids

Although it is the yeast in a sourdough culture that makes bread rise, it is the acids, produced by bacteria cultivated along with the yeast, that give bread raised with wild yeast its wonderful flavor.

While yeast is fermenting, producing the carbon dioxide that fills gluten cells and causes bread dough to rise, these bacteria, called lactobacilli, are producing lactic and acetic acids, which contribute a range of flavors from milky and buttery to sharply vinegary. In addition, these

Styles of Sourdough

Just as there are two styles of pre-ferment, the loose and liquidy sponge (similar to poolish) and the stiff pâte fermentée (similar to biga), so there are loose and stiff sourdough cultures. Both types will effectively raise bread.

There is no strict standard for what constitutes a liquid starter and what constitutes a stiff starter. Different bakers use different ratios of flour to water to create a starter with a consistency they prefer. But in general, a liquid starter will have at least as much water as flour, and sometimes more. When making a liquid sourdough, the key is to add enough water so that the mixture has more liquid qualities than solid ones. Liquid starters are extremely easy to mix and maintain. They tend to encourage the development of lactic over acetic acids, giving breads a mildly acidic flavor akin to yogurt or sour cream. They tend to produce doughs that are more extensible than elastic, which become exceedingly light and voluminous in the oven. If this is a bread style you favor, liquid starter may be for you.

A stiff dough starter will resemble a dough rather than a thick shake, and it performs much like a dough when fermenting. It is usually necessary to knead it for a minute or two before fermentation begins to make sure that all of the flour has been moistened. A stiff dough starter will produce more acetic acid than a liquid starter, resulting in a bread with a more pronounced sour flavor. If you prefer a more assertively flavored bread, this is one reason to use a stiff dough starter. I also like to use a stiff sourdough starter when converting a straight dough recipe to a sourdough because the consistency of the starter is similar to the consistency of bread dough, so there is no need to adjust the quantities of flour and water to compensate for extra liquid in the starter.

Either style of sourdough can be made with a variety of flours. Traditionally, sourdoughs cultivated in northern Europe were made with rye flour, which grows well in a colder climate. In France, Italy, and Spain, wheat sourdoughs were more common, since wheat thrives in a warmer climate and in less rocky soil. Sourdough can be cultivated with either white or whole rye or wheat flour.

acids bond with other by-products of fermentation to form dozens of flavor compounds that give sourdough bread its complexity.

Breads baked using the straight dough method, as well as many breads employing a quick-fermenting sponge, are unable to benefit from the bacterial fermentation. This is because lactobacilli ferment much more slowly than yeast, taking at least 8 hours to produce a quantity of acids that would make a difference in terms of flavor.

Many people mistakenly think that sourdough breads will have a sour taste. Although some sourdough breads are markedly acidic, sour flavor is by no means a foregone conclusion. If you taste an active, healthy sourdough culture, it *will* be flavored by these acids. Depending on the type of flour you've used, the ratio of flour to water, and the fermentation time, it can range from mildly tangy (French *levain* is an example of this style) to mouth-puckeringly tart (German rye *Sauerteig* tastes like this). But even the most acidic sourdough can produce a mild-tasting bread. How predominant the sour flavor will be depends upon a variety of factors, including the acid level of the starter, the ratio of starter to dough, and fermentation and proofing times and techniques. In fact, achieving a balance of flavors — wheaty, tangy, sweet, earthy — that is pleasing to you is the goal of sourdough baking. Learning to manipulate the starter and the dough as you work with them will help you achieve what you are after.

Sourdough Ingredients

Although there are recipes for sourdough that include yogurt, beer, or potato peels, the most efficient way to cultivate a sourdough starter is by using just two ingredients, flour and water. While yeast may be present in those former ingredients, the fact is that the best yeast for sourdough is the yeast that's already in your flour. This is the yeast that thrives on grain, and it is the yeast that is going to be present in your culture in the largest quantity from the beginning. Over time your culture will attract other strains of yeast that are in the environment, but to get it started you can rely on what's available in the flour. All that is needed to activate this yeast is water. When water comes into contact with flour, it will release the starches that the yeast feed on in order to multiply.

Although sourdough cultures can be grown using any type of flour, there are two types in particular that I find helpful in getting one going and then maintaining its strength. Rye flour, because it contains more starch than wheat flour, will encourage quick yeast growth. I've found that starting my culture with rye gives me a quick start.

The problem with a rye sourdough, however, is that it becomes acidic very quickly, because lactobacilli love to feed on the starches in rye as much as yeast does. In addition, rye doesn't have much gluten, so a starter made with rye won't contribute much to the structure of your finished

Signs of Sourdough Fermentation

How can you tell if your sourdough starter is ready to be put to work? It won't shout the news to you. Evaluate it with your other senses.

Look. An active culture will have increased in volume during a 24-hour period. A stiff doughlike starter will have doubled and developed a domed top, like risen dough. A liquid starter will become very bubbly, as if it were carbonated. If it has collapsed because of an extra-high rise, you will be able to see evidence of this: bits of starter clinging to the place in the container where it rose before falling.

Smell. When you activated your culture by mixing together flour and water, it had a rather neutral smell. After fermenting for several days, it will have an assertive fragrance — fruity, tangy, earthy, musty — that cannot be ignored. Don't be alarmed at the strength of this smell. Before you use your culture, you will refresh it and ferment it for only a short period, diluting

the acids that can sometimes produce a somewhat overpowering aroma.

Taste. Go ahead and take a taste. Is it tart from acetic acid? Does it have a slightly milky flavor due to the buildup of lactic acids? Your starter's flavor will tell you if the lactobacilli in the culture are fermenting vigorously.

Touch. A firm starter will be soft, not springy, to the touch, with visible dimpling on the surface from the air bubbles underneath. A liquid starter will be very stretchy. Dip a spatula into your culture, and then pull away. Is it extensible, with strands of gluten that can be pulled many inches above the surface? These are more signs of readiness.

bread. Once the rye has given the yeast and lactobacilli a quick start, it's a good idea to start feeding it with organic wheat flour, which has a larger proportion of enzymes for breaking down the flour's starches than does flour that's been grown with pesticides, sprayed, and in general processed more roughly. The more enzymes in the flour, the more starches they will make available to the yeast and the more quickly your culture will ferment.

One type of flour you should definitely avoid: bleached flour. During bleaching, nutrients essential to healthy yeast growth are destroyed. So bleached flour won't provide the nutritious environment required for building a healthy sourdough.

I have to admit that once, when I was too lazy to go to the store to buy spring water, I mixed my flour with tap water and had no problem whatsoever in activating some wild yeast. But on the off chance that your water contains minerals or an overabundance of chlorine that might inhibit yeast growth, it's best to stick with spring water until your culture is able to double in volume over a 24-hour period. After this point, when your starter is exhibiting signs of vigorous yeast activity, it's perfectly fine to feed it with tap water for the rest of its life.

Building a Starter

Before I actually cultivated (or built, as professional bakers like to say) my own starter, I read a lot about the different ways it could be done. The scientific language, complicated feeding schedules, and bizarre ingredients (grape skins, pineapple juice) said to aid in fermentation all terrified me. Some recipes demanded such frequent feedings and so much stirring between feedings that I'd need an alarm clock to keep me on schedule.

But if cultivating wild yeast is so difficult, how come it has been accomplished so successfully for thousands of years by people with no knowledge of the science behind it, no special equipment, and no other ingredients than the ones they had on hand to make bread?

This isn't to say that results are guaranteed or that it will always be smooth sailing. The first time I tried to cultivate a sourdough starter with wheat flour and water, I waited for days to see signs of yeast activity before scraping my would-be starter into the trash and starting over again. Who knows why the culture failed? Perhaps I introduced some type of yeast-killing bacteria or mold with my spoon when I stirred it. I was eventually able to get one going, after several tries, but then when I took the advice of several baking experts to start with rye flour instead of wheat flour, I was amazed at how effortlessly the yeast proliferated.

Because it has more starch than wheat, rye flour ferments more quickly and easily. So why not use rye to jump-start your culture? The recipe and technique are simple:

How to Use Your Sourdough Starter in Any Bread Recipe

Once you have had some success with the recipes in this chapter, you might wonder whether or not your sourdough culture can be used instead of instant yeast to raise the other breads in this book. Of course it can, if you are willing to pay attention to your dough and make some adjustments as you work.

An amount of 1.8/51 grams ounces (about ¼ cup) of active sourdough culture will raise a 1- to 2-pound loaf (or two 1-pound loaves). Eight to twelve hours before you bake, combine ¼ cup of your healthy culture with 2 ounces (¼ cup) water and 4 ounces/113 grams (about ½ cup) flour. Add this to your bread dough after letting it stand, deducting the same amounts of water and flour from the bread recipe. You may have to add a tablespoon or two of flour to your dough to compensate for the small amount of extra liquid you've added along with the sourdough. Wait and see how the dough feels.

Remember to allow extra time for bulk fermentation and to give the dough a turn after an hour to disperse excess carbon dioxide, even if your recipe doesn't call for this. And remember to proof your breads sufficiently in order to coax from them their highest rise possible.

1. Combine some rye flour and water in a bowl. Use a glass bowl, if possible, which will let you observe the fermentation that is going on at the bottom of the bowl as well as on the culture's surface.

2. Stir so that you have a smooth, sticky mixture, and then cover the bowl with plastic wrap.

3. Let it stand on the counter for 24 hours, stirring once or twice during that period to aerate the yeast.

4. After a day, you may be able to detect some early signs of fermentation: small bubbles that you can see when you look underneath the bowl, a mild acidic aroma, and even some increase in volume. Don't worry if you don't see any of these signs, however. It is still early.

5. On day 2, add more flour and water, to provide fresh food for the yeast. Let the culture stand, covered, for another day. Try to remember to stir it once or twice to give the yeast some oxygen.

6. On day 3, you will begin to notice some signs of fermentation: bubbles on the surface and even some increase in volume. The aroma of the mixture will be slightly acidic, and it will taste mildly sour. These are all signs that yeast and lactobacilli have begun to multiply and produce gases and acids. Once your culture shows these signs, you can start to feed it with wheat flour instead of rye.

7. At this stage, you'll throw away a portion of your starter before feeding the remaining portion. This accomplishes two things. It is possible that even at this early stage enough acid has built up to endanger the yeast. To make the environment safe, discard half of the culture before feeding it with fresh flour and water. Even if the environment isn't acidic, there's another reason to toss part of the starter away. If you kept refreshing the entire batch, after a week you'd have an unmanageable and impractical quantity of the stuff.

It may take just a few days, or it may take up to 2 weeks, but eventually your culture, thus jump-started with rye flour and regularly refreshed with wheat flour and fresh water, will display signs of readiness to raise bread. Congratulations: You have built an active starter. At this point, it is ready for the "final build."

The Final Build

You won't simply add this starter you've created to your other bread dough ingredients and proceed. First you have to perform what is called "the final build," feeding your starter one more time. This last step will give your yeast one last nutritional boost, diluting any excess acids that might inhibit your dough's rise. It will also give you just the right quantity of starter that you'll need for the bread you will be baking. Up until now, you've been letting your culture stand at room temperature for 24 hours. Fermentation time for the final build will be shorter, between 8 and 12 hours. This will give the yeast plenty of time to multiply before too much acid starts to weaken it.

Most sourdough bread recipes actually begin with instructions for making the final build, so if you have cultivated the starter from the recipe on page 166 for Foolproof Sourdough Starter, you can use it in any other sourdough recipe in place of the sourdough starter called for, making adjustments (adding flour or water to the dough as necessary) to account for any differences in starter hydration.

Easy Care and Maintenance

When you cultivate a starter, you'll make more of it than you can use. A portion of it will go to making the final build for your first batch of bread. What will you do with the extra? You'll scoop up a portion, refresh it, and refrigerate it for up to a week, so you have healthy sourdough for the next time you want to make bread, and then discard or give away the remaining portion. Next time you want to bake, you'll follow the same procedure: Make your final build and then refresh and refrigerate some of the left-over starter for next time.

Do not worry about becoming a slave to your sourdough. If a week elapses between feedings and you just don't have the time to bake, simply refresh and refrigerate a portion of your culture without making a final build. Discard whatever you don't need, or divide it among friends. Refreshment only takes minutes and requires just a few ounces of flour. For this small investment, you'll have your culture ready for baking, whenever that may be.

A Note on Yield

I decided I would never make a sourdough starter after reading a recipe that resulted in a bucket of the mixture so large that I realized I'd need an extra refrigerator to store it. Why would I want to keep so much sourdough around if I was only going to bake a loaf or two at a time? For that small quantity of bread, I'd need as little as ¼ cup of starter and no more than ½ cup. It wasn't until I found an economical recipe with a yield that could be stored in a pint container that I gave it a try.

The recipe on page 166 for Foolproof Sourdough Starter is designed to yield about 1 cup of starter, plenty to portion out for a very large bread while still having enough to refresh for the next week's baking. Individual recipes will instruct you on making the final build. Once you do so, you'll have plenty left over to refresh for your next breads.

Baking Sourdough Bread

Even after I had studied the science behind yeast and understood how, once activated by water and fed by the starches in flour, it was able to raise bread, I still looked upon the granules of instant yeast that I added to my dough as a magical substance. With yeast, my dough would become bubbly and light, alive with microorganisms that would help it expand in the oven. Without it, my dough would remain an inert lump, like last night's leftover mashed potatoes.

So it took a huge leap of faith to mix my first sourdough bread without this magical substance. Even though I could see the air bubbles in my sourdough starter, signaling that there was plenty of active wild yeast in my culture, and even though my bread dough rose in its dough-rising container (although not as much as my previous doughs had), I was nervous. I remember sliding the shaped baguettes into the oven and thinking, "Here goes nothing," ready to toss away some very hard, very large breadsticks if baking went badly.

But as soon as I had several successes under my belt, I started to see my sourdough culture in the same magical light that I had formerly viewed commercial yeast. It really does work, if you give it a chance.

Allowing sourdough to do its work takes faith and patience. The doughs mixed with a natural starter won't behave in quite the same way as doughs employing commercial yeast, and they'll take longer to ferment and proof. Pace yourself, using the following tips, to achieve the ultimate result in home bread baking.

Prepare the final build. To actually use the sourdough you've cultivated, you'll have to refresh it one last time — the final build — which ensures that you will have the right quantity of culture for the particular bread you are baking, as well as ensuring that when you do add the sourdough it will be at peak ripeness and fully able to raise bread. In addition to full volume, a fully ripe culture will contribute to a well-developed and shiny crust as well as superior flavor. Your recipe will instruct you about quantities. Don't forget to refresh the sourdough that remains, to store in the refrigerator for the next time you bake.

Give autolyse a chance. Traditional artisan breads made with sourdough are famously wet. You've taken the time to cultivate a starter, so take an extra 10 to 20 minutes to let your flour absorb some water before adding your starter and salt to the dough. Full absorption at this stage will give you a more workable, more extensible dough, which will result in a bubblier, higher-rising bread.

Take rising times with a grain of salt. If your water was exactly 78°F, your dough was the same temperature after kneading, your kitchen is a nice, warm 78°F, and you used instant yeast, then you'd reasonably expect fermentation to take place within the time frame suggested in the recipe. But if you replace instant yeast with sourdough, you won't know what to expect. Keep an eye on your dough, waiting patiently if it seems to be taking a lot longer than expected to reach that mark on your dough-rising container.

Turn the dough. Instead of kneading your wet dough until it passes the windowpane test (see page 71), allow it to develop gluten by giving it a turn. Turning accomplishes something else in sourdough breads. Because bulk fermentation takes 2 to 3 hours for these doughs (as opposed to 1½ hours or even less with most straight doughs and doughs mixed with pre-ferments), there is a danger that excess carbon dioxide will accumulate, ultimately interfering with the activity of the yeast. Turning disperses some of the gas so that your natural yeast can work effectively.

Fully bench proof. Here's one last step that requires some faith. Certified master baker Jeffrey Hamelman says that sourdough loaves aren't ready for baking until they "feel light, somewhat loose, somewhat weak." If you have prepared your dough well up until this point, mixing it with a strong starter, kneading and turning and fermenting it properly, and shaping it well, then "that seemingly weak dough will spring exuberantly in the chamber of the oven." In other words, resist the impulse to get the loaves into the oven while they're still somewhat bouncy and resilient, the opposite of what you would do if working with a straight dough. Here's one last place in the recipe where you can extend fermentation, so take the opportunity.

The Recipes

This section begins with the recipe for a sourdough starter, without which you won't be able to make the bread recipes that follow. Because the starter can take up to 2 weeks to become fully active (if you are at all in doubt about its readiness, it is better to continue to feed it for a few extra days, which can only strengthen it), why not begin to cultivate it while you explore other recipes in this book? Making some breads using yeasted pre-ferments (see chapter 5 for recipes) will give you an idea of how to make a dough in two stages. After a couple of weeks of baking, you'll have developed some feel for well-crafted bread dough. This will be great preparation for the adventure you are about to embark on with your newly cultivated sourdough.

Foolproof Sourdough Starter

Makes 7.3 ounces (about 1 cup)

Cultivating a sourdough starter from scratch takes very little effort but a large quantity of patience. There are several variables that will dictate how long the process will take. The flour, the water, and the air all factor in, as does the temperature of your kitchen. I've seen signs of fermentation in my starter in as little as a few hours, but occasionally it's taken up to 2 days. So there are no set amounts of flour and water that you will need. At the same time each day, you'll observe your culture to see how it is developing, and then add fresh water and flour so it can continue to ferment. When you notice that your culture has doubled in volume over the course of a 24-hour period, you can begin to convert it to a wheat starter (from a rye starter) by adding water and mostly wheat flour with just a touch of rye. You might only have to do this a couple of times before commencing baking — or it might take a week to 10 days.

Every time you use your starter to bake, you will reserve a portion of it for future loaves. Refreshed with water and flour, this portion will remain healthy in the refrigerator (for up to 1 week — then it will need fresh flour and water) until you want to bake another loaf.

Room temperature spring water (70 to 78°F)

Stone-ground dark or medium rye flour

Unbleached all-purpose flour, preferably organic

DAY 1
Combine 2 ounces (¼ cup) water and 2.6 ounces/74 grams (½ cup) rye flour in a medium glass bowl. Stir the mixture with a rubber spatula until it is smooth, with just a few lumps. Cover the bowl with plastic wrap and set it aside at room temperature for 24 hours.

DAY 2

You may see some bubbling on the surface of your culture and on the underside if you look at the bottom of the bowl. The mixture may have even risen slightly. But don't worry if it hasn't. Stir it with a spatula, and then stir in another 2 ounces (¼ cup) water and 2.6 ounces/74 grams (½ cup) rye flour. Cover it and let it stand at room temperature for another 24 hours.

DAY 3

By day 3, you will definitely notice some signs of fermentation: bubbling, an increase in volume, and a mild to strong acidic aroma. It may have even doubled in volume. At this point, you will begin to convert your rye starter to a wheat starter. Mix the starter with a spatula to deflate it and invigorate the yeast. Then discard half of it. Place the remaining half in a clean bowl and stir in 2 ounces (¼ cup) spring water, 2.6 ounces/74 grams (½ cup) unbleached all-purpose flour, and 2 teaspoons rye flour, making sure all of the flour is moistened. Cover it and let it stand at room temperature for 24 hours, stirring it once or twice to aerate the yeast. At this point, if the yeast is already very strong, it may have doubled in size. Or it may have slowed down considerably with the addition of wheat flour. In any case, repeat what you did on day 2: Discard half of the culture, place the remaining culture in a clean bowl, and stir in 2 ounces (¼ cup) spring water, 2.6 ounces/74 grams (½ cup) unbleached all-purpose flour, and 2 teaspoons rye flour. Cover and let the culture stand for 24 hours.

CONTINUED $\longrightarrow$

DAY 4 AND BEYOND

With the addition of wheat flour, fermentation will slow down, in some cases considerably. On day 4, repeat what you did on days 2 and 3. Repeat this procedure (it may take up to a week) until your starter has doubled in volume. If it has doubled this indicates that it is almost ready to use. Now, portion out what you need for your final build and proceed with your recipe.

Don't discard all of the remaining starter. You'll need it when you want to bake sourdough bread again. Measure out 3.6 ounces/102 grams (½ cup), discarding the rest, and place it in an airtight container. Stir in 2 ounces (¼ cup) water, 2.6 ounces/74 grams (½ cup) unbleached bread flour, and 2 teaspoons rye flour. There's no need, from here onward, to use spring water unless you prefer its taste to tap water. Let this culture stand at room temperature for 1 hour, and then refrigerate it for up to 3 days before using it. If you don't bake within 3 days, you'll have to refresh it again as just described and let it stand for 8 to 12 hours before baking.

To keep your starter in baking shape, refresh it once a week, whether you bake or not, as directed above.

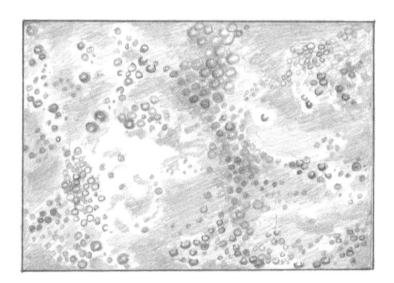

Bran-Flecked Sourdough Country Bread

Makes 1 large round

This country loaf is inspired by the giant, burnished *miches* made famous by Lionel Poilâne, France's legendary baker. Poilâne's bread is made with a special flour only available in France, primarily white but with some of the bran retained. Rather than blending white and whole-wheat flour to approximate this "gray" flour, as many American bakers do, I've used white flour and added a portion of wheat bran, which gives the dough good bran flavor while allowing it to rise high as only a white bread can.

This loaf is big, but not as big as a Poilâne loaf, which weighs about 2 kilograms. You can score it with 4 slashes in the shape of a number symbol (#), or you can attempt the Poilâne score, 2 interlocking curves that make a stylized *P*.

FOR THE FINAL BUILD:

3.6 ounces/102 grams (½ cup) Foolproof Sourdough Starter (page 166)

3.5 ounces/99 grams (⅔ cup) unbleached bread flour

0.3 ounce/8 grams (1 tablespoon) rye flour

2.5 ounces (⅓ cup) room temperature water (70 to 78°F)

FOR THE DOUGH:

23.4 ounces/663 grams (4½ cups) unbleached bread flour

1 ounce/28 grams (½ cup) wheat bran

13 ounces (1½ cups plus 2 tablespoons) room temperature water (70 to 78°F)

0.25 ounce/7 grams (1½ teaspoons) kosher salt or fine sea salt

CONTINUED →

1. Make the final build: Place the sourdough starter in a clean bowl, and stir in the bread flour, rye flour, and water (don't forget to refresh a portion of your leftover sourdough for the next time you want to bake). Cover and let the culture stand at room temperature for 8 to 12 hours.

2. Make the dough: Combine the bread flour, bran, and water in the bowl of a stand mixer or a large mixing bowl. Stir with a rubber spatula until a rough dough forms. Cover with plastic wrap and let stand for 20 minutes.

3. Add the salt and sourdough starter to the bowl and give the dough a few turns with the spatula to incorporate.

4. Knead the dough. By machine: With a dough hook, knead the dough on medium speed until it is smooth and stretchy and clears the sides of the bowl, 10 to 12 minutes. By hand: Turn the dough out onto a lightly floured countertop. Using steady, firm strokes, knead until it becomes smooth and stretchy, scraping it from the counter with a bench scraper as necessary to keep it from sticking, about 15 minutes, and taking breaks every 5 minutes or so to rest your hands and the dough.

5. Spray the inside of a dough-rising container or large mixing bowl with nonstick cooking spray and place the dough inside. Cover with plastic wrap and let rise for 1 hour.

6. Give the dough a turn: Slide your hands underneath the dough and pick it up from underneath, so that it droops over your hands. Then set it down again, on one of its drooping sides, back in the bowl. Cover the bowl with plastic wrap and let it rise for another hour. Give it another turn, and let it rise until it has increased in volume by 50 percent, another 1 to 1½ hours.

7. Shape the dough into a tight ball (see shaping rounds, page 88). Line a large bowl or colander with a clean kitchen towel and sprinkle the towel with flour. Place the loaf in the bowl, smooth side down. Lightly drape the bowl with plastic wrap. Let stand until it is pillowy and soft and almost doubled in volume, 2 to 3 hours.

8. One hour before baking, place a baking stone in the middle rack of the oven and a cast-iron skillet on the lower rack. Preheat the oven to 475°F.

9. Uncover the loaf, place a parchment-lined baker's peel or rimless baking sheet on top of the bowl, and invert the loaf onto the peel. Use a razor blade, lame, or sharp chef's knife to score the loaf, making four 4-inch cuts in a # shape, on top.

10. Slide the loaf, still on the parchment, onto the preheated baking stone. Drop ½ cup ice cubes into the cast-iron pan. Bake until the loaf is deep golden and an instant-read thermometer inserted into the center reads 205°F, 50 to 60 minutes.

11. Slide the loaf, still on the parchment, onto a wire rack. Let cool for 5 minutes, peel from the parchment, and then let cool to warm room temperature, about 2 hours, before slicing and serving.

Semolina, Golden Raisin, and Fennel Seed Sourdough Round

Makes 1 round

I tasted a bread similar to this one at Amy's Bread in New York City, and loved the combination of flavors. Semolina flour is milled from durum wheat, and gives this bread a lovely yellow color and sweetness. Although durum wheat is very high in protein, it doesn't form as strong of a gluten web as the wheat flour we usually use for bread. So bread baked with semolina should also include some bread flour for strength. Take care to buy finely milled flour (see Resources, page 273), and not the more coarsely ground semolina that's intended for home pasta making.

FOR THE FINAL BUILD:

1.8 ounces/51 grams (¼ cup) Foolproof Sourdough Starter (page 166)

2.25 ounces/64 grams (½ cup) unbleached all-purpose flour

0.2 ounce/6 grams (2 teaspoons) rye flour

2 ounces (¼ cup) room temperature water (70 to 78°F)

CONTINUED →

FOR THE DOUGH:

7 ounces/198 grams (1¼ cups) unbleached bread flour

7 ounces/198 grams (1 cup plus 2 tablespoons) semolina flour

8 ounces (1 cup) room temperature water (70 to 78°F)

0.2 ounce/6 grams (1¼ teaspoons) kosher salt or fine sea salt

¾ cup golden raisins

1 tablespoon fennel seeds

1. Make the final build: Place the sourdough starter in a clean bowl, and stir in the all-purpose flour, rye flour, and water (don't forget to refresh a portion of your leftover sourdough for the next time you want to bake). Cover and let the culture stand at room temperature for 8 to 12 hours.

2. Make the dough: Combine the bread flour, semolina flour, and water in the bowl of a stand mixer or a large mixing bowl. Stir with a rubber spatula until a rough dough forms. Cover with plastic wrap and let stand for 20 minutes.

3. Add the salt and the sourdough starter to the bowl and give the dough a few turns with the spatula to incorporate.

4. Knead the dough. By machine: With a dough hook, knead the dough on medium-low speed until it is smooth and supple and clears the sides of the bowl and is still a little rough and sticky, 8 to 10 minutes. Add the raisins and fennel seeds and mix on low speed to incorporate. By hand: Turn the dough out onto a lightly floured countertop. With floured hands, knead it with steady strokes until it becomes smooth and supple, 12 to 15 minutes, taking breaks if it resists or if your hands need a rest. Flatten the dough slightly and sprinkle the raisins and fennel seeds on top. Fold it in half and continue to knead for a minute or two until they're well distributed.

5. Spray the inside of a dough-rising container or large mixing bowl with nonstick cooking spray and place the dough inside. Cover with plastic wrap and let rise for 1 hour.

6. Give the dough a turn: Slide your hands underneath the dough and pick it up from underneath, so that it droops over your hands. Then set it down again, on

one of its drooping sides, back in the bowl. Cover the bowl with plastic wrap and let it rise until it has increased in volume by about 50 percent, 1 to 1½ hours.

7. Turn the dough onto a countertop lightly dusted with flour. Gently shape it into a rough round. Sprinkle with flour and drape with plastic wrap. Let stand until it has spread quite a bit (it won't rise much because of the slackness of the dough), 1½ to 2 hours.

8. One hour before baking, place a baking stone in the middle rack of the oven and a cast-iron skillet on the lower rack. Preheat the oven to 400°F.

9. Uncover the loaf and quickly shape it into a tight round (see page 88). Place it on a parchment-lined baker's peel or rimless baking sheet. Use a razor blade, lame, or sharp chef's knife to score the loaf, making an X on the top.

10. Slide the loaf, still on the parchment, onto the preheated baking stone. Drop ½ cup ice cubes into the cast-iron pan. Bake until the loaf is deep golden and an instant-read thermometer inserted into the center reads 205°F, 50 to 55 minutes.

11. Slide the loaf, still on the parchment, onto a wire rack. Let cool for 5 minutes, peel from the parchment, and then let cool to warm room temperature, about 2 hours, before slicing and serving.

Rye and Pumpkin Seed Pan Loaf

Makes 1 (9-inch) loaf

The final build for this flavorful sandwich loaf is made with rye flour to give the bread an extra boost of flavor, from the flour but also from the extra acids that rye flour produces in the starter. Soak the pumpkin seeds at the same time that you mix your final build. Soaking (see page 217) will soften them so that they don't rob the dough of moisture. You'll notice that, as is often the case with sourdough rye breads, a little bit of packaged yeast is added to the dough as insurance in case your starter over-ferments because you've added so much rye flour. This is a rather sticky dough, much easier to knead in the mixer than by hand. This bread is wonderful served with some farmstead cheddar cheese, hard salami, or cured ham.

FOR THE FINAL BUILD:

1.8 ounces/51 grams (¼ cup) Foolproof Sourdough Starter (page 166)

2.5 ounces/71 grams (½ cup) medium rye flour

2 ounces (¼ cup) room temperature water (70 to 78°F)

¼ cup hulled unsalted pumpkin seeds (pepitas)

FOR THE DOUGH:

7.48 ounces/212 grams (1½ cups) unbleached bread flour

3.5 ounces/99 grams (½ cup plus 2 tablespoons) medium rye flour

8 ounces (1 cup) room temperature water (70 to 78°F)

0.05 ounce/1.5 grams (½ teaspoon) instant yeast

1 ounce/3 grams (¾ teaspoon) kosher salt or fine sea salt

¼ teaspoon ground coriander

¼ teaspoon ground cumin

¼ cup hulled unsalted pumpkin seeds (pepitas)

1. Make the final build: Place the sourdough starter in a clean bowl and stir in the rye flour and water (don't forget to refresh a portion of your leftover sourdough for the next time you want to bake). Cover and let the culture stand at room temperature for 8 to 12 hours.

2. Soak the seeds: Place the pumpkin seeds in a small bowl and cover with water. Let stand at room temperature for 8 to 12 hours.

3. Make the dough: Combine the bread flour, rye flour, and water in the bowl of a stand mixer. Stir with a rubber spatula until a rough dough forms. Cover with plastic wrap and let stand for 20 minutes.

4. Drain the pumpkin seeds of excess water.

5. Add the yeast, salt, coriander, cumin, and sourdough starter to the bowl and give the dough a few turns with the spatula to incorporate. Knead the dough using the dough hook in a stand mixer on medium-low speed until it is smooth and firm and a little bit bouncy, about 8 minutes. Add the drained pumpkin seeds and knead for a minute or two to incorporate.

6. Spray the inside of a dough-rising container or large mixing bowl with nonstick cooking spray and place the dough inside. Cover with plastic wrap and let rise until it doubles in size, 1 to 1½ hours.

7. Turn the dough onto a countertop lightly dusted with flour. Gently shape it into a rough rectangle and fold the rectangle in half. Let the dough rest for 10 minutes.

8. Spray the inside of a 5- by 9-inch loaf pan with nonstick cooking spray. Shape the dough into a loaf (see page 89). Transfer it, seam side down, to the prepared pan. Lightly brush the top with some water and sprinkle with the unsoaked pumpkin seeds. Drape with plastic wrap. Let stand until almost doubled in size, 1 to 1½ hours. The dough should come almost to the top of the pan but not over the top! (If this happens, you've waited too long to get it into the oven — turn the dough onto a lightly floured countertop, reshape into a loaf, re-fit it into a clean and greased pan, and let stand until just doubled).

9. One hour before baking, place a baking stone on the middle rack and preheat the oven to 400°F. Uncover the loaf and bake until it is deep brown, the seeds are well toasted, and an instant-read thermometer inserted into the center reads 200°F, 35 to 45 minutes.

10. Turn the loaf out of the pan onto a wire rack, re-invert the loaf, and let cool at least 2 hours before slicing. Store cooled bread in a resealable plastic bag at room temperature for up to 2 days or in the freezer for up to 2 weeks.

Intensely Flavored Sourdough Baguettes

Makes 2 (14-inch) baguettes

Retarding these sourdough baguettes will give them a more intense flavor than baking them directly. It will also give them a uniquely beautiful crust, a mottled brown caused by the gelatinization of the numerous gas bubbles that form right underneath the surface during the long, cold fermentation. For more mildly flavored loaves, simply proof them at room temperature until they are pillowy and soft and have almost doubled in volume, about 2 hours.

FOR THE FINAL BUILD:

1.8 ounces/51 grams (¼ cup) Foolproof Sourdough Starter (page 166)

4.8 ounces/136 grams (¾ cup) unbleached bread flour

0.3 ounce/8 grams (1 tablespoon) rye flour

6 ounces (¾ cup) room temperature water (70 to 78°F)

FOR THE DOUGH:

11.72 ounces/332 grams (2¼ cups) unbleached bread flour

5 ounces (½ cup plus 2 tablespoons) room temperature water (70 to 78°F)

0.25 ounce/7 grams (1½ teaspoons) kosher salt or fine sea salt

1. Make the final build: Place the sourdough starter in a clean bowl, and stir in the bread flour, rye flour, and water (don't forget to refresh a portion of your leftover sourdough for the next time you want to bake). Cover and let the culture stand at room temperature for 8 to 12 hours.

2. Make the dough: Combine the bread flour and water in the bowl of a stand mixer or a large mixing bowl. Stir with a rubber spatula until a rough dough forms. Cover with plastic wrap and let stand for 20 minutes.

3. Add the salt and sourdough starter to the bowl and give the dough a few turns with the spatula to incorporate it.

4. Knead the dough. By machine: With a dough hook, knead the dough on medium-low speed until it is glossy and stretchy and passes the windowpane test (see page 71), 8 to 9 minutes. By hand: Turn the dough out onto a lightly floured countertop. With floured hands, knead with firm but gentle strokes until it is glossy and smooth and passes the windowpane test, 10 to 15 minutes. Use a bench scraper to scrape up the dough from the counter if it sticks, and take breaks every 5 minutes or so to let the flour in the dough absorb water and to give your hands a rest.

5. Spray the inside of a dough-rising container or large mixing bowl with nonstick cooking spray and place the dough inside. Cover with plastic wrap and let rise for 1½ hours.

6. Give the dough a turn: Slide your hands underneath the dough and pick it up from underneath, so that it droops over your hands. Then set it down again, on one of its drooping sides, back in the bowl. Cover the bowl with plastic wrap and let it rise until it has almost doubled in volume, another 1½ hours.

7. Turn the dough onto a countertop lightly dusted with flour. Divide the dough into 2 equal pieces. Shape each piece into a rough rectangle and fold each rectangle in half. Let the dough rest for 10 minutes.

8. Shape the dough into two 14-inch-long baguettes (see shaping baguettes, page 89). Transfer them, seam sides down, to a parchment-covered baker's peel or rimless baking sheet, positioning them so that they're about 3 inches apart on the paper. Pleat the paper in between the loaves to draw them together. Place a rolled-up kitchen towel underneath the paper on the sides of the loaves to support them and help them keep their shape as they proof. Sprinkle the baguettes with flour and drape with plastic wrap.

9. Place the peel in the refrigerator and retard the baguettes for at least 12 and up to 24 hours.

10. Two hours before you want to bake, take the loaves out of the refrigerator and let them come to room temperature on the countertop, keeping them covered. They won't rise noticeably.

11. One hour before baking, place a baking stone in the middle rack of the oven and a cast-iron skillet on the lower rack. Preheat the oven to 450°F.

CONTINUED →

12. Uncover the loaves, remove the towels, and pull the paper so it lies flat and the loaves are separated. Use a razor blade, lame, or sharp chef's knife to make three 3-inch-long diagonal cuts on each loaf.

13. Slide the loaves, still on the parchment, onto the preheated baking stone. Drop ½ cup ice cubes into the cast-iron pan. Bake until the baguettes are deep brown and an instant-read thermometer inserted into the center reads 205°F, 20 to 25 minutes.

14. Slide the loaves, still on the parchment, onto a wire rack. Let cool for 5 minutes, peel from the parchment, and then let cool to warm room temperature, another 10 minutes or so. Serve warm.

Sourdough Baking
Questions and Answers

Q For the health of the environment, I avoid buying bottled spring water, preferring to use what comes out of the tap. How can I make sure my tap water is safe to activate a sourdough culture?

A Chances are that your tap water will work just as well as bottled spring water in a sourdough culture. In moderate quantities, the minerals in tap water will not harm yeast. But if your water is very hard, meaning it is so full of minerals that you have difficulty getting soap to lather on your hands, these abundant minerals may inhibit or altogether arrest the growth of your starter. An inexpensive water filter such as the ones made by Brita (see Resources, page 273) will remove enough minerals to make your water effective for sourdough.

If your water has so much chlorine in it that it smells faintly of the YMCA, you will want to dechlorinate it before using it to activate and feed a sourdough culture. Doing so is simple. Chlorine gas dissipates quickly into the air. You need only pour your water into a measuring cup and let it sit uncovered for several hours.

Q My culture seemed to be thriving after 2 days, but when I added the wheat flour on day 3, it stopped exhibiting signs of life: no rising, no bubbling, no acidic aroma. I had to throw it out. What happened?

A Bread book author Peter Reinhart has discussed this phenomenon, which he says is occurring more and more frequently due to the increased presence in today's flour of a certain bacteria called *Leuconostoc*. This bacteria mimics yeast fermentation by producing abundant carbon dioxide and acids, but it actually suppresses yeast as it multiplies. At a certain point, it is killed off by its own acids. So on the third or fourth day of cultivation, fermentation appears to come to a grinding halt. In reality, the yeast hasn't even had a chance to begin fermenting. It is too bad that you discarded the culture, because if you had given it another few days, the yeast would have in all likelihood become more active and plentiful.

Reinhart has a few suggestions for preventing this and encouraging yeast to become active earlier. He says that if you use pineapple juice instead of water on days 1 and 2, you will create a pH-balanced environment that is hostile to the *Leuconostoc* and friendly to yeast. More appealing to me because it is simpler is his suggestion that stirring the culture vigorously once or twice each day will activate the yeast earlier. Yeast thrive on oxygen and will multiply more quickly when exposed to air, and they are more likely to overcome the *Leuconostoc* if strengthened this way.

What to do if you haven't added pineapple juice or stirred your culture, it is day 3, and you have a suddenly inert mass of flour and water on your hands? Start stirring today, and give it some time. Chances are good that the dormant yeast will ultimately be awakened by your patient attentions.

Q **My culture didn't cease to ferment when I began adding bread flour instead of rye flour, but it slowed down considerably. Why?**

A Wheat flour, because it is proportionately higher in protein than rye flour, has comparatively fewer starches, so it doesn't provide quite the same lavish banquet for yeast. Fermentation will slow down because of this. If you want a fast-fermenting wheat starter, try using organic flour, which has more enzymes that will convert starch to sugar, providing more food for your yeast.

Q **I am eager to bake sourdough bread but too impatient to wait 2 weeks for a homegrown culture to be ready. Do you recommend using dehydrated wild yeast as a shortcut?**

A There are a few shortcuts you can try, although none will give you the intense satisfaction of having cultivated your own yeast from scratch. King Arthur Flour (see Resources, page 273) sells dehydrated French sourdough starter, which works the same way as commercial yeast but contains a variety of strains of wild yeast, which give bread a more complex flavor. More intriguing to me is the fresh sourdough culture that the company sells. You can order a portion of the starter that King Arthur has been using in its own bread for years and refresh it the way you would a homegrown starter, and eventually it will take on the characteristics of the yeast from your kitchen and your flour. As long as it was handled properly during shipping, and you feed it within the time frame suggested on the package, you will save yourself some time while ending up in a month or two with a starter that is identical to one you would have made yourself.

Q When I took my starter out of the refrigerator, it had little puddles of water on its surface. Is this a bad sign?

A After obsessively watching your starter come alive and gain in strength over the course of one or several weeks, it's understandable that you might fret about small changes in its appearance or texture once you've had some success with it. But don't worry — the difficult part is over. Once a starter is well established, it is difficult to kill! Sometimes a liquid sourdough culture will separate as it stands. Just stir it well before you refresh it and it should behave as you expect during the final build.

Q I used my starter a week ago and it was fine, but when I took it out of the refrigerator to refresh it today, it had spots of what I assume is mold on the surface. It took me 2 weeks to cultivate this starter! Do I have to throw it out and start all over again?

A Don't panic. Simply scrape the visible mold off the starter with a spoon and refresh it as directed, feeding it several times during the next week instead of waiting a whole week. It should become healthy again with this extra care and feeding.

Q How can I convert my liquid starter to a firm starter?

A It may take 2 or 3 refreshments, but it's very simple to go from a liquid starter to a firm one. Simply change the proportions of flour to water when you refresh the starter, measuring out ½ cup starter and adding 4 ounces (½ cup) water and 6.8 ounces (1⅓ cups) flour to come up with a more claylike mixture. Remember, a stiff dough starter will require a minute or two of kneading, instead of stirring, to moisten all the flour.

Q Every time I refresh my starter, I get a little pang when I discard the small portion that I don't need for either my final build or my new batch of sourdough. Is there anything I can do with the rest (it's usually just a few tablespoons) instead of throwing it away?

A Do I have an idea for you! Why not use your extra sourdough to make waffle or pancake batter? In the evening, after you have made your final build and refreshed your starter, scrape the leftovers into a bowl and add the flour, sugar, and milk or buttermilk from your favorite waffle or pancake recipe. Stir well, cover the bowl with plastic, and then refrigerate the mixture overnight. Basically, you will be creating a wet sponge. The next morning, stir in the remaining ingredients — the melted butter, eggs, salt, and baking powder or baking soda — and cook. Your waffles will be lighter on the inside and crisper on the outside than you could have ever imagined, and I bet you will want to make use of your leftover sourdough culture in this way every time you refresh it.

Q **In other books, I've read about "six-build" or "five-build" or "two-build" sourdough systems. What does this mean? What kind of system do you recommend?**

A There are countless ways to "build" a sourdough starter. Some bakers start off with a small amount of a larger culture and continue to feed this culture with larger and larger amounts of flour and water until they reach a final build with just the right balance of yeast and acids for the breads they want to bake. Then they'll start building all over again, using a small amount of the original starter and taking it through as many builds as they need all over again. Building a starter in a number of stages provides the baker with the same number of opportunities to customize the flavor and texture of the bread. But it's not the most practical method for home bakers. Although less refined, the two-build system I use in these recipes is easier for the home baker who wants to give sourdough baking a try. Once a viable

culture is established, the baker uses it to mix the final build. From then onward, the starter goes through only two builds: First, it is refreshed and set aside for the batch of bread. Then, 8 to 12 hours before baking, it is used to make the final build. It's important to understand that you need not commit to a particular system forever and ever. Once you have built a healthy starter, you can use it as a first build in any other sourdough system that you read about.

Q **My final build fermented much more quickly than the 8 to 12 hours suggested in the recipe, becoming so acidic that I was afraid to use it in my dough. Why did this happen and what can I do to make it less active?**

A If your culture is maturing before you are ready to use it, either because it is exceptionally active (be happy that you have so much yeast!) or because your kitchen is exceptionally warm, you can make a couple of adjustments in the way you build it. You can use a smaller proportion of culture, say ⅓ cup instead of ½ cup, for the next final build that you mix. This will result in a less active, slower-fermenting starter. Or you can use cold instead of room temperature water, which will also slow down fermentation.

Q When I used my sourdough to bake bread, the bread was underrisen and damp on the inside. Did I jump the gun with my starter? How can I get it to ferment more quickly so I can get baking?

A Don't feel bad. Bakers new to sourdough don't always judge the readiness of their starter accurately, and in their eagerness often use it before it's ready. These are both signs that your dough didn't have enough active yeast to raise your bread. If your starter is at all active, time will take care of the problem. Just keep feeding your starter until it is ready. But if you are in a hurry, you can do a couple of things to speed up the fermentation process.

Instead of feeding the starter every 24 hours, feed it twice a day, giving it just half the amount of food and water each time. (If you are following the recipe on page 166, that would mean stirring together ½ cup starter with ½ cup all-purpose flour, 1 teaspoon rye flour, and ¼ cup water.) Doubling up on feedings, even though you are giving it the same amount of food overall, should help. You could also add water that's a little warmer than 78°F but no warmer than 85°F. A little warmth at the beginning of each feeding will stimulate the yeast.

Q Is it ever appropriate to add commercial yeast to bread dough made with a sourdough starter?

A Sourdough purists might balk, but there are sometimes good reasons for using commercial yeast along with the wild yeast. In doughs with a large proportion of starchy rye flour, commercial yeast is often added as a hedge against all of the yeast-destroying acids produced by the fast-fermenting grain.

For bakers who want the flavor of sourdough bread without the long fermentation time that some of these breads require, adding some commercial yeast can speed up the process considerably. For example, if you add ¾ teaspoon instant yeast to the Bran-Flecked Sourdough Country Bread (page 169) dough along with the sourdough starter, you can cut bulk fermentation time and the proofing time in half.

Q Can I use a sourdough starter in place of a yeasted pre-ferment such as poolish?

A Yes, and it couldn't be easier. Use a loose sourdough starter in place of a sponge or poolish, and use a firm sourdough starter in place of a biga or stiff dough levain. Use the same weight of sourdough starter as the weight of pre-ferment called for in the recipe. You can skip commercial yeast altogether as long as you give your dough adequate time to ferment and proof, or you can add some commercial yeast to the dough to keep the fermentation times the same as in the original recipe.

Q **I was surprised at how mildly flavored my sourdough bread came out. How can I make my breads more distinctly sour tasting?**

A There are several ways to get a more pronounced sour flavor. You could ferment your sourdough culture longer than usual, taking care that acid buildup doesn't compromise the yeast. To do this, let it stand on the countertop for the recommended 8 to 12 hours after refreshing, and then instead of using it directly, refrigerate this mixture overnight to build up more acids without killing the yeast. Let the culture come to room temperature for an hour or two before proceeding with the recipe.

Alternatively, you could retard your loaf (see page 85) once it's been shaped. Refrigerate it for up to 24 hours, and then let it sit at room temperature for several hours before baking. Remember, when considering this option, that it works best with wheat breads. The weaker gluten structure of rye breads won't be able to support this extra-long, cool proofing.

Q **I just saw a picture of a Poilâne loaf with its distinctive slash, and I'd like to "sign" my bread in a similarly attractive way. But I'm afraid my slashing skills are very primitive, and I'm not up for attempting to carve a G (my initial) in my bread. Any suggestions?**

A The conventional scoring pattern for a large round loaf — 4 slashes that make a square or parallelogram on top of the bread — provides an excellent frame for a bread stencil. Draw your initial (or your whole name, if it will fit) on a piece of parchment paper and then cut out the letter or letters. Place the stencil on top of the bread just before scoring it and sift some flour over it, using a fine strainer. Carefully lift the paper from the bread, score the 4 slashes around your stencil to frame it, and bake. You don't have to limit yourself to monograms. I often use a stencil in the shape of a whale, the symbol of the seaside town where I live, when I'm baking what I like to think of as my Sag Harbor Sourdough Country Bread.

Q I've fermented my baguette dough, but it seems rather sluggish. Will it ferment sufficiently overnight in the refrigerator, even if it hasn't shown much activity up to now?

A Remember, doughs raised with wild yeast will not always rise in the bowl in the same way as doughs raised with instant yeast. But if your kitchen is particularly cold or your culture a little less active than you'd like, you can let your shaped loaves stand on the countertop for up to 1 hour before retarding them. Take care not to leave them out for too long. Even in a 40-degree refrigerator, bread dough will accumulate quite a lot of acids during a 24-hour period. If it is already acidic when it goes into the refrigerator, it may overproof, even if left to stand at such a low temperature.

Q Why can't I place my chilled baguettes in the oven directly from the refrigerator, if they are fully proofed?

A If, when you take them out of the refrigerator, your loaves have that soft, puffy, almost slack feel to them that indicates they're fully proofed, by all means bake them. If you let them sit at room temperature past this point, you risk the chance of baking under-risen baguettes. But most loaves will need to come to room temperature to reach this stage of readiness. As with every aspect of home bread baking, the baker's judgment, aided by experience, is a better guide than a recipe when it comes to coaxing the best bread from a lump of dough.

Q What is San Francisco sourdough? Is it better than the sourdough I've cultivated in my own kitchen?

A San Francisco sourdough is characterized by its particularly tangy flavor, chewy crust, and moist crumb. Its flavor is uniquely regional. It contains acids produced by *Lactobacillus sanfrancisco*, a microorganism local to the Bay Area. While fans may prefer its flavor, there is nothing inherently better about a starter cultivated in San Francisco than one cultivated in, say, Minneapolis. Breads made with these starters will have flavor differences discernible to connoisseurs and local boosters, of course. But as long as the starter from Minneapolis is healthy and well cared for, it will raise and flavor bread just as well as a San Francisco sourdough.

Q I'm going on vacation for 3 weeks. Will my starter die in the refrigerator while I'm away?

A To keep your culture ready for baking, it's a good idea to refresh it once a week. But I've left my sourdough in the refrigerator for far longer than that, without refreshment, and have always been able to revive it. The fact is that even if your starter has soured beyond belief, separated so that a grayish liquid has floated to the top of the container, and/or is growing visible mold, there is almost certainly live yeast in there somewhere that can be invigorated. Refresh the culture as you would after 1 week, let it stand at room temperature for 8 to 12 hours, and see what happens. It may bounce back immediately, or it may show weakened signs of life. If it's not quite as bubbly and well risen as it was before your vacation, refresh it again. Continue to do so until it is behaving in a way that tells you it is ready to raise bread.

Chapter 7
Yeasted Flatbreads

ALTHOUGH WE MAY THINK of baguettes as ancient, this style of loaf is a relatively recent tradition. Invented to be baked in the new gas-fired deck ovens of the mid-nineteenth century, they really took hold after 1920, as a help to Parisian bakers, who were forbidden by law to begin work before 4 AM and who thus needed a supply of quick-baking loaves for early-morning customers who couldn't wait for larger boules to be ready.

If you really want to bake an ancient bread, you can do much better than this. While unleavened flatbreads can be dated as far back as 5,000 years, the first known yeasted breads were baked in ancient Egypt sometime around 2650 BC, after some clever or very lucky Egyptians discovered that when they left a mixture of flour and water (or yeasty beer, more likely) to stand for a while rather than baking their dough right off, it would bubble up rather than remain flat. Lacking proper ovens, Old and Middle Kingdom Egyptian bakers made bread molds of pottery and set these molds atop glowing embers. They then draped dough over the heated molds to bake. New Kingdom bakers slapped disks of yeasted bread dough onto the preheated walls of newly invented hearth ovens.

Ancient Egyptian bread mold

These and other ancient bread traditions continue today, well beyond the borders of Egypt. Not only are breads such as Afghan naan, Middle Eastern pita, and Italian pizza served in bakeries and restaurants run by natives of Afghanistan, Syria, and Italy, but they are also baked more and more frequently at home by adventurous American bakers looking to expand their repertoire to include these fun and accessible breads.

This chapter has some of my favorite recipes for yeasted flatbreads from around the world. These breads are called "flat" because of their shape rather than because they don't rise. (For suggestions about baking unleavened flatbreads, see below.)

Yeasted flatbreads have much in common with more conventionally shaped breads. Everything you've learned about gluten development and yeast activity, about sponges and poolish, can be applied to flatbreads. Indeed, crafting an exceptional yeasted flatbread requires knowledge, experience, and technique similar to what is necessary when making an exceptional baguette.

Unleavened Flatbreads

An entire book could be written on unleavened bread, and there are several very good bread books that cover the subject extensively (see page 278 for titles). These flatbreads, often made with grains other than wheat, as well as with ground beans and mashed tubers, are outside the scope of our discussion. But they are well worth investigating for their variety and cultural significance, whether you are a serious student of bread or have a serious fear of yeast!

Many unleavened flatbreads are indeed as flat as a tortilla. This isn't to say that unleavened flatbreads don't rise. Some of the most delectable examples are puffy and beautifully shaped. They get their structure and sometimes an ethereal airiness from techniques that don't involve fermentation.

Here are descriptions of some of the most popular and/or interesting unleavened flatbreads, if you are interested in pursuing the subject.

Corn tortillas. When I was growing up, tortillas were a mythical food, as they were entirely unavailable in New Jersey. Now there probably isn't a child at my old elementary school who hasn't eaten a taco or some chips made with this staple of Mexican cooking. Homemade corn tortillas are so far superior to commercial examples that it is almost your duty as a home baker to try making them. You will need a tortilla press (an inexpensive item that can easily be found online) and some masa harina (a flour made with lime-soaked ground corn, available in most supermarkets) and little else.

But there are a few issues unique to flatbreads that you'll want to consider before baking pita breads or a pizza of your own, including shaping techniques, proofing, and baking your breads on surfaces other than a baking stone inside your oven. A quick study of these issues will get you ready for a wonderfully gratifying baking experience.

Flatbreads Are Breads, Too

Flatbreads are among the simplest and most forgiving bread recipes in existence. Many are free-form in shape, so there's no need to worry about rolling out a perfect baguette and scoring it just so. Since they're often enjoyed warm from the oven (or griddle or grill), it's not necessary to

Dosas. These crêpelike southern Indian flatbreads made with rice flour and urad dal (split small black beans similar to mung beans) are eaten at every meal and in between. Filled with potato curry or lightly fried red onions, they are an exotic but delicious breakfast.

Lefse. This is a Norwegian flatbread made with mashed potatoes, butter, cream, and flour, rolled with a special corrugated pin to deflate any air bubbles in the dough. In Norway, freshly griddled lefse are spread with butter or lingonberry jam before being folded up like crêpes, or served with lutefisk. In Minnesota and other parts of the United States with a considerable Norwegian-American population, lefse are served this way but are also used to wrap ham and eggs or peanut butter and jelly.

Matzoh. Author Rose Levy Beranbaum argues that matzoh shouldn't be relegated to its symbolic presence on the Passover table (it represents the unleavened bread made by Jews fleeing Egypt, prepared in haste because they didn't have time to let dough rise), and she provides a rosemary-flavored version in *The Bread Bible.*

Poori. These delicious cumin-spiced flatbreads from northern India puff up when fried in hot oil.

Poori

cultivate a sourdough starter for them the way you might if you wanted to extend the shelf life of a giant boule.

But flatbreads are breads just the same. Give some consideration to your ingredients and technique, as you would when getting ready to bake a baguette or a boule, and your breads will be as worthy of the "artisan" label as those two classic French breads.

Flour. I use bread flour when I want to give a heavy dough, such as Sunflower Seed Bread (page 136), a boost. But the breads in this chapter don't need to rise high. All-purpose flour has just enough protein to give them character without making them too crusty or hard.

Developing gluten. Even though flatbreads don't rise high the way a sandwich loaf or boule does, they still require some gluten to give them structure. All-purpose flour has enough protein to make pitas puff up or to give lavash its bubbly texture, but only if that protein is developed into a good gluten web. When developing these recipes, I utilized some of the gluten-building techniques discussed in previous chapters to give breads their shape, with an eye toward convenience: Pizza dough isn't kneaded. Instead, it's allowed to sit for up to 18 hours, giving the gluten time to organize itself into a web all on its own. English muffin dough is retarded in the refrigerator overnight, accomplishing the same goal, just in time for breakfast in the morning.

Fermentation — or not. The equation that we discussed in chapter 5, long fermentation equals flavorful bread, applies to flatbreads as well. To extend fermentation, you can use any trick in the book, from employing the no-knead method (during which dough ferments for almost a day) to retarding your dough (again, extending fermentation overnight) to building your dough in two stages by using a pre-ferment. Any of these methods will result in a wonderfully flavored flatbread. But keep in mind that many flatbreads are meant to be enjoyed with flavorful fillings, dips, or toppings. Pita bread, scallion pancakes, and Turkish gözleme are examples of simple doughs that get a lot of flavor from extra ingredients, in which case there's no great need to build a dough's flavor in two steps or through an extra-long fermentation. With these breads, you can enjoy the ease of straight dough baking.

Bench rest. Unlike thicker, heavier doughs, most of these flatbreads require just a few minutes' rest after shaping before they go into the oven (or onto the grill or into the skillet). They'll do most of their rising as they bake.

"Baking" Flatbreads

Bakers made flatbreads before ovens were invented. Early examples were baked over an open fire, on stones heated over coals, and even on the hot sand of the Sahara Desert. Today, flatbreads are steamed, grilled, or fried when they're not baked in an oven. Take into consideration the following when getting ready to "bake." Once you have some experience with flatbreads, you might try an alternative cooking method with a favorite recipe to see what kind of results you might get.

Baking. Like other hearth breads, oven-baked flatbreads such as No-Knead Roman Pizzas (page 193), Pita Bread (page 195), and Lavash (page 202) benefit immensely if baked on a preheated baking stone. When their bottom crusts make contact with the superheated stone, they'll get all of the oven spring they need to puff or bubble up beautifully. But unlike most other hearth breads, flatbreads usually don't require steam to keep their crusts moist, since they either get moisture from a wet topping (as in the case of pizza) or bake too quickly for the steam to have an impact (as with pita and lavash).

Griddle. A nonstick surface is not essential, but it is nice insurance that you will be able to lift your flatbread easily from the pan and flip it if necessary. For doughs that are relatively thick, such as those for English muffins or Turkish gözleme, set the heat to low to allow them to bake through before the exterior burns.

Grilling. Grilling is a great way to add some charred flavor to your bread. Preheat your gas grill adequately before baking, for the best "oven spring" outdoors. A clean cooking surface is important, for clean flavor and also to prevent the dough from sticking, so scrape your grill grids well when the grill is hot. Oil either the grill grids or the bottom surface of the flatbreads so that they'll come away easily when they're done baking.

Frying. Who doesn't like fried bread? From doughnuts and beignets to Navajo fry bread to lángos (sometimes called Hungarian pizza), there are many examples of yeasted dough that is deep-fried rather than baked. The result is a spectacularly rich bread with a delicate but crisp outer crust and a wonderfully most interior. For safety's sake, fry your bread in a deep pot such as a Dutch oven, filling it with only an inch or two of vegetable oil. Use a long-handled slotted spoon or tongs to put your dough into the pot and to remove it. The key to good fried bread is temperature control. Use a deep-frying thermometer to gauge the temperature. Wait until the oil reaches 325°F before beginning. And watch the thermometer carefully during cooking. It is easy to burn bread dough if the oil gets too hot. Drain your bread briefly on a paper towel–lined baking sheet before serving in order to remove excess grease. And eat your fried treats right away, because this is one type of bread that won't keep well past cooking.

The Recipes

Part of the appeal of these breads is their wonderful diversity. There's a flatbread recipe here for everyone — the Anglophile (Overnight English Muffins, page 200), the ethnic food maven (Scallion Pancakes, page 204, or Spinach and Feta Gözleme, page 207), the picky kid (No-Knead Roman Pizzas, page 193). There's also something new to learn about bread in every single recipe, whether it is how to stretch pizza dough, how to keep lavash soft, or why most commercial pita breads are dry and how to make moist homemade ones.

No-Knead Roman Pizzas

Makes 4 (10-inch) pizzas

My favorite pizza dough requires kneading on high speed in an electric mixer for up to 20 minutes. I wondered if, using the same proportion of flour and water, I could save my motor by using the no-knead method. The recipe adapted beautifully, resulting in pizza crust that was crisp and bubbly with a wonderful softness. The easiest way to shape the individual pizzas is to stretch each piece of dough into a long rectangle.

15 ounces (1¾ cups) room temperature water (75 to 78°F)

0.25 ounce/1 gram (¼ teaspoon) instant yeast

16.25 ounces/461 grams (3¼ cups) unbleached all-purpose flour

0.25 ounce/7 grams (1½ teaspoons) kosher salt or fine sea salt

1 (15-ounce) can diced tomatoes, drained

8 ounces fresh mozzarella cheese, shredded

¼ cup extra-virgin olive oil

¼ cup finely chopped fresh basil leaves

Freshly ground black pepper

1. Combine the water, yeast, flour, and salt in a large mixing bowl. Stir the mixture with a rubber spatula until it comes together into a rough dough. Cover the bowl with plastic wrap and let the dough stand at room temperature for 8 to 18 hours.

2. One hour before baking, place a baking stone on the middle rack. Preheat the oven to 500°F.

3. Heavily dust the countertop with flour. Turn the dough out onto the counter and heavily dust the top of the dough with flour. Use a bench scraper or sharp chef's knife to divide the dough into 4 equal pieces.

4. Line a baker's peel with parchment paper and sprinkle with flour. Transfer one of the dough pieces to the peel and, with floured hands, gently stretch and pull it into a 4- by 12-inch rectangle. Repeat with a second dough piece so you have two pieces side by side, with about 1 inch between them. Drape the remaining dough pieces with plastic wrap.

CONTINUED →

5. Scatter half of the tomatoes and then half of the cheese over the two stretched dough pieces. Slide the pizza, still on the parchment, onto the baking stone and bake until the crust is golden brown and the cheese is bubbling, about 15 minutes. Drizzle each pizza with a tablespoon of olive oil and sprinkle with 1 tablespoon of the basil. Let stand for 5 minutes on a cutting board before slicing and serving.

6. Line the peel with a fresh piece of parchment and repeat with the remaining dough pieces and topping ingredients.

Where Is It From? Varieties of Pizza

Scholars and people on the street have been debating the origins of this worldwide favorite and the merits of its various styles. Once you know something about customizing bread dough, you can perhaps attempt a bake-off of your own.

Detroit. A square deep-dish pie notable because it is baked twice, once to crisp the crust and once to cook the toppings.

Chicago. A deep-dish pie with a tall edge (which is sometimes brushed with melted butter) that is important for containing large quantities of sauce, cheese, and other toppings.

Neapolitan. Stretched by hand and baked in a wood-fired oven. There are only two sanctioned toppings: marinara (tomatoes, oregano, garlic, and olive oil) and Margherita (tomatoes, mozzarella cheese, and basil).

New Haven. Pizza in the Neapolitan style, but with a larger variety of toppings. Most famously made in the brick ovens at the competing New Haven pizza parlors Pepe's and Sally's.

New York. A greasier, thicker, more heavily sauced version of Neapolitan pizza.

St. Louis. This very regional specialty has a yeastless crust and is topped with local Provel cheese, a mix of cheddar, Swiss, and provolone that is sold only in the St. Louis area.

Sicilian. Sicilian pizza has a thick (about 1 inch) crust and cheese that's placed underneath the tomato sauce.

Pita Bread

Makes 8 (6-inch) pitas

When my children ate fresh pitas at a local Middle Eastern restaurant, they were amazed at how soft and moist the breads were in contrast to the thin, dry pitas from the supermarket. It's all in the timing — most commercial pitas are overbaked (they shouldn't brown at all) and stale (these are best eaten on the day they're made). You may substitute 8 ounces (1¾ cups) whole-wheat flour for the white flour, but you may need up to an additional ¼ cup water for proper hydration.

Sometimes a pita won't balloon properly because the air pocket inside isn't seamless. These pitas will still taste great and can still be sliced in half and filled, or cut them into wedges for dipping into hummus or baba ghanoush.

10 ounces (1¼ cups) warm room temperature water (78°F)
0.2 ounce/6 grams (2 teaspoons) instant yeast
16 ounces/454 grams (3 cups) unbleached all-purpose flour
0.25 ounce/7 grams (1½ teaspoons) kosher salt or fine sea salt
2 tablespoons olive oil

1. Combine the water, yeast, flour, salt, and olive oil in the bowl of a stand mixer or in a large mixing bowl. Stir with a rubber spatula until a rough dough forms.

2. Knead the dough. By machine: With a dough hook, knead the dough until it is smooth and soft and passes the windowpane test (see page 71), about 10 minutes on medium-low speed. By hand: Turn the dough out onto a lightly floured countertop. Flour your hands and knead the dough with firm strokes until it is smooth and soft, 12 to 15 minutes.

3. Spray the inside of a dough-rising container or large mixing bowl with nonstick cooking spray and place the dough inside. Cover with plastic wrap and let rise until the dough has more than doubled in size and when poked with a fingertip doesn't spring back, 2 to 3 hours.

CONTINUED $\rightarrow$

4. One hour before baking place a baking stone on the bottom rack of the oven and preheat the oven to 475°F. Turn the dough out onto a lightly floured countertop and divide into 8 equal pieces. Shape each piece into a ball (see page 88), flatten into a disk, sprinkle lightly with flour, drape with plastic wrap, and let stand for 20 minutes.

5. Use a rolling pin to roll each piece of dough into a ¼-inch-thick circle. Let the pieces rest, uncovered, for 10 minutes.

Uses for Day-Old Flatbread

When our baguettes and sandwich breads are a day or two old, we generally toast them, make bread crumbs or croutons, or feed them to the birds.

Many flatbreads, in contrast, are deliberately dried after baking and set aside to be consumed at a later (sometimes much later) date. In Armenia, the birthplace of lavash, great quantities would be baked in the fall, dried, and stored in stacks for consumption throughout the winter. Dried lavash was softened by sprinkling it with water and covering it with a cloth for a half hour. You could try softening your lavash this way, or do as modern-day Armenians do: Tear it into pieces and mix it into a soup or stew. Or use it as you would a partially baked pizza crust, topping it with tomato sauce, vegetables, and/or cheese and heating it in the oven for a few minutes for a quick lunch or weeknight dinner.

If you find yourself with leftover pita bread, you might use it in fattoush, a traditional Lebanese bread salad (along the lines of Italian panzanella) that makes good use of day-old bread. Traditionally, it is flavored with powdered sumac, a lemony spice made from ground berries of the sumac bush that is used often in Lebanese and Turkish cooking. In fact, it is often used in conjunction with lemon juice, as it is here. Look for it in the spice aisle of your supermarket, or buy it online (see Resources, page 273).

Here is a simple recipe:

6. Lightly brush the tops of 2 of the dough rounds with water and place them, moistened side down, on the baking stone. Bake just until the pitas inflate and are just barely golden on their undersides, about 3 minutes. Remove to a wire rack and repeat with the remaining pitas. Serve immediately, or wrap them in a clean kitchen towel and serve within 4 hours.

Fattoush
Serves 4

2 leftover pita breads

Olive oil

Fine sea salt

2 tablespoons fresh lemon juice

1 small garlic clove, finely chopped or crushed

1 tablespoon ground sumac

Freshly ground black pepper

1 small head romaine lettuce, torn into bite-size pieces

6 radishes, trimmed and sliced

6 scallions (white and light green parts), chopped

1 cucumber, peeled, seeded, halved, and thinly sliced

2 tomatoes, cored and cut into 8 wedges each

¼ cup finely chopped fresh flat-leaf parsley leaves

¼ cup finely chopped fresh mint leaves

1. Preheat the oven to 350°F. Split the pitas and cut each half into ¼-inch-wide strips. Place on a baking sheet, mist with olive oil, sprinkle with sea salt, and bake until just golden, 7 to 10 minutes. Let cool completely.

2. Whisk together ¼ cup olive oil, the lemon juice, garlic, sumac, ½ teaspoon salt, and ground black pepper to taste in a small bowl.

3. Just before serving, combine the lettuce, radishes, scallions, cucumber, tomatoes, parsley, mint, and pita strips in a large mixing bowl. Drizzle the dressing over the salad and toss to coat.

Yeasted Flatbreads from Around the World

If pizza from Italy is the most well-known yeasted flatbread in America, other breads are gaining in popularity every day. In addition to Pita Bread (page 195), Lavash (page 202), Spinach and Feta Gözleme (page 207), and Naan (page 205), here are some common and less common examples worth baking and eating.

Fougasse. A Provençal flatbread, often made with olives, and shaped distinctively by making cuts in the flattened dough and then pulling on the dough to open up those cuts. This shaping gives the bread an unusually high crust-to-crumb ratio.

Pissaladière. This onion and anchovy pizza also hails from Provence.

Injera (Ethiopian sponge bread). Made with teff flour, milled from an ancient grain related to millet, this light and bubbly bread is made in a shallow clay pan set over an open fire (American bakers can use a nonstick skillet set over a burner). It gets so bubbly because the batter is allowed to sour at room temperature over several days, producing lots of gas bubbles. It is perfect for scooping up traditional meat and legume stews.

Khachapuri (Georgian cheese bread). These yeasted flatbreads from the Republic of Georgia are filled with fresh cheese such as goat cheese and sometimes topped with a raw or fried egg.

Malooga. To make this flatbread from Yemen, roll out a piece of yeasted dough, brush with clarified butter, fold, and repeat several times. When baked the bread rises not only because of the yeast, but also because of the steam created when the butter melts, as with puff pastry.

R'ghayef. In Morocco, yeasted dough is flattened, filled with a mixture of sautéed onions, butter, and spices, and then folded and flattened again before being cooked on a griddle.

Olive fougasse

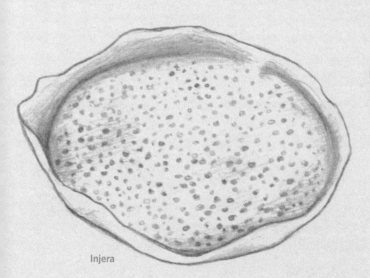

Injera

R'ghayef

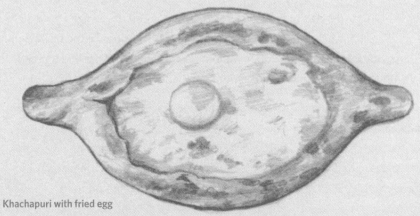

Khachapuri with fried egg

Overnight English Muffins

Makes 12 muffins

Retarding the dough overnight in the refrigerator allows flavor to build; it also allows you to have freshly baked muffins shortly after you wake up. Be sure to let the muffins cool for 10 minutes before eating. During this time they will continue to bake, so when you finally do eat them their centers will be cooked, not doughy.

20 ounces/567 grams (4 cups) unbleached all-purpose flour
10 ounces (1¼ cups) warm whole milk (110°F)
2 ounces (¼ cup) warm water (110°F)
0.2 ounce/6 grams (2 teaspoons) instant yeast
0.5 ounce/14 grams (1 tablespoon) sugar
0.35 ounce/10 grams (2 teaspoons) kosher salt or fine sea salt
2 tablespoons unsalted butter, melted and cooled, plus more for greasing the pan
1 large egg, at room temperature
Cornmeal for dusting

1. Combine the flour, milk, water, yeast, sugar, salt, butter, and egg in the bowl of a stand mixer or in a large mixing bowl. Stir with a rubber spatula until a rough dough forms.

2. Knead the dough. By machine: With a dough hook, knead the dough on medium-low speed until it is smooth and shiny and just clears the sides of the bowl, about 10 minutes. By hand: Turn the dough out onto a lightly floured countertop and knead with steady strokes until it is smooth and shiny, 12 to 15 minutes.

3. Spray the inside of a dough-rising container or large mixing bowl with nonstick cooking spray and place the dough inside. Cover with plastic wrap and let rise until the dough has doubled in size, about 1½ hours. Gently press down on the dough, fold it in half, flip it over in the bowl, re-cover the bowl with plastic, and refrigerate until chilled and firm, at least 2 hours and up to 24 hours.

4. Sprinkle the countertop liberally with cornmeal. Turn the dough out onto the countertop, pat it into a ½-inch-thick rectangle, and sprinkle the top with cornmeal. Use a rolling pin to roll the dough to a ½-inch thickness. Use a floured 3-inch biscuit cutter to cut the dough into circles. Cover the rounds loosely with plastic wrap and let stand for 20 minutes.

5. Heat a large skillet over medium-low heat. Brush lightly with melted butter. Place the muffins in the skillet, at least 1 inch apart, and cook, turning once, until both sides are lightly browned, 8 to 10 minutes total. Transfer to a wire rack to cool for 10 minutes. Serve warm, or let cool to room temperature, store in a resealable plastic bag for up to 2 days, and slice and toast before serving.

Armenian Hummus

Serve traditional hummus with your lavash (see the recipe on page 202), either when it is freshly baked and soft or when it is toasted and broken into pieces. This is flavored with a blend of allspice, fenugreek, cumin, and paprika that gives Armenian cooking its distinctive flavor.

1 (14-ounce) can chickpeas, rinsed and drained

¼ cup water

¼ cup well-stirred tahini

3 tablespoons fresh lemon juice

2 tablespoons olive oil

½ teaspoon salt

½ teaspoon paprika

¼ teaspoon ground cumin

¼ teaspoon ground allspice

¼ teaspoon cayenne pepper

¼ teaspoon ground fenugreek

2 tablespoons finely chopped fresh flat-leaf parsley leaves

Place the chickpeas, water, tahini, lemon juice, olive oil, salt, paprika, cumin, allspice, cayenne, and fenugreek in the work bowl of a food processor and process until smooth, scraping down the sides of the bowl several times as necessary. Add the parsley and pulse once or twice. Scrape the hummus into a bowl and serve immediately, or cover with plastic wrap and refrigerate for up to 1 day before serving.

Fennel and Black Pepper Lavash

Makes 6 (10-inch) flatbreads

Lavash is a thin, yeast-raised flatbread that originated in Armenia and is now popular in a much wider area that includes Turkey, Georgia, and Iran. Bakeries in Armenia produce lavash in huge sheets, sometimes measuring 4 or 5 feet across. Smaller sheets of dough are laid over a convex iron plate set over an open fire to bake. To mimic this method at home, you can lightly grease the outside of a large metal wok, set it over a burner upside down, and heat the wok over medium-high heat before draping the dough over it and baking until golden on the underside, 3 to 4 minutes. Don't overbake them — you want them to be soft, not crisp. Or just bake them on a preheated baking stone, as directed in the recipe. You will get a very similar result.

This recipe starts off with a sponge, to extend fermentation and help the lavash stay fresh for several days. The idea of adding fennel seeds and black pepper comes from Peter Reinhart's recipe in *Crust and Crumb*. For a more traditional seeded lavash, substitute poppy or sesame seeds for the fennel. For plain lavash, omit the fennel and pepper.

Just-baked lavash is soft and pliable and can be used to wrap stews or grilled meats and vegetables. Once baked, the lavash will dry out and crisp up quickly. Use crispy lavash to accompany soups, or soften it by misting lightly with water.

FOR THE SPONGE:

3 ounces (6 tablespoons) room temperature water (75 to 78°F)

0.05 ounce/1.5 grams (½ teaspoon) instant yeast

4 ounces/113 grams (¾ cup) unbleached all-purpose flour

FOR THE DOUGH:

9 ounces (1 cup plus 2 tablespoons) room temperature water (75 to 78°F)

0.025 ounce/1 gram (¼ teaspoon) instant yeast

12.8 ounces/363 grams (2½ cups) unbleached all-purpose flour

0.5 ounce/14 grams (1 tablespoon) sugar

0.17 ounce/5 grams (1 teaspoon) kosher salt or fine sea salt

2 teaspoons fennel seeds

½ teaspoon freshly ground black pepper

2 teaspoons olive oil

1. Make the sponge: Combine the water, yeast, and flour in a medium bowl and stir to combine. Cover with plastic wrap and let stand at room temperature until it is very bubbly and has a mild acidic aroma (it won't rise much, because it is so loose), 3 to 5 hours.

2. Make the dough: Combine the water, yeast, flour, sugar, salt, fennel seeds, pepper, olive oil, and sponge in the bowl of a stand mixer. Stir with a rubber spatula until a rough dough forms.

3. Knead the dough using the dough hook until it is soft and elastic and passes the windowpane test (see page 71), 5 to 7 minutes on medium speed.

4. Spray the inside of a dough-rising container or large mixing bowl with nonstick cooking spray and place the dough inside. Cover with plastic wrap and let rise until the dough has doubled in size and when poked with a fingertip doesn't spring back, about 1 hour.

5. One hour before baking, place a baking stone on the middle rack of the oven and preheat the oven to 475°F. Turn the dough out onto a lightly floured countertop and divide into 6 equal pieces. Shape each piece into a ball (see page 88), flatten into a disk, sprinkle lightly with flour, drape with plastic wrap, and let stand for 20 minutes.

6. Working with one at a time, stretch each dough disk into a rough 10-inch square. Bake the lavash, one at a time, until lightly browned on the bottom, about 2 minutes. Don't overbake them — you want them to be soft, not crisp. As they come out of the oven, fold them in half, place them on a plate, and keep covered with a kitchen towel to keep them soft. Serve them immediately, or let them cool completely.

Scallion Pancakes

Makes 8 (4-inch) pancakes

Stirring the flour with boiling water before mixing the dough is a traditional Chinese technique that encourages the starch molecules in the flour to swell (they will only do this in the presence of water and heat), giving the pancakes their moist, almost spongy texture and a pleasant sweetness.

8 ounces (1 cup) boiling water
7.55 ounces/214 grams (1½ cups) unbleached all-purpose flour
3 tablespoons vegetable oil, plus more if necessary
0.05 ounce/1½ grams (½ teaspoon) instant yeast
0.17 ounce/5 grams (1 teaspoon) sugar
0.17 ounce/5 grams (1 teaspoon) salt
¾ cup finely chopped scallions

1. Combine the boiling water and flour in a large bowl and mix with a rubber spatula until a rough dough forms. Let cool slightly.

2. Add 2 tablespoons vegetable oil, the yeast, sugar, and salt to the bowl, and fold it into the dough with the spatula. Turn the dough onto a lightly floured countertop and knead by hand until smooth and supple, 2 to 3 minutes.

3. Spray the inside of a dough-rising container or large mixing bowl with nonstick cooking spray and place the dough inside. Cover with plastic wrap and let rise until the dough has doubled in size and when poked with a fingertip doesn't spring back, 30 to 45 minutes.

4. Turn the dough out onto a lightly floured countertop and divide into eight 1½-inch pieces. Form each piece into a ball. Let stand on the countertop for 10 minutes to relax.

5. Preheat the oven to 200°F and place a baking sheet on the middle rack. One by one, use a rolling pin to roll each ball into a 5-inch round. Scatter some scallions over a round and roll it, jellyroll-style, into a tight cylinder. Then coil the cylinder into a snail-shaped round. Repeat with the remaining balls, keeping the rolled-up

dough pieces under a piece of plastic while you work so they won't dry out.

6. Heat the remaining 1 tablespoon oil in a large skillet over medium-high heat. On a lightly floured countertop, position 2 or 3 of the dough pieces on end, and roll out into 4-inch circles. Transfer them to the pan and cook until golden brown, turning once, 4 to 6 minutes total. Transfer to the baking sheet to keep warm. Repeat with the remaining pancakes, and then serve immediately.

Coil the cylinder into a round.

Grilled Whole-Wheat Naan

Makes 6 (5-inch) naan

Traditionally, Afghan naan is baked in a beehive-shaped tandoor oven that is heated on top of hot coals. The baker uses a special peel to slap the dough onto the oven's preheated clay walls. In just a few minutes, the bottom crust becomes well browned because of the direct contact with the hot clay, while the top crust firms up but stays soft, cooked by the hot air moving upward from the coals. Grilling the dough is a simple way to get a similar effect: a charred bottom crust, a moist interior, and a soft top crust. Serve them with chicken or lamb kabobs and grilled vegetables for an exotic summer dinner that you can cook entirely outdoors.

"Baking" naan on the grill

FOR THE SPONGE:

6 ounces (¾ cup) room temperature water (75 to 78°F)

4 ounces (½ cup) plain whole-milk yogurt

0.1 ounce/3 grams (1 teaspoon) instant yeast

8 ounces/227 grams (1½ cups) unbleached all-purpose flour

CONTINUED →

FOR THE DOUGH:

4.5 ounces/128 grams (1 cup) stone-ground whole-wheat flour

1 tablespoon olive oil

0.17 ounce/5 grams (1 teaspoon) kosher salt or fine sea salt

3 tablespoons sesame seeds

Olive oil for grilling

1. Make the sponge: Combine the water, yogurt, yeast, and all-purpose flour in a medium bowl and stir to combine. Cover with plastic wrap and let stand at room temperature until it is very bubbly, 1 hour.

2. Make the dough: Combine the whole-wheat flour, olive oil, salt, sesame seeds, and sponge in the bowl of a stand mixer. Stir with a rubber spatula until a rough dough forms.

3. Knead the dough with the dough hook until it is soft and elastic and passes the windowpane test (see page 71), 5 to 7 minutes on medium speed.

4. Spray the inside of a dough-rising container or large mixing bowl with nonstick cooking spray and place the dough inside. Cover with plastic wrap and let rise until the dough has doubled in size and when poked with a fingertip doesn't spring back, about 1 hour.

5. Turn the dough out onto a lightly floured countertop and divide into 6 equal pieces. Shape each piece into a ball (see page 88), flatten into a 5-inch round disk, sprinkle lightly with flour, drape with plastic wrap, and let stand for 20 minutes.

6. Preheat a gas grill to medium. Oil one side of each dough round and place them, oiled side down, on the grill. Cover and cook until the undersides are golden with dark grill marks, 3 to 5 minutes. Remove from the heat and serve immediately.

Spinach and Feta Gözleme

Makes 4 stuffed flatbreads

These traditional Turkish flatbreads get their name from *göz*, the Turkish word for "eye," because as they cook in the pan brown spots that look like eyes appear on the surface of the dough. Gözleme can be filled with ground meat, eggs, cheese, vegetables, or a combination of these. You can also make sweet gözleme filled with honey, nuts, and fruit. Baby spinach and crumbled feta cheese is a delicious but simple combination. Gözleme dough is quite wet, so let it rest for 10 minutes after mixing to allow the flour to fully absorb the water before kneading. Use a mixer to knead it unless you are up for the challenge of working with a wet dough.

FOR THE DOUGH:

10.6 ounces (1⅓ cups) warm room temperature water (78°F)

16 ounces/454 grams (3 cups) unbleached all-purpose flour

0.2 ounce/6 grams (2 teaspoons) instant yeast

0.17 ounce/5 grams (1 teaspoon) kosher salt or fine sea salt

0.17 ounce/5 grams (1 teaspoon) sugar

⅓ cup olive oil

FOR THE FILLING:

1 tablespoon olive oil

1 small onion, finely chopped

4 ounces baby spinach, coarsely chopped

8 ounces feta cheese, crumbled

1 tablespoon finely chopped fresh mint

Salt and freshly ground black pepper

Olive oil

Lemon wedges

CONTINUED →

1. Combine the water, flour, yeast, salt, sugar, and olive oil in the bowl of a stand mixer. Stir with a rubber spatula until a rough dough forms. Let stand uncovered for 10 minutes.

2. Knead the dough using the dough hook until it is smooth and soft and passes the windowpane test (see page 71), about 10 minutes on medium speed.

3. Spray the inside of a dough-rising container or large mixing bowl with nonstick cooking spray and place the dough inside. Cover with plastic wrap and let rise until the dough has doubled in size and when poked with a fingertip doesn't spring back, 30 minutes to 1 hour.

4. Turn the dough out onto a lightly floured countertop and divide into 4 equal pieces. Shape each piece into a ball (see page 88), flatten into a disk, sprinkle lightly with flour, drape with plastic wrap, and let stand for 20 minutes.

5. While the dough is resting, make the filling: Heat the oil in a medium saucepan over medium heat. Add the onion and cook until softened, 3 to 5 minutes. Add the spinach and cook, stirring, until just wilted, about 1 minute. Transfer to a bowl to cool, then stir in the feta cheese, mint, and salt and pepper.

6. Use a rolling pin to roll one of the pieces of dough into a 6-inch circle. Place one-quarter of the spinach and feta mixture on half of the dough. Fold the dough closed and pinch the edges to seal. Repeat with the remaining dough pieces.

7. Heat a large skillet over medium heat. Brush the bottom of two of the gözleme lightly with olive oil and cook until puffed and golden on both sides, turning once, 4 to 6 minutes total. Transfer to a plate and repeat with the remaining gözleme. Serve immediately with lemon wedges on the side.

As the gözleme cook in the pan, brown spots appear on the surface.

Sugar-Dusted Beignets

Makes about 12 beignets

These fried dough squares, a specialty of New Orleans, are traditionally dusted with loads of confectioners' sugar. They're difficult to eat without getting the sugar all over your face, but that's part of the fun.

FOR THE POOLISH:

0.05 ounce/1.5 grams (½ teaspoon) instant yeast

2 ounces (¼ cup) room temperature water (75 to 78°F)

2.25 ounces/64 grams (½ cup) unbleached all-purpose flour

FOR THE DOUGH:

1 ounce (2 tablespoons) milk

0.025 ounce/1 gram (¼ teaspoon) instant yeast

3.36 ounces/95 grams (¾ cup) unbleached all-purpose flour

0.75 ounce/21 grams (1½ tablespoons) sugar

0.025 ounce/1 gram (¼ teaspoon) kosher salt or fine sea salt

1 tablespoon unsalted butter, melted

1 large egg yolk

½ teaspoon pure vanilla extract

Vegetable oil for frying

½ cup confectioners' sugar

1. Make the poolish: Combine the yeast, water, and flour in a small bowl and stir with a rubber spatula to combine. Cover with plastic wrap and let stand on the counter for 1 hour. Gently stir with a spatula to deflate, re-cover, and refrigerate overnight.

2. Make the dough: Combine the milk, yeast, flour, sugar, salt, butter, egg yolk, vanilla, and poolish in the bowl of a stand mixer. Stir with a rubber spatula until a rough dough forms.

CONTINUED →

3. Knead the dough using the dough hook until it is smooth and soft, 5 to 7 minutes on medium-low speed.

4. Spray the inside of a dough-rising container or large mixing bowl with nonstick cooking spray and place the dough inside. Cover with plastic wrap and let rise until the dough has doubled in size and when poked with a fingertip doesn't spring back, about 1 hour.

5. Turn the dough out onto a lightly floured countertop and gently roll it out with a rolling pin into a rectangle measuring about 4½ inches by 7½ inches. Use a pizza

A Beignet by Any Other Name?

Fried dough is a treat enjoyed around the world. But don't tell a resident of New Orleans that beignets are just the buñuelos of the Big Easy. Different doughs, shaping techniques, and serving styles distinguish the following favorites:

Buñuelos. This Latin American fried bread often has anise seeds incorporated into the dough. Shaped into balls, pancakes, or twisted strips, buñuelos are often topped with sugar or honey. In Mexico, buñuelos are made with wheat flour, but in other countries mashed tubers like yuca are sometimes added to the dough.

Doughnuts. As the witty blogger Mr. Breakfast has put it, "Doughnuts have been around for centuries. Archaeologists turned up several petrified fried cakes with holes in the center in prehistoric ruins in the Southwestern United States." In fact, the origin of America's favorite fried dough item is disputed, with some historians arguing that it was brought to the United States by Dutch settlers in the eighteenth century, and others celebrating Hansen Gregory, a young American sailor who claimed to have invented the doughnut while cooking in the galley of a lime-trading ship. The Salvation Army claims to have popularized the doughnut, its volunteers preparing them for American soldiers at the front in France during World War I. What is accepted: Doughnuts are pieces of sweetened dough, shaped either into rings or filled with jam or custard, that are deep-fried.

Funnel cake. Funnel cake is made by pouring cake batter through a funnel into a pot of bubbling oil. Originally a specialty of the Pennsylvania Dutch region, it has become a carnival favorite all over the country. Funnel cake batter is an eggy wheel or sharp paring knife to cut the dough into twelve 2-inch squares. Lightly drape the cut squares with plastic wrap and let stand for 10 minutes.

6. Place 1 inch vegetable oil in a large Dutch oven. Heat the oil to 325°F. Cook the beignets in batches, turning once, until they are golden brown on each side, 1 to 1½ minutes total (if they get too dark too soon, lower the heat). Transfer the cooked beignets to a paper towel–lined baking sheet to drain briefly.

7. When all of the beignets are cooked, dust them heavily with confectioners' sugar and serve immediately.

mixture, leavened by the steam that is created when the moisture evaporates from the cakes as they cook. It is an unleavened bread, not to be confused with its carnival compatriot, fried dough; it's known by various names, including beaver tails, elephant ears, and frying saucers, depending upon the amusement park, rodeo, or seaside resort at which it is served.

Navajo fry bread. Although fried bread had been made by Native Americans before, this particular version was made by Navajos interned at Bosque Redondo in southern New Mexico after they were forced by the American army to leave their land. The ingredients — flour, sugar, salt, lard, powdered milk, and yeast — were chosen from the supplies provided by the United States government. Since then, it is commonly prepared at powwows to commemorate the sad course of events leading to its invention.

Sopapillas. This is the name for fried dough specialties made in parts of South America as well as the American Southwest. New Mexican sopapillas are the most well-known to us. Made with a wheat dough, leavened with baking powder, and pressed into a round shape like a small tortilla, a New Mexican sopapilla is then deep-fried until crisp and puffy. They are served sweet, sprinkled with confectioners' sugar or drizzled with honey, or opened and filled with ground beef, beans, or other savory fillings.

Sopapillas with honey

Flatbreads
Questions and Answers

Q Can the No-Knead Roman Pizza dough recipe be used with any type of pizza topping?

A Roman-style pizza is a showcase for the puffy, flavorful crust. In fact, in Rome, this type of pizza is often just topped with a drizzle of olive oil and a sprinkling of sea salt. That said, with common sense you can certainly adapt the recipe to suit your taste. You'll notice that my recipe calls for drained diced tomatoes, which gives good tomato flavor without making the crust soggy. In general, avoid overly heavy or wet toppings, which might prevent the crust from fully baking or make it damp.

Q I have the same problem with my Roman pizza and lavash: they bubble up unevenly in the oven, and sometimes there are huge bubbles right in the center of the breads. How can I prevent this?

A There is nothing like a large air bubble to "unflatten" your flatbread. In fact, flatbread stamps that eliminate large air bubbles in the dough before baking are a common baker's tool across central and western Asia, where flatbread is the daily bread. No need to buy a special tool to accomplish this, however. Either prick the center of the dough with a fork before baking or keep an eye on it for the first few minutes after you put it in the oven and prick it then if you see large bubbles forming.

Q In addition to naan, what other flatbreads can be made on a gas grill?

A The No-Knead Roman Pizza (page 193) and Lavash (page 202) recipes both work well on the grill. To make grilled pizza, liberally brush both sides of the dough with olive oil. Grill over medium heat for a minute or two to set the bottom crust, and then flip the dough and put the toppings on the set, flat side before covering and baking. As in the oven, lavash need not be turned. The grill will brown the underside while the hot air circulating around the dough will cook the top.

Q **Can flatbreads be cooked over an open fire?**

A Like nomadic bakers of many cultures, you can certainly bake flatbreads over a campfire. A well-seasoned cast-iron skillet is essential for this task. Good choices would include Overnight English Muffins (page 200; great for a camping trip), Pita Bread (page 195), and Lavash (page 202).

Q **I like the look of the lavash recipe, but am wondering if I could make 12 small breads instead of 6 large ones.**

A Most flatbread recipes, including the one for the lavash, are adaptable and forgiving. By all means, divide your dough into smaller pieces if it suits you. Be sure to adjust the baking time if necessary. Small breads will bake even more quickly than the larger ones.

Q **I don't have a candy thermometer. Is there any other way to tell if my oil is hot enough for frying my beignets?**

A Drop a small piece of dough into the pot when you think it is ready. If the oil bubbles and the dough immediately begins to puff and color, then go ahead and fry your beignets. By the same token, watch your beignets carefully as they cook, and adjust the temperature if they become very dark in a matter of seconds.

You don't want to burn their exteriors before the interiors are fully cooked. A beignet should take a minute or two to cook. Longer than this and it will be heavy and greasy. Shorter, and it will be bitter on the outside and raw on the inside.

Q **What is the best way to reheat frozen flatbreads?**

A It depends on how flat the flatbreads are. Thin breads, such as pita bread and lavash, can be reheated in a skillet over medium-high heat directly from the freezer. Thicker breads, like English muffins and naan, do better in a preheated 350°F oven, where they can be warmed through. Thicker breads should also be defrosted on the countertop before being reheated. Reheated flatbreads taste great but should be eaten right away. Once they cool, they will quickly lose moisture and become stale.

Chapter 8
Whole-Grain Breads

THERE ARE MANY REASONS to bake whole-grain breads. Medical research suggests that a diet rich in whole grains carries with it valuable health benefits. Whole grains can help us lose weight and reduce blood cholesterol, lowering our risk of heart disease and diabetes. A diet rich in whole grains may also prevent certain types of cancers. The nutrients contained in whole grains include dietary fiber (a digestive aid that can prevent or reverse diverticulitis), B vitamins (which help us metabolize protein, fat, and carbohydrates), folic acid (important in forming red blood cells and proven to prevent birth defects during fetal development), iron (the cure for anemia), and magnesium and selenium (which build bones and strengthen the immune system).

While true wheat allergies are very rare (less than 0.5 percent of the population will have a severe, sudden, and potentially deadly autoimmune response to wheat), wheat sensitivity or intolerance is on the rise. Some research suggests that as many as one in seven people have trouble digesting wheat and suffer from chronic gastrointestinal pain, eczema, and a host of other ailments as a result. For these people, whole-grain breads that contain less gluten than white wheat breads can be part of a healthy lower-gluten diet.

But for me, the primary reason to add whole-grain breads to my repertoire is for the variety and interest they bring to my table at every meal. The nutty flavor of whole wheat, the herbal taste of buckwheat, the earthiness of rye: Depending on what I'm eating, these can be appealing alternatives to white bread.

This is a good time to be a home baker in search of whole-grain flours. Retailers have responded to the growing demand for healthy whole-grain foods by stocking spelt flour, oat flour, barley flour, and several varieties of rye flour. Walk into any natural foods store, browse a baking supply website, or even take a stroll down the natural foods aisle at your supermarket and you will see flours and seeds that weren't available to the home baker just a decade ago. This array of products now available, many of them certified organic, opens up a world of bread that you might not have considered when you were making your first white baguette.

But baking with whole grains is not a matter of simply substituting the new flour you've purchased for the white flour called for in a recipe. First of all, whole flour milled from spelt, rye, buckwheat, barley, and other grains tastes dramatically different from white flour. For a population that's grown up on white bread, these flavors may take some getting used to. In addition, getting the most flavor from these grains may require different techniques from the ones you've used with wheat flour.

And then there is the issue of gluten. The protein in whole-wheat flour, oat flour, and spelt flour (spelt is a grain closely related to wheat) is more difficult to transform into gluten than the protein in white flour. Many nonwheat flours, including rye, buckwheat, and corn, have little or no protein. Since gluten provides the structural skeleton of most breads, its absence creates a serious challenge to the baker determined to bake a high-rising loaf (or a loaf that rises at all!) with whole grains.

In this chapter, I'll first show you some strategies for overcoming the challenges that whole-grain flours present to bread bakers, with a focus on three of the most popular whole-grain flours in the bread baker's pantry. Then I'll show you how to bake some wonderful whole-grain breads. Whole-Wheat and Honey Boule with Hazelnuts (page 222), Eight-Grain-and-Seed Pan Loaf (page 225), Rye Loaf with Rye Berries (page 233), and Spelt *Bâtardes* (page 228) are not just prescriptions for good health — they are also loaves that can stand beside any white loaf as full-flavored, well-crafted homemade breads.

Getting the Most out of Whole-Grain Breads

In *Whole Grain Breads,* award-winning baker Peter Reinhart cuts right to the heart of why white bread became Americans' favorite bread at least 100 years ago and continues to please the majority of eaters: "White flour is, after all, essentially sugar, in the guise of starch, with a little protein. We love sugar, in whatever form it comes in; our taste buds never seem to get enough of it." During fermentation and baking, enzymes in bread dough easily break down some of the starches in white flour, converting them into sugars. As we eat our bread, even more of those starches turn into sugar as we chew. These enzymes also cause starch molecules to gelatinize, holding on to water so that the resulting bread stays moist. White bread is comforting and satisfying (some might even say addictive) because it delivers this naturally pleasing nutrient in such an appealing package.

Techniques for Improving Flavor

The sugar in milled whole wheat, spelt, rye, oats, and corn is more difficult to access, but the project is not impossible. There are ways to make whole-grain breads just as deeply satisfying as white breads. In general, the following strategies for unlocking the flavor of grain apply to whole-wheat and other whole-grain breads:

Extend fermentation. For the best flavor, enzymes in bread dough must have sufficient time to break down the sugars trapped in starches. Since this takes longer and is more difficult with whole-grain flours, it makes sense that a longer fermentation period will be necessary. Longer fermentation is also helpful in building flavorful acids in the dough, which balance the sometimes bitter flavor of the bran and germ in whole grains. For the most flavorful bread, when you are choosing a whole-grain recipe, look for one that takes into consideration fermentation time.

Just as with white breads, there are several ways to extend fermentation. Using a tiny bit of yeast, you can let your dough ferment at room temperature for up to 18 hours (the no-knead method). This method works best with whole-wheat doughs and doughs made with grains related to wheat, such as spelt. Very starchy grains such as rye will produce so much sugar during this type of room temperature fermentation that the yeast will be compromised, resulting in a flavorful but low-rising and dense bread.

Using a large amount of pre-ferment is another option, which may serve you better if you are using grains other than wheat. A sponge or pâte fermentée will allow those flavorful acids to develop in a part of the dough without the danger that they will inhibit the yeast in the dough as a whole.

Try a soaker. Presoaking some of the whole grains and/or seeds before adding them to your bread dough is another way of unlocking the flavor of these ingredients. A soaker is different from a pre-ferment in that it contains no yeast, so there is no fermentation taking place. What presoaking does accomplish is to activate some of the enzymes in these ingredients so that they can break down the starches, releasing sugar. Employing a soaker has the added advantage of softening some of the tougher grains and seeds, making the final bread more tender and palatable.

Sweeten and enrich. The flavor of certain whole-grain breads can be greatly enhanced by adding just a little bit (we're talking a teaspoon or two) of granulated sugar, brown sugar, or honey to the dough. Likewise, substituting milk or buttermilk for some or all of the water in a whole-grain bread recipe will lend a mellow flavor to the bread.

Techniques for Improving Texture

Breads made with whole-wheat, spelt, rye, and other low- or no-gluten flours tend to have a tighter, smaller crumb than white breads. This is because it is more difficult to develop a strong gluten structure in doughs made with flours that are either low in protein (such as rye) or don't have the optimum ratio of glutenin to gliadin (such as spelt) to form a strong gluten web. In the case of whole-wheat flour, which has the same ratio of glutenin to gliadin as white flour, bits of bran get in the way of the formation of gluten strands, inhibiting the dough's rise. But there are ways to help these breads rise to a pleasing height.

Custom kneading. Breads made with a large proportion of whole-wheat flour contain plenty of gluten-forming proteins. The problem with whole-wheat doughs is that it takes a longer time than with white wheat doughs to develop that gluten. Underrisen bread is a common problem when using whole-wheat flour, and underkneading the dough is often to blame. Remember when working with whole-wheat dough to knead for a few minutes longer than you would when using white flour. It is difficult to overknead whole-wheat breads. More is better when you're trying to develop gluten in whole-wheat dough.

In contrast, flours that don't contain a lot of protein (such as rye) or whose ratio of glutenin to gliadin isn't the optimal 1 to 1 of white flour (such as spelt) should be handled gently, so as not to destroy what gluten has already been developed.

Take some vitamins. Yeast functions better in the presence of ascorbic acid, which is another name for vitamin C. Ascorbic acid also has a strengthening effect on gluten. Because one of the goals when baking whole-grain breads is to encourage the highest rise possible, adding a little bit of crushed vitamin C (no more than ⅛ teaspoon for every 3 to 4 cups of flour) may help.

Add a little fat. Adding a tablespoon or two of olive oil, vegetable oil, or melted butter to the dough won't inhibit its rise (the way, say, adding a stick of butter would), but it will give the bread some tenderness and moisture.

Special Considerations: Whole Wheat

The watchword when baking 100 percent whole-wheat breads is *patience.*

Kneading. Be patient during kneading. It takes longer to develop gluten during kneading if you are using whole-wheat flour.

Rising and proofing. Doughs made with whole-wheat flour generally take longer to rise than doughs made with white flour. Make sure to give your dough the time it requires during bulk fermentation and bench proofing to develop as much yeast and gluten strength as possible. Many beginning bakers worry about overproofing shaped doughs, wanting to avoid letting them rise too high before getting them into the oven. But it is much more likely that you will underproof your dough, in which case it will never reach its potential height.

Turning. Turning the dough mid-fermentation (you can even turn it two or three times) will slow down its rise a bit, but turning can change its gluten structure dramatically and ultimately will help it rise to greater heights in the oven. So don't hurry through fermentation if you can extend it this way.

Enhancements. Finally, think about how to enhance your whole-wheat dough's flavor, by either adding a bit of sugar, enriching it with some olive oil, or stirring in some chopped nuts. These additions will not change the bread's nutritional profile significantly, but they can add a great deal in terms of mouth appeal.

Special Considerations: Spelt

Spelt is an ancient variety of wheat that originated in Iran. It has been used to make bread for at least 6,000 years. Spelt kernels have a hard covering that makes them more difficult to hull than wheat kernels. This is probably one of the reasons why spelt never caught on with American farmers, who preferred the easier-to-hull wheat. European farmers, in contrast, have a long tradition of cultivating spelt, and its nutty flavor is especially beloved in Germany, where it is known as *Dinkel,* and in Italy, where its name is *farro.* Because spelt bread is lower in gluten than wheat breads, it is well tolerated by people who are sensitive to gluten. While it is still difficult to find spelt flour in the United States (see page 273 for resources), there is growing interest in spelt breads in this country.

Spelt has more protein than wheat, but its gluten to gliadin ratio is 1 to 3. This means that for every gliadin molecule that links up with a gluten molecule, there are 2 gliadin molecules left over. The resulting gluten web is considerably weaker than the gluten web of a dough made with the same amount of wheat flour. In addition, since gliadin is responsible for bread dough's extensibility (its ability to stretch), it will stretch but won't easily bounce back into shape, making it difficult to work with.

It is possible to develop enough gluten in a spelt dough to bake a bread with good volume and a reasonably open crumb. But there are some possible pitfalls, and if you don't take care to avoid them you can wind up with an underrisen loaf with a tight, dry crumb.

Use the right amount of water. You must use the correct amount of water. Too much and the dough will be sticky and weak and unable to hold the gases that are produced during the fermentation process. Too little and the dough will be dry and dense; it will not rise properly because the water will never fully get into the protein and there will be nothing to hold the loaf up. Also, the dense loaf will be too tight to allow the yeast gases to expand the loaf. Let experience be your guide when making spelt bread. Take notes as you mix your dough. If your first loaf is too dry, next time add more water. If your next dough is too slack to shape, add a little more flour next time. Soon you will be able to tell by sight and touch when you have achieved the right balance.

Knead carefully. Too little kneading will result in underdeveloped gluten that can't support a reasonable rise. Too much kneading will destroy the gluten that you *have* managed to develop. I've found that mixing the dough and then letting it stand for 10 minutes before kneading (to let the flour absorb the water) cuts down on kneading time, which shouldn't last more than 5 minutes on medium-low speed in a stand mixer.

Special Considerations: Rye

Rye flour does contain protein, but not the kind that forms gluten. Instead of gliadin and glutenin, it contains gliadin and glutelin (what a difference one letter makes!). These two proteins combine during kneading, but they don't form the strong bonds that gliadin and glutenin do. Doughs made with rye flour won't have the same protein web that can support expanding gases as a dough rises.

What rye does have, in abundance, is starch, along with a lot of active enzymes. While the starches in rye soak up huge amounts of water, making for some very moist bread, they can also make your bread unpleasantly sticky when digested by the enzymes too quickly.

To bake a well-risen rye loaf with a moist but not overly sticky crumb, try these tricks:

Use bread flour to add gluten. Rye flour must be mixed with some wheat flour to make a dough that will rise. For the best rise along with the best rye flavor, use the highest-gluten wheat flour you can buy. The higher the gluten in the wheat flour, the less you will need in your rye dough. And the more rye flour you use, the stronger your rye flavor will be.

Let acids work for you. Whether it is a sourdough starter, a pre-ferment, or a crushed tablet of vitamin C, adding an acidic component to the dough will keep the abundant enzymes in rye flour from gobbling up all of the starches and turning them into sugars. A little bit of acidity will ensure that you wind up with a pleasantly moist, nicely risen loaf rather than a sticky and dense one.

Guard against overproofing. The delicate gluten structure of most rye doughs won't allow for a sustainable rise during proofing. Take care to get your loaves into the oven before they've risen so high that they will collapse when touched or moved. Don't expect or wait for them to double in volume. Instead, check that they are ready by looking and touching. They should have spread slightly and have a pillowy look. When you press a fingertip into the dough, it should spring back slowly.

Use steam. You want to employ every trick in the book to get your bread to rise, and steam is the last one on the checklist. Abundant steam will keep the crust soft, allowing the bread to rise as much as possible in those early minutes of baking. Use steam even if you are baking your bread in a loaf pan, to keep the top crust moist.

The Recipes

Virtually every bread book out there (including this one) can supply you with recipes for breads that include a portion of whole-grain flour. My goal was to develop recipes for a few really good 100 percent whole-grain breads, plus a rye bread with a high percentage of whole rye. By employing the techniques discussed previously — delayed fermentation, a soaker — I've been able to bake whole-grain breads with the delightful sweetness, moist crumb, and chewy crust that are valued in white breads. But I've also been able to highlight the flavors of these grains, not disguise them, in order to fully enjoy all that whole-wheat, rye, and other whole-grain flours have to offer.

Whole-Wheat and Honey Boule with Hazelnuts

Makes 1 large round

I hadn't baked a 100 percent whole-wheat loaf since I was a teenager, working from a straight dough recipe in a vegetarian cookbook from the 1970s. I was so disappointed with my low-rising, heavy, bitter-tasting brick of a loaf that I avoided all breads that contained more than 30 percent whole-wheat flour for years. When I finally decided to develop my own 100 percent whole-wheat recipe, I was careful to employ several techniques that I thought might make my bread rise higher and taste better than my earlier disastrous attempt.

First, I used a pre-ferment, a pâte fermentée, to extend the bread's fermentation time. Adding a large percentage of "old dough" to the new was a quick way to add gluten, along with a tangy flavor. Next, I kneaded the dough with care, taking a 5-minute break in the middle to let the flour absorb the water before finishing up, another effortless strategy for gluten enhancement. In the middle of bulk fermentation I gave the dough a turn, knowing from previous experience with white breads that this simple step can have dramatic results in terms of rise. As for improving flavor, I followed the advice of many bakers of whole-wheat breads before me and added a touch of honey to the dough, which balances the strong (and sometimes bitter) flavor of the wheat. I added a cup of toasted, chopped hazelnuts, which provide richness as well as enhancing the wheat's nutty flavor.

To skin hazelnuts, place them on a baking sheet and bake them in a preheated 350°F oven until fragrant, about 10 minutes. Immediately wrap the hot nuts in a warm kitchen towel. Allow them to steam for 10 minutes, and then rub the nuts with the towel to remove the skins (it's okay if bits of skin stick to the nuts).

FOR THE PÂTE FERMENTÉE:

3 ounces (6 tablespoons) room temperature water (75 to 78°F)

0.05 ounce/1.5 grams (½ teaspoon) instant yeast

4 ounces/113 grams (¾ cup plus 2 tablespoons) whole-wheat flour

0.08 ounce/2 grams (½ teaspoon) kosher salt or fine sea salt

FOR THE DOUGH:

12 ounces/340 grams (2¾ cups plus 2 tablespoons) whole-wheat flour

0.17 ounce/5 grams (1 teaspoon) kosher salt or fine sea salt

0.08 ounce/2 grams (¾ teaspoon) instant yeast

9 ounces (1 cup plus 2 tablespoons) room temperature water (75 to 78°F)

2 teaspoons honey

2 tablespoons unsalted butter, softened

1 cup toasted and skinned hazelnuts, finely chopped

1. Make the pâte fermentée: Combine the water, yeast, whole-wheat flour, and salt in a bowl and use a rubber spatula to stir until a rough dough forms. Use the spatula to press any loose flour or stray bits of dough into the larger mass. The pâte fermentée won't be smooth. Cover with plastic wrap and let stand at room temperature until it is puffy and increased slightly in volume, about 1 hour. Gently deflate it by pressing down on it with the palm of your hand and then folding it in half. Re-cover and refrigerate until it has doubled in size, 8 to 12 hours.

2. Make the dough: Tear the pâte fermentée into pieces and place in the bowl of a stand mixer or a large mixing bowl. Add the whole-wheat flour, salt, yeast, water, honey, and butter. Stir with a rubber spatula until a rough dough forms.

3. Knead the dough. By machine: Using the dough hook, knead on low speed until the dough comes together into a rough mass. Turn the mixer to medium-low speed and knead until the dough becomes soft and a little tacky, but not very sticky, 4 to 5 minutes. Let the dough sit in the mixer for 5 minutes, and then knead again on medium-low speed until the dough can pass the windowpane test (see page 71), another 2 to 3 minutes. Knead in the nuts until incorporated. By hand: Turn the dough out onto a lightly floured countertop. Knead with careful strokes, scraping up the dough from the countertop as necessary with

CONTINUED $\longrightarrow$

a bench scraper, until it is soft and just a little bit tacky, 5 to 7 minutes. Let it rest for 5 minutes, and then continue to knead until it is smooth and can pass the windowpane test, another 5 minutes. All the while, resist adding extra flour. Flatten the dough and sprinkle the nuts on top. Fold the dough in half and continue to knead until the nuts are well distributed.

4. Spray the inside of a dough-rising container or large mixing bowl with nonstick cooking spray and place the dough inside. Cover with plastic wrap and let rise until the dough has increased in volume by about 50 percent, about 1 hour.

5. Give the dough a turn: Slide your hands underneath the dough and pick it up from underneath, so that it droops over your hands. Then set it down again, on one of its drooping sides, back in the bowl. Cover the bowl with plastic wrap and let it rise until it has again increased in volume by about 50 percent, 45 minutes to 1 hour.

6. Turn the dough out onto a countertop lightly dusted with flour. Gently shape it into a rough round. Let the dough rest for 10 minutes.

    One hour before baking, place a baking stone on the middle rack of the oven and a cast-iron skillet on the lower rack. Preheat the oven to 500°F.

7. Shape the dough into a tight ball (see shaping rounds, page 88). Line an 8-inch round bowl with a clean kitchen towel and sprinkle the towel with whole-wheat flour. Place the loaf in the bowl, smooth side down. Lightly drape the bowl with plastic wrap. Let stand until increased in volume by about 1½ times, 45 minutes to 1 hour.

8. Uncover the loaf, place a parchment-lined baker's peel or rimless baking sheet on top of the bowl, and invert the loaf onto the peel. Use a razor blade, lame, or sharp chef's knife to score the loaf, making two 4-inch cuts in an X shape on top.

9. Slide the loaf, still on the parchment, onto the preheated baking stone. Drop ½ cup ice cubes into the cast-iron pan. Bake for 10 minutes. Without opening the oven, turn the heat down to 450°F and bake until the crust is dark and an instant-read thermometer inserted into the center reads 205°F, 30 to 40 minutes longer.

10. Slide the loaf, still on the parchment, onto a wire rack. Let cool for 5 minutes, peel from the parchment, and then let cool to warm room temperature, about 2 hours, before slicing and serving.

Eight-Grain-and-Seed Pan Loaf

Makes 1 (8-inch) loaf

With this recipe, I wanted to make a simple health loaf that tasted like bread, not medicine! To improve this 100 percent whole-grain bread's flavor, I used a couple of tricks. First, I made a soaker, a mixture of grains and seeds soaked overnight in water to release the sugars in these ingredients. Then, I used mostly milk instead of water to hydrate the dough. Slightly enriching the bread this way adds flavor and tenderness.

Because the bread is made with 100 percent whole wheat, I worked extra hard to develop the flour's gluten by letting the hydrated dough stand for 10 minutes before kneading, kneading it for a full 10 minutes in a machine, and giving it a turn halfway through bulk fermentation. This is supposed to be a wet dough, but it should clear the sides of the bowl at the end of kneading. Whole-wheat flour varies greatly in its ability to absorb liquid, so if your flour is less absorbent than mine you might want to add a little more, 1 tablespoon at a time, midway through kneading, just until the dough comes together.

FOR THE SOAKER:

1 ounce/28 grams (3 tablespoons) stone-ground yellow cornmeal

0.75 ounce/21 grams (3 tablespoons) rolled oats

0.25 ounce/7 grams (2 tablespoons) wheat bran

2 tablespoons pumpkin seeds

2 tablespoons sesame seeds

2 tablespoons sunflower seeds

2 tablespoons flax seeds

4 ounces (½ cup) room temperature water (75 to 78°F)

CONTINUED →

FOR THE DOUGH:

10 ounces (1¼ cups) room temperature milk (75 to 78°F)

2 ounces (¼ cup) room temperature water (75 to 78°F)

0.2 ounce/6 grams (2 teaspoons) instant yeast

13.5 ounces/383 grams (3 cups) whole-wheat flour

0.25 ounce/7 grams (1½ teaspoons) kosher salt or fine sea salt

1. Make the soaker: Combine the cornmeal, oats, bran, pumpkin seeds, sesame seeds, sunflower seeds, flax seeds, and water in a medium bowl. Cover with plastic wrap and let stand at room temperature for at least 8 and up to 24 hours.

2. Make the dough: Combine the milk, water, yeast, whole-wheat flour, salt, and soaker in the bowl of a stand mixer. Stir with a rubber spatula until a rough dough forms. Let the dough stand for 10 minutes to absorb the water.

3. Knead the dough using the dough hook on medium-low speed until the dough just clears the sides of the bowl and is still a little lumpy, 7 to 10 minutes. Adjust it if necessary, adding more flour or water 1 tablespoon at a time.

4. Spray the inside of a dough-rising container or large mixing bowl with nonstick cooking spray and place the dough inside. Cover with plastic wrap and let rise until the dough is increased in volume by about 50 percent, 45 minutes to 1 hour.

5. Give the dough a turn: Slide your hands underneath the dough and pick it up from underneath, so that it droops over your hands. Then set it down again, on one of its drooping sides, back in the bowl. Cover the bowl with plastic wrap and let it rise until it has increased in volume by about 50 percent, 45 minutes to 1 hour.

6. Turn the dough out onto a countertop lightly dusted with flour. Gently shape it into a rough rectangle and fold the rectangle in half. Let the dough rest for 10 minutes.

7. Spray the inside of a 5- by 9-inch loaf pan with nonstick cooking spray. Shape the dough into a loaf (see page 89). Transfer it, seam side down, to the prepared pan. Lightly spray the surface with nonstick cooking spray and lightly drape with plastic wrap. Let stand until almost doubled in size, 1 to 1½ hours. The dough should come almost to the top of the pan but not over the top! (If this happens, you've waited too long to get it into the oven. Turn the dough out onto a lightly

floured countertop, reshape into a loaf, place in a cleaned and greased pan, cover, and let ferment again until almost doubled in size.)

8. One hour before baking, place a baking stone on the middle rack and preheat the oven to 425°F. Uncover the loaf and bake (make sure there's enough room above so that the rising bread doesn't bump into the upper rack) for 10 minutes. Without opening the oven, turn the heat down to 375°F and bake until the top is golden brown and an instant-read thermometer inserted into the center reads 190°F, 25 to 30 minutes longer.

9. Turn the loaf out onto a wire rack, re-invert the loaf, and let cool completely, at least 2 hours, before slicing.

The Myth of Scalded Milk

Very often when a bread recipe includes milk, it will direct you to scald the milk and then bring it back to room temperature before going on to mix the dough. What purpose does scalding serve, and is this step really necessary?

Raw milk contains plentiful numbers of active enzymes, including proteases, which attack gluten and can compromise a dough's structure. The idea behind scalding milk, then, is to denature the enzymes, allowing the gluten to remain strong and the bread to rise high.

If you are using raw milk right from the cow, go ahead and scald it. But if you are using milk you've purchased at the grocery store, there's no need. Ultra-pasteurized milk has already been heated to a high temperature, denaturing those enzymes in the process.

Do take the time, however, to bring your milk to room temperature, or your dough will be chilly rather than warm; chilly dough will throw off the expected fermentation time.

Spelt Bâtardes

Makes 2 (10-inch) torpedo-shaped loaves

This is a low-gluten bread with all of the satisfying flavor and texture of a white baguette. The tricks: Using a biga extends the fermentation time, allowing gluten to develop. Whole-wheat flour adds extra gluten, but not as much as white flour would. A tiny bit of ascorbic acid (a crushed vitamin C tablet) strengthens the dough's fragile gluten structure.

FOR THE BIGA:

2 ounces (¼ cup) room temperature water (70 to 78°F)

0.1 ounce/3 grams (1 teaspoon) instant yeast

2.3 ounces/65 grams (½ cup) whole spelt flour

FOR THE DOUGH:

12 ounces (1½ cups) room temperature water (70 to 78°F)

12.3 ounces/349 grams (2¼ cups) whole spelt flour

5.2 ounces/147 grams (1 cup) whole-wheat flour

0.25 ounce/7 grams (1½ teaspoons) kosher salt or fine sea salt

0.25 ounce/7 grams (1½ teaspoons) sugar

⅛ teaspoon ascorbic acid from a crushed vitamin C tablet

1. Make the biga: Combine the water, yeast, and spelt flour in a bowl and use a rubber spatula to stir until a rough dough forms. Use the spatula to press any loose flour or stray bits of dough into the larger mass. The biga won't be smooth. Cover with plastic wrap and let stand at room temperature for 1 hour, and then refrigerate until it has doubled in volume, 8 to 16 hours.

2. Make the dough: Tear the biga into pieces and place in the bowl of a stand mixer or a large mixing bowl. Let stand for 15 minutes to warm up. Add the water, spelt flour, whole-wheat flour, salt, sugar, and ascorbic acid. Stir with a rubber spatula until a rough dough forms.

3. Let the dough stand for 10 minutes, allowing the flour to absorb the water.

4. Knead the dough. By machine: With a dough hook, knead the dough on medium-low speed until it just clears the sides of the bowl, 5 to 7 minutes. By hand: Turn the dough out onto a lightly floured countertop and knead with steady strokes until it comes together into a coherent mass, about 10 minutes, using a bench scraper as necessary to scrape it from the counter if it sticks.

5. Spray the inside of a dough-rising container or large mixing bowl with nonstick cooking spray and place the dough inside. Cover with plastic wrap and let rise until the dough has doubled in size, 1½ to 2 hours.

6. Turn the dough out onto a countertop lightly dusted with flour. Use a bench scraper or sharp chef's knife to divide the dough into 2 equal pieces. Gently shape each piece into a rough rectangle and fold each rectangle in half. Lightly drape with plastic wrap and let the dough pieces rest for 20 minutes.

7. One hour before baking, place a baking stone in the middle rack of the oven and a cast-iron skillet on the lower rack. Preheat the oven to 450°F.

8. Shape each piece into a 10-inch bâtarde (see page 88). Transfer them, seam sides down, to a parchment-covered baker's peel or rimless baking sheet, positioning them so they're about 3 inches apart on the paper. Pleat the paper in between the loaves to draw them together. Place a rolled-up kitchen towel underneath the paper on the outer side of each loaf to support them and help them keep their shape as they proof. Sprinkle the bâtardes with flour and drape with plastic wrap. Let stand until puffy and almost doubled in size, 1 to 1½ hours.

9. Uncover the loaves, remove the towels, and pull the paper so it lies flat and the loaves are separated. Use a razor blade, lame, or sharp chef's knife to make a diagonal slash down each of the loaves.

10. Slide the loaves, still on the parchment, onto the preheated baking stone. Drop ½ cup ice cubes into the cast-iron pan. Bake for 15 minutes, lower the heat to 400°F without opening the oven door, and continue to bake until the bâtardes are evenly browned, 15 to 20 minutes longer.

11. Slide the loaves, still on the parchment, onto a wire rack. Cool for about 5 minutes, and then peel them off the parchment paper. Let the loaves cool completely, about 1 hour, before slicing and serving.

Lower-Gluten Bread

In addition to spelt, there are several old and new wheat varieties that can be used to bake lower-gluten breads. These grains all contain gliadin and glutenin, the proteins that link up together during kneading (also during autolyse and fermentation) to form a gluten web. Glutenin gives dough its elasticity, while gliadin contributes extensibility.

White flour has a ratio of 1 to 1, allowing every glutenin molecule to link up with a gliadin molecule, resulting in a strong gluten web with a balance of elasticity and extensibility that is best for bread. But the ratio of gliadin to glutenin varies among the different wheat varieties. Doughs made with these varieties might be either too elastic or too extensible, depending on the ratio. All of them have a less developed gluten web because of the imbalance of glutenin and gliadin in the flour.

Understanding the limits of gluten development that this ratio puts on bread dough made with these grains will help you bake with them more successfully, if you'd like to try (see page 273 for sources).

Einkorn. Einkorn is widely considered to be the first cultivated grain, grown as far back as 10,000 years ago in the Fertile Crescent. Although it is higher in total protein than wheat, einkorn has a gliadin to glutenin ratio of 2 to 1, similar to spelt. This means that the gluten web formed in a dough made with einkorn flour will have considerably less strength than the gluten web in a wheat dough, and breads made with this flour will rise less than breads made with wheat flour. But there is a reason for some bakers to continue to experiment with this grain: Recent studies suggest that even though it is related to wheat, it may be consumed safely by people with celiac disease. If this proves true, einkorn might be the alternative grain to watch in the future.

Emmer. Similar to spelt, but much older, emmer is very likely the grain that Egyptians used to make the first leavened bread. With a gliadin to glutenin ratio of 6 to 1, doughs made with emmer flour produce extremely extensible, sticky doughs that are difficult to work with. Emmer has one thing going for it: its sweet and nutty flavor, which can be used to offset the bitterness of whole-wheat flour. Emmer flour is just being discovered by some small United States millers, but it could grow in popularity as bakers search for ways to make palatable lower-gluten breads.

Kamut. Legend has it that a Montana farmer, returning from battle after World War II, brought home with him some

Einkorn　　　　Emmer　　　　Kamut　　　　Triticale

seeds of an ancient Egyptian wheat, which he was told had come from the tomb of King Tut. The crop — eventually named *kamut*, the Egyptian word for wheat — has gained attention from nutritionists for its healthy profile: Kamut is high in protein, minerals such as magnesium and zinc, B and E vitamins, and healthy unsaturated fats. Because it has not been genetically modified or improved, the way high-yielding strains of modern wheat have been, it retains its natural resistance to pests and disease and is generally hardy, making it a good choice to grow organically. It is tolerated well by people with wheat allergies and works reasonably well when substituted for wheat flour in recipes for cookies, crackers, crêpes,

and cereal. Used this way, it can be a boon for people on wheat-free diets. As far as bread baking goes, kamut can be used to make lower-gluten breads when combined with wheat flour, but it won't develop enough gluten on its own to raise a 100 percent kamut bread to acceptable heights.

Triticale. Triticale is a crossbreed of rye and wheat, developed in Scotland in the late nineteenth century to take advantage of rye's ability to thrive in that country's cool, damp climate while providing the population with a grain suitable for bread baking. It has a lot of good rye flavor, with some (but not all) of wheat's gluten-forming capability.

Rye Chops, Flakes, Flours, and Berries

Whole rye, like whole wheat, is processed into a number of products, the variety of which can be bewildering to the uninitiated. While German, eastern European, and northern Italian bakers are well acquainted with this grain in all its forms, most Americans will need the following primer to understand what rye products are available and how they are used.

Bohemian rye flour. Traditional mills sometimes sell this ready-to-use blend of rye and wheat flours, which contains enough rye for good rye flavor and enough wheat gluten for a good rise.

Cracked rye. Cracked rye is just what it sounds like: rye berries that have been slightly cracked between millstones or by machine. Added to bread dough, cracked rye adds a texture similar to cracked wheat.

Rye berries. This refers to the entire hulled kernel of rye, including the endosperm, germ, and bran.

Rye chops. A synonym for cracked rye.

Rye flakes. These are rye berries that have been cut, cooked, and rolled into flakes. Rye flakes can be used just like rolled oats — as cereal or mixed into bread dough.

Rye flavoring. A combination of rye flour and natural and artificial flavoring ingredients, rye flavoring is often used in commercial rye breads to enhance their flavor. But there are more natural ways to give your rye breads authentic flavor.

Rye meal. Coarsely ground rye flour, similar in texture to pumpernickel, rye meal has had the germ and bran sifted out.

Pumpernickel flour. The rye equivalent of whole-wheat flour, pumpernickel flour retains all of the germ and bran. It is used for the darkest, most robust rye breads.

Medium rye flour. This is a finely ground rye flour that retains some of the germ and bran, used to make hearty rye breads.

White rye flour. Like white wheat flour, white rye flour consists of the ground endosperm, the germ and bran having been removed. It is used to make more refined light rye breads.

Rye Loaf with Rye Berries

Makes 1 loaf

This moist loaf gets texture and great rye flavor from soaked rye berries. The relatively quick sponge is a good way to extend fermentation time without allowing too much starch breakdown in the dough. Bread flour supplementing the rye gives the dough the extra strength that it needs to rise. Even with the bread flour, you will see how fragile the gluten is when you turn the fermented dough out onto the countertop. It's difficult to knead by hand, so use a mixer if you have one, and then shape the dough gently. It should be proofed and baked in a loaf pan, which will provide some support as it rises.

FOR THE SOAKER:

2.4 ounces/68 grams (⅓ cup) whole or cracked rye berries

3 ounces (6 tablespoons) boiling water

FOR THE SPONGE:

3 ounces (6 tablespoons) room temperature water (70 to 78°F)

0.05 ounce/1.5 grams (½ teaspoon) instant yeast

3 ounces/85 grams (11 tablespoons) unbleached bread flour

FOR THE DOUGH:

6 ounces (¾ cup) room temperature water (70 to 78°F)

6.1 ounces/173 grams (1 cup plus 2 tablespoons) unbleached bread flour

2.6 ounces/74 grams (½ cup) pumpernickel (whole) rye flour

0.025 ounce/1 gram (¼ teaspoon) instant yeast

0.17 ounce/5 grams (1 teaspoon) salt

⅛ teaspoon ascorbic acid, from a crushed vitamin C tablet

CONTINUED →

1. Make the soaker: Place the rye berries in a heatproof bowl and pour the boiling water over them. Let stand, uncovered, at room temperature until the berries have absorbed most of the water, 3 to 5 hours.

2. Make the sponge: Combine the water, yeast, and bread flour in a medium bowl and stir to combine. Cover with plastic wrap and let stand at room temperature until it is very bubbly and has a mild acidic aroma (it won't rise much, because it is so loose), 3 to 5 hours.

3. Make the dough: Drain and discard any excess water from the rye berries. Combine the water, bread flour, rye flour, yeast, salt, ascorbic acid, rye berries, and sponge in the bowl of a stand mixer. Stir with a rubber spatula until a rough dough forms.

4. Knead the dough with the dough hook until it is smooth and stretchy, but still sticking to the sides of the bowl, 5 to 7 minutes on medium-low speed.

5. Spray the inside of a dough-rising container or large mixing bowl with nonstick cooking spray and place the dough inside. Cover with plastic wrap and let rise until the dough has increased 1½ times in volume, 1½ to 2 hours.

6. One hour before baking, place a baking stone on the middle rack of the oven and preheat the oven to 400°F.

7. Turn the dough out onto a countertop lightly dusted with flour. Gently shape it into a rough rectangle and fold the rectangle in half. Let the dough rest for 10 minutes.

8. Spray the inside of a 4- by 8-inch loaf pan with nonstick cooking spray. Shape the dough into a loaf (see page 89). Transfer it, seam side down, to the prepared pan. Lightly spray the surface with nonstick cooking spray and lightly drape with plastic wrap. Let stand until increased in volume by 50 percent, 45 minutes to 1 hour. The dough should just come to the top of the pan. Take care not to over-proof, or your dough may collapse on its way into the oven or shortly afterward.

9. Gently slide the pan onto the preheated baking stone. Bake until the loaf is deep brown and an instant-read thermometer inserted into the center reads 180°F, 35 to 40 minutes.

10. Turn the loaf out of the pan onto a wire rack, re-invert the loaf, and let cool completely, at least 2 hours, before slicing.

Whole-Grain Breads
Questions and Answers

Q I'd like to start baking with whole-wheat flour, but I don't know if I'm ready to tackle a 100 percent whole-wheat bread. Can I start by substituting a portion of whole-wheat flour for white flour in a favorite recipe? Are there guidelines for doing this?

A Most bread recipes can be adapted to use some whole-wheat flour, between one-third and one-fifth of the total flour in the recipe, with a good result. Begin your baking knowing that your new bread will be a bit heavier and denser than a 100 percent white bread (although not unacceptably so). Something else to remember: Whole-wheat flour is generally more absorbent than white flour, so you might find you have to add more liquid to your recipe, 1 tablespoon at a time, until your dough is properly hydrated. If your original recipe does not call for added sugar, you might think about adding a teaspoon or two to balance the flavor of the whole grain. Once you've had success with this substitution, you can increase the proportion of whole-wheat flour in later attempts, seeing how high you can go while still meeting your expectations for good bread.

Q I made the Whole-Wheat and Honey Boule with Hazelnuts recipe, and while it had a better flavor than the last 100 percent whole-wheat bread I baked, it was still a little bitter for my taste. Do you have any suggestions for improving it further?

A You could always substitute some bread flour for some of the whole-wheat flour, which will sweeten your bread. But if you are determined to make a 100 percent whole-wheat bread that is sweeter than this one, you could do a few things. The easiest: Add a cup or so of raisins or other sweet dried fruit. I find that the addition of raisins to any whole-wheat bread increases its palatability dramatically without changing the molecular structure of the dough. Or you could try something that Peter Reinhart proposes in his book *Whole Grain Breads,* which is soaking the whole-wheat flour in the water before mixing your dough. Although soakers are usually made using whole or coarsely ground grain, there's a good reason to try this technique with your regular whole-wheat flour. An extended soak (mix together the flour and the water and let them stand, covered, for an hour or two before making your dough) will allow the flour's enzymes to break down starches into simple sugars, not only making more food available for your yeast and enhancing fermentation but also sweetening the dough in the process.

Q I made a moist and delicious whole-grain loaf, but the crumb was more compact near the bottom crust than in the upper portions. Why did this happen, and how can I get a more even crumb next time?

A It sounds like your bread did not get as strong of an oven spring as is ideal. This is a common problem with whole-wheat breads for several reasons. Did you place the loaf pan on a preheated baking stone? Delivering an intense blast of heat to the bottom crust this way, even if the loaf is in a pan, is a good way to get things going. Or it could be that the dough's gluten structure was not quite what it should have been. Next time you might try kneading a few minutes longer, or giving the dough an extra turn during bulk fermentation, to strengthen the gluten. A final possibility is that your dough was slightly over-proofed, which will result in a weakened gluten structure and less even rising in the oven.

Q I would like to experiment with making a kamut or emmer bread. Is there a good recipe to start with?

A Einkorn, emmer, and kamut can all be substituted for spelt in the recipe for Spelt Bâtardes. Or use the guidelines outlined on page 235 for substituting whole-wheat flour for white flour in a favorite recipe. Go slowly, substituting an increasing percentage of the new flour each time, so that you wind up with a bread you are happy with in terms of volume, flavor, and gluten level. Start by substituting 25 percent to 30 percent of a new flour for an equal portion of white flour. Keep an eye on your dough — your new flour may absorb more or less water than wheat flour, so you'll have to adjust accordingly. Once your bread is baked, evaluate its taste and texture. Did the substitution have any adverse impact on the result? Could even more of the new flour be added next time without detriment to the bread's texture or flavor? Depending on the answers to these questions, you can adjust further the next time you bake.

Q What is vital wheat gluten? Should I be adding it to my lower-gluten breads?

A Vital wheat gluten is the protein that has been extracted from wheat, hydrated to activate the gluten, and then processed and dried and ground into a powder. It is sometimes used by bakers to strengthen whole-wheat, rye, spelt, and other lower-gluten doughs so that they will rise higher when baked. You can add vital wheat gluten to any of the recipes in this chapter, 1 tablespoon for every 2 to 3 cups of flour.

Although vital wheat gluten will improve the texture of your bread (sometimes markedly so, sometimes only subtly), it will also boost the bread's gluten content. So if your aim is to produce a lower-gluten bread, you will of course want to skip it and try the other techniques discussed in this chapter for coaxing your lower-gluten whole-grain breads to rise high.

Q I'd like to make a 100 percent sourdough spelt bread. Can I use whole spelt in my sourdough culture?

A Absolutely, as long as you adjust your expectations about how quickly and vigorously it will ferment compared to white flour. Because you are using whole-grain flour, there will be fewer starches available to the yeast than there would be with white spelt flour. It might take some extra time for your culture to gain enough strength to raise bread. Just follow the instructions in chapter 6. And don't forget to continue adding a little bit of rye flour with every feeding, which will spur fermentation.

Q Is it possible to knead rye doughs by hand, or are they just too sticky?

A It is possible and can be enjoyable, as long as you adjust your expectations of what a well-kneaded dough should feel like! Because rye flour has less gluten and more starch than wheat flour, doughs made with rye flour will be softer and stickier than doughs made with 100 percent wheat flour. Bakers inexperienced with the feel of rye tend to add too much flour during kneading, with the desire to make the dough smooth and bouncy like wheat dough. But the fact is that a well-kneaded rye dough will remain sticky until the end, and adding too much flour will result in a tough, dry loaf. To resist the temptation to add flour while kneading by hand, oil your hands with olive oil or vegetable oil or flour them frequently, and use a bench scraper to scrape sticky dough from the countertop as you knead. Eventually it will come together in a coherent mass.

Q **My rye dough isn't rising! What did I do wrong?**

A It's possible that the yeast you used was past its expiration date, and so your dough really isn't rising. But more likely it is just rising more slowly and to a lesser volume than wheat doughs you've worked with before. Remember, rye dough will not expand into a bouncy, balloonlike mass. When fully fermented, it will be spongy and delicate to the touch, with perhaps only a 50 percent to 75 percent increase in volume.

Q **My rye bread was delicious, but it didn't taste anything like the bread I buy at the kosher deli, which is what I was expecting. Why not?**

A Most "Jewish rye bread" sold commercially actually contains very little rye flour, and the rye flour it does contain is in all likelihood white rye flour, from which the flavorful bran and germ have been sifted out. Chances are, that bread was mixed, fermented, and baked in less than 2 hours, giving it very little time to develop the flavor of the grain. To compensate for the lack of flavor, commercial bakeries often add artificial flavoring to the dough. Because Jewish rye bread traditionally had caraway seeds both mixed into the dough and sprinkled on top, the artificial flavor added at the bakery was more likely artificial caraway than artificial rye! If you want to bake a purer version of the bread you are describing, you can grind 1 tablespoon of caraway seeds in a spice grinder and add it to the dough. Just before baking, brush the loaf lightly with water and sprinkle some whole seeds on top. These two steps will give you real, rather than artificial, caraway flavor to complement the real rye taste of your bread.

Chapter 9
Bread Machine Baking

YOU MIGHT WONDER WHY it is even necessary to include a chapter on bread machine baking in this book, if the purpose of using a machine is to sidestep all of the mystery (not to mention all of the work) involved in home bread baking. But for the thoughtful baker, the bread machine can be more than a convenience. It can be a valuable tool for crafting excellent loaves. The more you know about bread baking, and the more you know about your machine, the better your bread machine loaves will be.

Carefully read the sections in this book on ingredients and techniques. The ingredients that you use for bread machine baking will be the same ones you use in conventional recipes. It isn't even necessary to buy special "bread machine yeast," because instant yeast, the kind I recommend throughout this book, works the same way, without having to be rehydrated before being added to flour. Although mixing and kneading techniques won't be necessary when you use the bread machine, it's still important to know the hows and whys of mixing and kneading, if only so you can choose the proper settings for the particular bread you are baking in the machine. If you choose to make your dough in the machine and then remove it to hand-shape it before baking it in a regular oven, you'll need to understand those steps. But even if you want to make a loaf start to finish in the machine, understanding what happens to bread dough once it is kneaded and while it is baking will help you figure out how to tinker with the settings on your machine to make each successive loaf better than the last one.

Once you have a basic understanding of how bread is made, you'll be ready to think about buying a bread machine if you don't already own one. I hope I'll be able to answer some questions about this not-inexpensive

Bread machine varieties

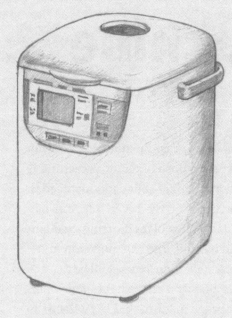

Zojirushi: makes loaf-shaped loaves

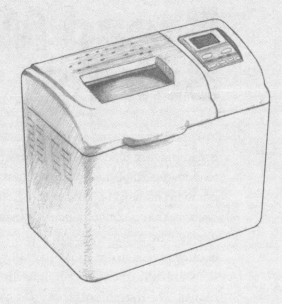

Zojirushi Mini: makes 1-lb loaves

Black & Decker Deluxe: makes 3-lb loaves

Panasonic: makes square loaves

purchase: Is it necessary to buy the one with the highest price tag? Which special features are necessary, and which ones aren't worth the trouble or the added cost?

When you have chosen (or been given, or inherited) your machine, you'll need to understand its two primary settings. The Dough setting can be used to mix, knead, and ferment dough that you will later shape by hand and bake in your own oven. I'll tell you how you can adapt your favorite bread recipes to take advantage of the machine's powerful kneading blade and temperature-controlled interior, which is perfect for fermentation.

The Bake setting allows anyone to throw some ingredients into the bread machine's baking pan and wind up, a few hours later, with some hot, fresh bread. I'll discuss how to wind up with the best bread possible when using the machine from start to finish.

This chapter ends with recipes developed specifically with the strengths of the bread machine in mind. Bread Machine Brioche (page 250), *Pane alla Cioccolata* (page 252), and Overnight Oatmeal Bread (page 254) are all loaves I'd make even if they weren't so easy. They are that enjoyable.

Selecting a Bread Machine

I don't subscribe to the belief that every bread machine requires a different recipe for the same bread. Although machines vary from brand to brand, they all basically perform the same functions, kneading and baking dough. Your pumpkin bread may come out looking different if you bake it in a Zojirushi machine rather than a Panasonic machine, because these machines have different-shape pans, but each machine can accommodate the same dough and bake it successfully without changes to the recipe. As long as your pan is large enough to accommodate the quantity of dough you are making, there's no need to worry about which brand of machine you have and then to tinker with the recipe accordingly. Use the machine you already own — any machine will do — and it is possible to get great results.

That said, if you are in the market for a new machine, you might consider the options before making the best choice for yourself. The first

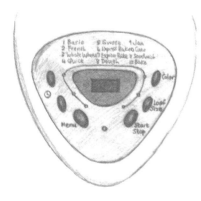

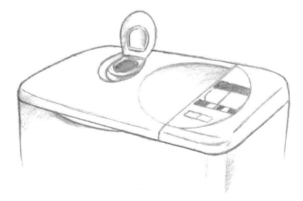

Bread machine control panel

Bread machine yeast dispenser and control panel

thing you'll need to decide is what size loaves you'd like to bake. Are you a single person who doesn't want a lot of leftover bread around? Then the Zojirushi Mini, which bakes 1-pound loaves, might be right for you. If you have hungry teenage boys who want bread morning, noon, and night, Black and Decker's Deluxe model will bake a 3-pound loaf in a few hours. Note that there are several machines on the market that can be programmed to bake small, medium, and large loaves, and it may be worth it to choose one of these for the sake of flexibility.

Beyond size, what is important? It is nice to have a pan that is removable, for ease of filling. Pans that don't come out of the machine will make extracting the baked bread a pain and cleanup a chore. The heaviness of the pan will determine how dark and crusty your loaves will get when baked in the machine. For chewier crusts, a heavier, darker pan is better. For light and tender crusts, go with a lighter pan.

A Raisin Bread setting will sound an alarm when it is time to add raisins, olives, nuts, or other additional ingredients that would be crushed or otherwise damaged if added at the beginning of the mixing cycle. But this isn't absolutely necessary, as long as your machine will keep running if you open the lid to add ingredients. This ability is also important if you want to check on your dough after it's been kneaded for a few minutes, to see if it is properly hydrated. Some machines will turn off automatically when opened, driving you crazy when you have to reset them at the right time to continue with the recipe.

A machine with a Crust Color setting is also nice. While lean doughs can tolerate the high heat required for a very dark crust, enriched and sweetened doughs may burn unless baked on a gentler, lighter setting.

If you plan on baking with whole grains, buy a machine with a Whole Grain setting. On this setting, the machine will knead and ferment the dough longer, which is very important if you want a whole-grain loaf that is light and well risen.

Some of the more expensive machines have many more settings than this, so that you can customize the preparation of your dough much the way you would when making a dough by hand. There is even a machine that allows you to program settings that you've designed yourself, for the loaves you make most frequently. It is up to you to decide how much of this customizing ability you will need. Since I use my own machine only for the simplest loaves, I'm happy with a Sandwich Bread, a Whole Grain, and a Raisin Bread setting, which give me enough flexibility to bake with a variety of flours and add-in ingredients to make a nice assortment of fragrant and moist pan loaves.

My current machine has a few settings that I wish I hadn't had to pay extra for. I would never dream of using the Bake Only option, which is for baking cakes. Nor would I use the Rapid Bake setting, which does bake a loaf in less than 2 hours, as opposed to the Basic Bake setting's 4 hours. It takes, at the very least, 4 hours to make a decent-tasting loaf of bread. Rapidly baked bread is, to my taste, so characterless that it's not worth eating. I could also live without the automatic yeast dispenser. (I'll never forget the first time I used the machine, when I failed to tightly close the dispenser's lid. It was only when I lifted the hard, bricklike bread from the pan that I noticed the yeast granules scattered all over the counter, where they had been blown outward through the crack between the lid and the machine instead of being dropped into the baking pan. Now I'm afraid to use it, and I just put the yeast in the machine first, under a thick blanket of flour so that it doesn't become activated before the machine is ready to knead.) Last, there is the power saver feature. If there is a power failure while my machine is on and then the power is restored in 10 minutes or less, the machine will pick up where it left off. Maybe my electrical service is remarkably reliable, but I've never had to depend on this feature to finish baking a loaf of bread.

Before Baking: Read Your Manual!

You can read every article, book, and blog post ever written about bread machine baking, but if you don't study your own machine's manual carefully you will inevitably make small mistakes that can have a negative effect on your bread. All bread machines work in basically the same way, but each one has its own particular design, programming vocabulary, and programs for bread baking. Understand how long it will take your machine to knead, ferment, and bake your bread. Figure out how the Raisin Bread cycle works — the way the machine alerts you and the amount of time you have to add extra ingredients will vary depending on the machine. Make sure you understand how to set your machine's timer for delayed baking, so that you don't wake up to a lump of unbaked dough or a loaf that's been steaming inside the machine for half the night. You get the idea.

Using the Dough Setting

Every bread machine on the market has a Dough setting, which will allow you to mix and knead your ingredients and then ferment the kneaded dough in the temperature- and humidity-controlled environment of the sealed machine. For busy bakers who want hand-shaped hearth breads without too much hassle, this can be a godsend. There's no kneading, no worry about the temperature or draftiness of your kitchen, no fretful judgment of whether or not the dough has fermented long enough. Just add the ingredients, press a button, and when the timer goes off you are ready to shape, proof, and bake. There are other considerable benefits:

Bread machines love wet doughs. As discussed in earlier chapters, adding too much flour during kneading is a major reason for dry, dense bread. When you are simply dumping your ingredients into the pan of the bread machine, there is no need to worry that you'll make an error in judgment and add extra flour to what only looks like a too-wet dough, or that you won't be able to resist adding too much flour if you are kneading by hand. The machine will force you to use some self-restraint.

It provides a nice, warm environment for yeast. One recent winter, when my husband and I were trying to save energy and money by keeping the house cool, I had a tough time with my bread. Although many recipes advise a long, cool rise, fermenting bread dough on my countertop was more like retarding it in the refrigerator! Sometimes it took my dough forever to double in volume, and sometimes my dough never made it to the doubling mark at all! When I decided to knead and ferment my doughs in the bread machine, I got consistently good results every time. Now I use my bread machine frequently in the winter, almost like a temperature-controlled proofing box or chamber in a bakery, to help me predict and assess my dough's progress.

Shaping becomes a nonissue. When you make a loaf start to finish in a bread machine, you know what it will look like when it's baked: It will have the same shape, whether it's a square, a rectangle, or a cylinder, as the baking pan. So easy! And there are no worries about overhandling the dough, deflating it while rolling it into a baguette shape, or rounding it insufficiently so it bubbles up inelegantly on one side in the oven. If, on the other hand, you enjoy shaping slim baguettes, perfectly rounded boules, or more complicated wheat sheaf and fougasse shapes, then you will want to consider shaping by hand and baking in the oven as an alternative to baking in the machine.

Bread machine bread pans come in different shapes.

But there are a few downsides. Be aware, when you choose the Dough setting, that you will be giving up quite a bit of control over your dough and possibly several opportunities to improve your bread, as follows:

No gargantuan Poilâne-style miches. With a bread machine, you limit the size of your breads to the size of the machine's bread pan, even though you will be using your oven for baking. Small machines, with a 1-pound loaf capacity, can only accommodate breads made with 2 cups of flour or less. Larger machines that bake 1½- to 2-pound loaves are limited to accommodating recipes using 3 to 4 cups of flour.

Making adjustments is difficult. When you are kneading by hand or using a stand mixer, it is easy to stop and add a tablespoon of extra flour or extra water if you can see and feel that your dough is too wet or too dry. With a bread machine, making this kind of small but sometimes crucial adjustment is difficult and must be done with care, since you'll have to open the lid of the machine while it is kneading to do so. Bakers experienced with their bread machines say they are able to tell by the sound the machine makes as it kneads whether or not the dough is too dry. Perhaps with experience you will be able to intuit your dough's hydration level similarly!

One-size-fits-all kneading. Although the more expensive machines have several different kneading settings for different types of breads (my Panasonic machine has different knead cycles for whole-wheat bread, sandwich bread, and French bread), there's no way to customize kneading the way you can with a KitchenAid stand mixer, using

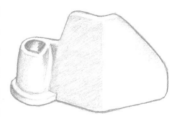

Kneading blade

different speeds (very wet ciabatta dough likes a high speed) and kneading times (bread baked with spelt flour shouldn't be kneaded for too long, to preserve fragile gluten strands) to get just the right result.

No opportunity to turn the dough. If you want to build gluten by turning the dough midway through fermentation, you are out of luck. When using the bread machine, you'll have to rely on its kneading powers alone to build gluten.

Adapting a Bread Recipe for Your Machine

You'll have to use some math and a little common sense to adapt your favorite bread recipes to the bread machine.

First, look at your recipe and see if your bread machine's pan is big enough to accommodate the dough. Depending on the make and model, your machine might have a 1-pound pan, a 1½-pound pan, or a 2-pound pan. A 1-pound pan can accommodate doughs made with no more than 2 cups of flour. A 1½-pound pan can hold doughs made with 3 cups of flour. A 2-pound pan can hold doughs made with 4 cups of flour, but no more.

Then ask yourself which setting, Dough or Bake, would be appropriate for the bread you'd like to bake. Choose the Dough setting for breads that are going to require special shaping or loaves that need a superheated baking stone to reach their potential height and crusty exterior. The Bake setting is fine for pan loaves that are supposed to have a more tender crust and softer crumb.

Does your recipe have a pre-ferment? Whether you will be using the Dough setting or the Bake setting, you will have to mix your sponge or biga first and then let it ferment for the recommended amount of time before proceeding with the recipe. If the pre-ferment stands at room temperature, you can mix it right in the bread pan and then add the other ingredients when it is ready. If you are going to do this, add the remaining wet ingredients first and then the dry ingredients, the opposite of what you would do with a straight dough, to keep the wet separate from the dry while the machine brings everything to warm room temperature before mixing and kneading the dough.

You can make certain types of sourdough breads in your machine, but save the crusty hearth breads for the oven. Flavorful sourdough pan loaves are a better bet (try the Rye and Pumpkin Seed Pan Loaf, page 174). Use the same method as with a pre-ferment: Mix your final build right in the bread machine pan. Add the wet ingredients and then the dry. With the bread machine, you won't be able to use some of the techniques that I prefer for sourdough baking, like the 20-minute autolyse. But the fact is that your bread will get some of the benefits of autolyse simply because while the machine brings the ingredients up to warm room temperature, your flour and water will sit together for some time (in my machine the rest-before-knead period can take as long as 45 minutes) before kneading commences.

Because sourdough breads often require a longer fermentation time than breads made with packaged yeast, it's a good idea to program an extra hour or two of fermenting and proofing into the machine if you can. If not, set the machine to its longest setting (usually the Whole Grain setting) and see what happens. If your bread is underrisen, you might think about supplementing the wild yeast with ¾ teaspoon of packaged yeast next time. Your bread will still get all of the benefits of your sourdough starter's flavor, with a quicker rise from the packaged yeast.

Some bread machine manufacturers claim that you can actually make a sourdough culture in the bread machine in a matter of hours. Don't believe it! The "sourdough" they are referring to is simply a pre-ferment, made with commercial yeast and allowed to ferment in the bread machine's pan. You can certainly cultivate a real sourdough starter in the machine's pan and ferment it in the machine, as long as you don't plan on using your machine for several days, and sometimes for up to 10 days, while your wild yeast develops. But I just don't see the point. It's easier and less messy to do it the old-fashioned way, as outlined in chapter 6.

Bread on Demand:
Using the Bread Machine's Timer

One of the really fun things about a bread machine is its timer, which allows you to assemble your bread ingredients before you go to bed and wake up just as your loaf is ready to come out of the "oven." It's very important when using the timer that you have some experience with the recipe and know that it won't require tinkering with during mixing, since instead of standing by to add 1 tablespoon of flour or 2 teaspoons of water, you'll be asleep, dreaming about breakfast. For the same reason, take extra care to weigh or measure your ingredients accurately.

You can make a variety of loaves using this setting, but there are some types that you can't make on time delay. Breads that have raisins or other dried fruits, nuts, or other add-in ingredients such as chocolate chips can't be baked using the timer, because the baker needs to be standing by to add the extra ingredient just as kneading is ending, so that the ingredients can be distributed throughout but not crushed.

Breads that contain perishable ingredients such as eggs and milk shouldn't be baked on time delay either, for a much more serious reason. Out of the refrigerator, these ingredients will spoil quickly and may cause food poisoning.

The Recipes

If you are in the mood for a crusty artisan loaf, you will be well served by the machine's Dough setting, a stand mixer, or your own two hands in creating one from scratch. The bread machine simply can't compete with a home oven fitted with a baking stone when it comes to giving these types of dough the energetic oven spring and intense heat required for a superior crust.

But softer, more yielding pan loaves bake wonderfully in the bread machine. Remember, the longest bread machine cycle takes only about 4 hours, so bread machine breads are not going to ferment long enough to allow the lactobacilli in the dough to develop flavorful acids. It's a good idea to add flavor with other ingredients when you can. Doughs enriched with butter, some eggs, or even bacon grease do well in the machine. Doughs with ingredients such as candied fruit, nuts, or cooked bacon (but not in the same loaf!) are also good. My machine bakes loaves that can be cut into uniform squares or rectangles, perfect for sandwiches. So it's fun to think of new and interesting sandwich loaves for favorite sandwich fillings. Grilled cheese is great on Cornmeal Loaf with Bacon and Thyme (page 255). Shrimp or lobster salad is superb on toasted Bread-Machine Brioche (page 250).

These are the types of recipes I've included below: a sandwich rye, a flavorful and tender oatmeal loaf, a traditional Italian pane alla cioccolata. They can all take their place in your repertoire alongside your crusty baguettes. Once you get the hang of it, it's easy to create your own interestingly flavored loaves. Substitute dried cranberries and chopped sage for the bacon and thyme. Add chopped apricots and cinnamon to the brioche or raisins and caraway seeds to the rye. You get the idea.

Bread-Machine Brioche

Makes 1 loaf

Brioche is a good choice for the bread machine, as it can be tricky to work with by hand because of its high butter content. The pan shape of most machines works well for this bread, too, which can then be cut into uniformly square slices. For the best gluten development, wait to add half of the butter until the end of the kneading cycle. If you add it all in the beginning, the fat molecules may coat the proteins and prevent a sufficient number of them from linking up to form a strong gluten web.

17.63 ounces/500 grams (3½ cups) unbleached bread flour
2.12 ounces/60 grams (⅓ cup) sugar
0.25 ounce/7 grams (1½ teaspoons) kosher salt or fine sea salt
6 large eggs
2 ounces (¼ cup) water
1 cup (2 sticks) unsalted butter, at room temperature, cut into small pieces
0.25 ounce/7 grams (2¼ teaspoons) instant yeast

1. Place the flour, sugar, and salt in the bread machine pan. Add the eggs, water, and ½ stick (4 tablespoons) of the butter.

2. Place the bread pan in the machine, making sure it snaps into the machine properly. Close the top lid.

3. Place the yeast in the yeast dispenser and close the lid. (If your machine doesn't have a yeast dispenser, place it in the machine first, before the remaining dry ingredients.)

4. Make your selections on the control panel of your machine. Depending upon how many options your machine has, choose the following: a bread program (Basic), a bake program (Bake), and a crust color (Light). Press Start.

5. Ten minutes into the kneading cycle, open the lid and add the remaining 1½ sticks butter, a few pieces at a time, until it is all incorporated. Close the lid and let the machine finish kneading the bread.

6. When the machine signals that the bread is baked, promptly open the lid and remove the bread pan, using oven mitts. Overturn the bread out of the pan onto a wire rack. If the kneading blade remains in the bread, remove it with metal tongs.

7. Turn the bread upright and cool completely before slicing and serving. Or wrap in plastic and store for up to 2 days at room temperature.

Other Recipes for Your Bread Machine

In addition to the recipes in this chapter, you might try the following bread recipes in your machine if you are so inclined:

Ricotta Loaf (page 35): Bake on the Sandwich setting, and choose the medium crust color.

Cheddar Cheese Boule (page 119): You can bake this in a loaf shape in your machine, adding the cheese when kneading is almost completed (use the Raisin Bread setting if your machine has one) and choosing the darkest crust color.

Sunflower Seed Bread (page 136): In the bread machine, this will bake up as a sturdy sandwich loaf rather than as a rustic seeded boule. Use the Whole Grain setting, add the sunflower seeds when kneading is almost completed (use the Raisin Bread setting if your machine has one), and skip sprinkling the extra sunflower seeds on top.

Pain de Mie (page 142): This classic white sandwich bread bakes beautifully in the bread machine.

Eight-Grain-and-Seed Pan Loaf (page 225): Prepare the soaker right in the bread pan, 8 to 12 hours before you bake. Then add the remaining wet ingredients, and then the dry ones, set the machine to Whole Grain, and press Start.

Rye Loaf with Rye Berries (page 233): This is another great whole-grain bread for the bread machine.

Pane alla Cioccolata

Makes 1 loaf

You can bake this loaf in the bread machine, or you can use the Dough mode. If you do this, shape the loaf into a braid (see page 118), place it on a parchment-lined baking sheet, sift some cocoa powder over it, drape with plastic wrap, let rise until doubled, and bake in a 350°F oven until the interior registers 190°F on an instant-read thermometer. When it cools, you can drizzle it with some melted chocolate: Dip the tines of a fork into the chocolate and then wave the fork back and forth over the bread to make a decorative pattern.

Choose the Raisin Bread option if your machine has one, so that the chocolate chips can be added toward the end of kneading. If your machine doesn't automatically add extra ingredients like raisins and chocolate chips at the right time, add the chips 3 minutes before kneading is done so they won't get crushed. Set crust color to Light, or else the sugar in the dough will cause the crust to burn.

Leftovers are very good toasted and spread with cherry preserves. Or use the bread to make a sensational chocolate bread pudding.

11.25 ounces/319 grams (2¼ cups) unbleached all-purpose flour
2 ounces/57 grams (4 tablespoons) sugar
0.8 ounce/23 grams (¼ cup) unsweetened Dutch-process cocoa powder
0.1 ounce/3 grams (¾ teaspoon) salt
6 ounces (¾ cup) cold water (55 to 65°F)
1 large egg yolk
1 tablespoon unsalted butter
0.15 ounce/4 grams (1¼ teaspoons) instant yeast
¾ cup bittersweet chocolate chips or chunks

1. Place the flour, sugar, cocoa powder, and salt in the bread machine pan. Add the water, egg yolk, and butter.

2. Place the bread pan in the machine, making sure it snaps into the machine properly. Close the top lid.

3. Place the yeast in the yeast dispenser and close the lid. (If your machine doesn't have a yeast dispenser, place it in the machine first, before the remaining dry ingredients.)

4. Make your selections on the control panel of your machine. Depending upon how many options your machine has, choose the following: a bread program (Basic), a bake program (Raisin Bread, or Bake if your machine doesn't have a Raisin Bread cycle), and a crust color (Light). Press Start.

5. If your machine has a Raisin Bread program, add the chocolate chips when alerted by the machine. If not, add the chocolate chips a minute or two before the kneading cycle is completed.

6. When the machine signals that the bread is baked, promptly open the lid and remove the bread pan, using oven mitts. Overturn the bread out of the pan onto a wire rack. If the kneading blade remains in the bread, remove it with metal tongs.

7. Turn the bread upright and cool completely before slicing and serving. Or wrap in plastic and store for up to 1 day at room temperature.

Overnight Oatmeal Bread

Makes 1 large loaf

This is a great breakfast bread, perfect to put together in the evening to be ready for the next morning. Then use what remains for sandwiches at lunch. Pour the water right on top of the oatmeal, so that it soaks overnight. This will soften the oats and release some of their bread-friendly enzymes that will help break down the starches in the grains, enhancing fermentation.

16 ounces/454 grams (3½ cups) unbleached bread flour

2.65 ounces/75 grams (⅞ cup) rolled oats

0.25 ounce/7 grams (1½ teaspoons) kosher salt or fine sea salt

12 ounces (1½ cups) cold water (55 to 65°F)

2 tablespoons honey

2 tablespoons unsalted butter, chilled, cut into bits

0.08 ounce/2 grams (¾ teaspoon) instant yeast

1. Place the flour, oats, and salt in the bread machine pan. Add the water, honey, and butter.

2. Place the bread pan in the machine, making sure it snaps into the machine properly. Close the top lid.

3. Place the yeast in the yeast dispenser and close the lid. (If your machine doesn't have a yeast dispenser, place it in the machine first, before the remaining dry ingredients.)

4. Make your selections on the control panel of your machine. Depending upon how many options your machine has, choose the following: a bread program (Multigrain), a bake program (Sandwich), and a crust color (Medium).

5. Set the timer for the time tomorrow morning when you want your bread to finish baking. Press the Start button.

6. When the machine signals that the bread is baked, promptly open the lid and remove the bread pan, using oven mitts. Overturn the bread out of the pan onto a wire rack. If the kneading blade remains in the bread, remove it with metal tongs.

7. Turn the bread upright and cool completely before slicing and serving. Or wrap in plastic and store for up to 1 day at room temperature.

Cornmeal Loaf with Bacon and Thyme

Makes 1 large loaf

Cornmeal gives this bread a pleasant crunch, and bacon bits not only give it great flavor but also extend its shelf life.

11.25 ounces/319 grams (2½ cups) unbleached bread flour

2 ounces/57 grams (⅓ cup) yellow cornmeal

1 ounce/28 grams (2 tablespoons) sugar

0.08 ounce/2 grams (½ teaspoon) kosher salt or fine sea salt

6 ounces (¾ cup) room temperature water (70 to 78°F)

2 tablespoons bacon grease

1 large egg

0.2 ounce/6 grams (2 teaspoons) instant yeast

4 ounces (4 slices) bacon, cooked crisp and crumbled

1 tablespoon finely chopped fresh thyme leaves

1. Place the flour, cornmeal, sugar, and salt in the bread machine pan. Add the water, bacon grease, and egg.

2. Place the bread pan in the machine, making sure it snaps into the machine properly. Close the top lid.

CONTINUED $\longrightarrow$

3. Place the yeast in the yeast dispenser and close the lid. (If your machine doesn't have a yeast dispenser, place it in the machine first, before the remaining dry ingredients.)

4. Make your selections on the control panel of your machine. Depending upon how many options your machine has, choose the following: a bread program (Basic), a bake program (Raisin Bread or Bake), and a crust color (Medium). Press Start.

5. If your machine has a Raisin Bread program, add the bacon and thyme when alerted by the machine. If not, add them a minute or two before the kneading cycle is completed.

6. When the machine signals that the bread is baked, promptly open the lid and remove the bread pan, using oven mitts. Overturn the bread out of the pan onto a wire rack. If the kneading blade remains in the bread, remove it with metal tongs.

7. Turn the bread upright and cool completely before slicing and serving. Or wrap in plastic and store for up to 1 day at room temperature.

Poppy Seed and Onion Rye Bread

Makes 1 large loaf

Sautéed onions baked right into this bread add moisture and give it incredible flavor. Poppy seeds provide the crunch. Try this bread as an alternative to bagels, sliced and topped with cream cheese and thin slivers of smoked salmon. Or spread slices with mustard and pile with corned beef, turkey, or pastrami.

1 tablespoon olive oil

1 small onion, finely chopped

2 tablespoons poppy seeds

9 ounces/255 grams (2 cups) unbleached bread flour

4.5 ounces/128 grams (1 cup) medium rye flour

0.25 ounce/7 grams (1½ teaspoons) kosher salt or fine sea salt

0.5 ounce/14 grams (1 tablespoon) light brown sugar

6 ounces (¾ cup) room temperature water (70 to 78°F)

½ cup full-fat sour cream or yogurt

0.25 ounce/7 grams (2¼ teaspoons) instant yeast

1. Heat the oil in a small skillet over medium heat and add the onions. Cook until softened, about 5 minutes. Remove from the heat, scrape into a small bowl, stir in the poppy seeds, and let cool.

2. Place the bread flour, rye flour, salt, and brown sugar in the bread machine pan. Add the water, sour cream, and onion mixture.

3. Place the bread pan in the machine, making sure it snaps into the machine properly. Close the top lid.

4. Place the yeast in the yeast dispenser and close the lid. (If your machine doesn't have a yeast dispenser, place it in the machine first, before the remaining dry ingredients.)

CONTINUED →

5. Make your selections on the control panel of your machine. Depending upon how many options your machine has, choose the following: a bread program (Basic), a bake program (Bake), and a crust color (Medium). Press Start.

6. When the machine signals that the bread is baked, promptly open the lid and remove the bread pan, using oven mitts. Overturn the bread out of the pan onto a wire rack. If the kneading blade remains in the bread, remove it with metal tongs.

7. Turn the bread upright and cool completely before slicing and serving. Or wrap in plastic and store for up to 1 day at room temperature.

Pumpkin Bread

Makes 1 large loaf

This recipe, adapted for the bread machine from a King Arthur Flour recipe I copied down years ago, makes a lovely fall bread. Serve it throughout the holidays as part of a larger breadbasket. For fantastic day-after-Thanksgiving sandwiches, toast leftover slices and top them with cranberry sauce, turkey, and gravy.

14.6 ounces/414 grams (3¼ cups) unbleached all-purpose flour

2 ounces/56 grams (¼ cup) dark brown sugar

0.17 ounce/5 grams (1 teaspoon) kosher salt or fine sea salt

¼ teaspoon ground ginger

¼ teaspoon ground cardamom

5 ounces (½ cup plus 2 tablespoons) warm room temperature water (70 to 78°F)

2 large eggs

¾ cup canned pumpkin purée (not pumpkin pie filling)

1 tablespoon unsalted butter

0.25 ounce/7 grams (2¼ teaspoons) instant yeast

1. Place the flour, brown sugar, salt, ginger, and cardamom in the bread machine pan. Add the water, eggs, pumpkin purée, and butter.

2. Place the bread pan in the machine, making sure it snaps into the machine properly. Close the top lid.

3. Place the yeast in the yeast dispenser and close the lid. (If your machine doesn't have a yeast dispenser, place it in the machine first, before the remaining dry ingredients.)

4. Make your selections on the control panel of your machine. Depending upon how many options your machine has, choose the following: a bread program (Basic), a bake program (Bake), and a crust color (Medium). Press Start.

5. When the machine signals that the bread is baked, promptly open the lid and remove the bread pan, using oven mitts. Overturn the bread out of the pan onto a wire rack. If the kneading blade remains in the bread, remove it with metal tongs.

6. Turn the bread upright and cool completely before slicing and serving. Or wrap in plastic and store for up to 1 day at room temperature.

Making Meat Loaf in Your Bread Machine and Other Crazy Ideas

Bread machine fanatics, encouraged by overzealous marketers, sometimes attempt to make items other than bread in their bread machines. These items range from the plausible (tea cakes) to the messy (jam or bread pudding) to the just plain gross (meat loaf). I personally reserve my bread machine for bread baking, if only because my oven does a very good job with banana bread, thank you very much, and I'd rather not have my next brioche loaf carry the faint aroma of garlicky ground chuck and seasoned bread crumbs.

CONTINUED →

Panettone

Makes 1 large loaf

Panettone, an Italian holiday bread filled with candied orange peel and sometimes chocolate, is just the right kind of bread for the bread machine — soft and tender. If you have a machine with a pan in the shape of a tall cylinder, panettone's traditional shape, all the better, although this bread is a treat no matter what its shape. Serve it with sweetened cream cheese or mascarpone, and slice leftovers for toast or French toast. This bread is rich like brioche, so it requires bread flour to counteract the weakening effect of the fat on the gluten.

14 ounces/397 grams (3 cups) unbleached bread flour
2 ounces/57 grams (¼ cup) sugar
0.25 ounce/7 grams (1½ teaspoons) kosher salt or fine sea salt
4 large eggs
2 ounces (¼ cup) milk
1 teaspoon pure vanilla extract
½ teaspoon pure almond extract
1¼ cups (2½ sticks) unsalted butter, at room temperature, cut into small pieces
0.25 ounce/7 grams (2¼ tablespoon) instant yeast
1 cup mini chocolate chips
1 cup chopped candied orange peel
½ cup coarsely chopped almonds

1. Place the flour, sugar, and salt in the bread machine pan. Add the eggs, milk, vanilla and almond extracts, and ½ stick (4 tablespoons) of the butter.

2. Place the bread pan in the machine, making sure it snaps into the machine properly. Close the top lid.

3. Place the yeast in the yeast dispenser and close the lid. (If your machine doesn't have a yeast dispenser, place it in the machine first, before the remaining dry ingredients.)

4. Make your selections on the control panel of your machine. Depending upon how many options your machine has, choose the following: a bread program (Basic), a bake program (Raisin Bread or Bake), and a crust color (Light). Press Start.

5. Ten minutes into the kneading cycle, open the lid and add the remaining 2 sticks of butter, a few pieces at a time, until it is all incorporated. Close the lid and let the machine continue to knead.

6. If your machine has a Raisin Bread program, add the chocolate chips, orange peel, and almonds when alerted by the machine. If not, add them a minute or two before the kneading cycle is completed.

7. When the machine signals that the bread is baked, promptly open the lid and remove the bread pan, using oven mitts. Overturn the bread out of the pan onto a wire rack. If the kneading blade remains in the bread, remove it with metal tongs.

8. Turn the bread upright and cool completely before slicing and serving. Or wrap in plastic and store for up to 2 days at room temperature.

Bread Machine Baking
Questions and Answers

Q When I'm using my bread machine, should my ingredients be at room temperature, the way they should be for baking conventionally?

A If your bread machine doesn't have a resting period during which it brings ingredients to the proper temperature for kneading, then the answer is yes: Use room temperature water, take your flour out of the refrigerator or freezer (if that's where you store it) and allow it to come to room temperature, remove eggs from the refrigerator, and soften butter before adding them to the baking pan. But even if your machine will do this work for you, it's best to start with room temperature ingredients so that it can get more quickly to the work of kneading and fermenting.

Q Your recipes call for adding the dry ingredients to the machine before adding the wet ingredients, but my manual says to do the opposite: Add the wet ingredients and then the dry. Which directions should I follow?

A It is really an arbitrary choice. The important thing is to keep the yeast separate from the liquid until mixing commences, so that the fermentation times that the machine calculates aren't thrown off while the ingredients are brought to temperature before kneading. Of course, if your machine doesn't have a resting cycle during which ingredients are brought to room temperature, then it makes no difference how you load them in, since they will be combined immediately in any case.

Q What are the differences between the Sandwich Bread, Whole Wheat, and French Bread cycles on my machine?

A The cycles differ in their particulars from machine to machine, but basically they offer different combinations of kneading and fermenting times, each designed to result in a typical sandwich, whole-wheat, or French bread (and some machines have many more cycles than these three). A Whole Wheat cycle will include longer kneading and fermenting times than a Sandwich Bread cycle. A French Bread cycle will have a shorter kneading time and a longer baking time, for an extra-crisp crust. For details, consult your owner's manual.

Q My machine has a Crust Color setting. What are the guidelines I should follow when choosing Light, Medium, or Dark?

A For many breads, you can answer with your preference. If you prefer a lighter, more yielding crust, choose Light. If you like a crisper, more colored crust, choose Dark. But also keep in mind the ingredients in your dough. If it contains sugar or another sweetener that will cause caramelization, choose a lighter color to prevent burning. If it is a lean dough that needs all the help it can get to brown properly, choose Dark.

Q My bread did not rise to the top of the bread pan. What did I do wrong?

A The answer may very well be nothing. Some recipes will fill the pan, while others will produce smaller loaves, depending on the quantity of ingredients used and the texture and density that the final bread is supposed to have. That said, if you find that the same bread didn't rise as high this time as last time, think about what might have caused this lower rise. Did you substitute whole-wheat flour for some of the white flour? Was your yeast well taken care of, stored in a cool, dry place in an airtight container? Did you add more or less liquid this time around? Did you place the salt and yeast one on top of the other, causing the salt to inhibit the yeast's growth? Is the temperature in your kitchen a lot cooler than it was the last time you baked? Did you open the pan numerous times, letting heat from the machine escape? The bread's low rise could be caused by any one of these.

Q My bread rose so high that the top crust stuck to the inside of the bread machine lid. What did I do wrong?

A The problem may have been as simple as baking too large a loaf for the size of your machine's bread pan. Check your ingredient quantities and see if this might be the case (see page 247 for guidelines). If your loaf has an exceptionally fluffy texture, more like cotton candy than bread, you may be baking with too much yeast. Sometimes the bread machine, which is warmer than the typical kitchen, encourages more yeast activity than is actually desirable, resulting in too-tall loaves. Make a note, and next time you bake with this recipe cut the yeast quantity by 30 percent and see what happens.

Q My loaf is gnarled and twisted like an old tree trunk! What happened?

A It sounds like your dough was too dry, which caused it to clump together into separate pieces, which then baked up into the compact, twisted bread you describe. Next time, don't be afraid to open the top of the machine and peek in during kneading. Add more water, 1 tablespoon at a time, if your dough isn't coming together into a smooth mass.

Q Mid-cycle, my machine just shut down. I checked the power source, and I still have electricity. Has the motor burned out?

A Bread machines, especially the more expensive ones, have powerful motors designed to knead bread. They also have protective sensors that detect stress on the motor and an automatic shutdown feature that stops the machine before the motor burns out. After a cooling-off period of about 30 minutes, the motor will restart. If your motor has shut down because your dough is too stiff or there is too much of it, remove the dough and discard it. Then, start over with a smaller quantity or with a dough that has a more manageable texture.

Q There is smoke coming from the bread machine. Is my bread burning? Is the machine on fire?

A Do not call 911 quite yet. Sometimes bread dough will leak onto the heating element through a small space where the kneading blade attaches to the pan. Or sometimes, after repeated use, crumbs from previous breads will start to burn. These are the most likely causes of smoke. Let your current bread bake, and when the machine is cooled, remove the bread pan and use a small handheld vacuum to clean the debris from the bottom of the machine.

Q The "ready" alarm went off on my machine, and when I opened the lid, there was an unbaked lump of dough. What happened?

A This happened to me once, and it took me a few minutes to figure out what I had done wrong. I had pressed Dough instead of Bake. No harm done. I simply programmed the machine to pick up where it left off and finish the process.

Q I've just removed a loaf of bread from the machine, and I can't wait to bake another one. Do I have to let my machine cool down before I begin again?

A If your first loaf is successful, it is tempting to throw some more ingredients in the machine right away, but it is important to let the machine cool down before beginning again. If the machine is too warm from baking, it will make your ingredients too warm for proper fermentation — either destroying the yeast with heat or making the dough rise too rapidly and thus throwing off the machine's timing. Many machines have an indicator light that will tell you when it is safe to bake again, but if yours doesn't, let it sit with the lid open for at least 30 minutes. The interior should be no warmer than warm room temperature before you start.

Q **My machine has an automatic cooldown cycle that runs for an hour after my bread is baked. Is it better to leave the bread in the machine to cool down, or should I remove it as directed in your recipes?**

A An automatic cooldown cycle is a great thing if you are going to be out of the house or possibly sleeping when your bread is done baking. The machine's internal fan will run, preventing the crust from getting too soggy even while it is encased in the pan. But if you are able to remove your bread from the pan right away, that is ideal because cooling it outside the pan on a wire rack, with air circulating all around it, is the best way to encourage starch retrogradation (see page 91), which is necessary for optimal crumb and crust.

Q **What's the best way to clean my bread machine pan?**

A Your nonstick bread pan should be washed by hand with a sponge and mild dish soap. Don't put it in the dishwasher or use an abrasive scrubber because you may damage the nonstick surface, causing the bread to stick to the pan the next time you bake.

Q **After baking my last loaf, I noticed that the kneading blade seems to be baked onto my pan. How should I remove it?**

A If dried dough is gluing the blade to the pan, pour some warm water into the pan and let it stand for 15 minutes. The water should loosen the baked-on dough, allowing you to remove the blade.

Q **Sometimes liquid leaks out of the pan and onto the bottom of the machine and dries, leaving debris. How do I clean the inside of the machine?**

A Sometimes ingredients will wind up in the bottom of the bread maker, outside of the pan. If this happens, wipe the interior with a clean, dry cloth to remove debris. Never use a wet cloth or submerge the machine in water; you will damage its electrical parts.

Converting Volume to Weight Measurements

Almost every bread recipe published nowadays by a reputable bread baker includes both weight and volume measurements. Professional bakers will strongly encourage you to choose weight over volume for the sake of consistency when you make bread. What to do if you have older recipes that only give volume measurements? I suggest penciling in the following equivalents, so that every time you bake you'll wind up with a consistently great result. Here are the commonly recognized equivalents, if you'd like to update old recipes to use weight measurements:

INGREDIENT	VOLUME	WEIGHT
All flours	3½ cups	16 ounces/454 grams
	1 cup	4.5 ounces/128 grams
Fine sea salt	6 teaspoons	1 ounce/28 grams
	1½ teaspoons	0.25 ounce/7 grams
Kosher salt	6 teaspoons	1 ounce/28 grams
	1½ teaspoons	0.25 ounce/7 grams
Table salt	4 teaspoons	1 ounce/28 grams
	1 teaspoon	0.25 ounce/7 grams
Instant yeast	3 tablespoons	1 ounce/28 grams
	2¼ teaspoons	0.25 ounce/7 grams
	1 teaspoon	0.11 ounce/3 grams
Granulated sugar	2 tablespoons	1 ounce/28 grams
	1½ teaspoons	0.25 ounce/7 grams
Butter, oil, water, milk	1 cup	8 ounces/227 grams
	2 tablespoons	1 ounce/28 grams
Honey	1½ tablespoons	1 ounce/28 grams
Eggs	1 large egg	1.65 ounces/47 grams
Raisins	2⅓ cups	16 ounces/454 grams
	1 cup	6 ounces/170 grams
Nuts (coarsely chopped)	3⅓ cups	16 ounces/454 grams
	1 cup	4.8 ounces/136 grams

Bread Baker's Glossary

Acetic acid. One type of acid produced by lactobacilli during fermentation, which lends to the dough a decidedly tart taste. Acetic acid favors cooler conditions and a stiffer pre-ferment such as biga or a stiff sourdough starter such as levain.

Active dry yeast. Dried commercial yeast that needs to be soaked in water or another liquid in order to become active before being added to the dough.

Altes Brot. An old German technique for flavoring bread by adding bits of old bread to the dough.

Ash content. Ash contains the minerals that remain after a sample of flour has been incinerated. The quantity of ash is an indicator of how high the level of minerals is in a batch of flour (high mineral content is generally a good thing for bread). It also indicates how much of the germ and bran have been sifted out, since whole-grain flours and minimally milled flours have higher ash content than white flours and industrially milled flours, which contain primarily the endosperm.

Autolyse. A technique, promoted by French bread baking expert Raymond Calvel, for mixing together the flour and water in a bread recipe and letting it rest for at least 20 minutes and up to 1 hour, giving time to the flour to become thoroughly hydrated and the proteins in the flour to begin to organize themselves into a gluten web before kneading begins.

Baguette. A long, thin loaf of French bread. In France, there are actually legal guidelines that define its shape and size, which should be 5 to 6 centimeters in diameter and up to 1 meter in length, with a typical weight of 250 grams. Home bakers will have difficulty crafting such long baguettes, which won't fit in the typical home oven, but in the United States our standards for bread are less strict than they are in France!

Baker's percentage. The standard used by professional bakers to calculate the ratio of ingredients in a dough. Flour is always 100 percent, and then the other ingredients are given a value based on their weight in relation to the weight of the flour. Baker's percentages make it easy for the professional baker (or the home baker, for that matter) to easily change the yield of a recipe without altering the formula.

Baking stone. A heavy rectangular or round plate of stone used to duplicate the effect of baking bread in a brick oven.

Banneton. A traditional woven willow basket, sometimes lined with linen, used to proof breads. A bowl or colander lined with a floured kitchen towel can be used to get a similar result.

Bâtarde. A torpedo-shaped bread, wider and shorter than a baguette, but shaped using the same technique.

Benching. The period of rest between bulk fermentation and shaping that is sometimes allowed the dough once it is turned out of its dough-rising container.

Biga. An Italian-style yeasted pre-ferment, a biga usually has a stiff, dough-like consistency.

Boule. A loaf shaped into a round.

Bran. Bran is the outermost layer of the wheat kernel, edible but containing minerals and indigestible cel-lulose; it adds to a bread's fiber and mineral content.

Bread machine yeast. Another term for instant yeast, bread machine yeast is commercial dried yeast that doesn't need to be rehydrated before being mixed into dough.

Bromate. A chemical additive that hastens the aging process of flour, making it ready for baking earlier than natural aging would.

Bulk fermentation. The period of fermentation and rising that takes place after kneading and before shaping.

Compressed yeast. Another term for fresh yeast.

Couche. The French term for the folded cloth used to support baguettes, bâtardes, and other oblong doughs as they rise. A couche can easily be improvised by the home baker using a piece of parchment paper and some kitchen towels.

Crumb. The interior of the bread, crumb can be loose and large (typical of artisan breads raised with sourdough) or tight and small (softer white breads and many whole-grain breads have a tighter crumb structure).

Dimpling. A technique of pressing the fingertips into the surface of a shaped bread to control its rise in the oven;

used on many Italian breads, such as focaccia and ciabatta.

Direct dough. Another term for the straight dough method of mixing dough in one stage rather than in two.

Durum. A type of hard wheat with a yellow color, most often used to make dried pasta but sometimes finely milled to make semolina flour for bread.

Einkorn. An ancient variety of wheat, believed to be used in Egypt to bake some of the earliest yeasted breads.

Elasticity. A dough's ability to bounce back when stretched. Glutenin, one of the gluten-forming proteins in wheat flour (along with gliadin), is responsible for a dough's elasticity.

Emmer. Another ancient wheat, similar to spelt, that was also used in ancient breads.

Endosperm. The innermost portion of the wheat kernel, the endosperm contains the wheat's starch molecules and gluten-forming proteins.

Extensibility. A dough's ability to stretch without springing back. Gliadin, one of the gluten-forming proteins in wheat flour (along with glutenin), is responsible for a dough's extensibility.

Fermentation. The process by which yeast breaks down flour's starches, producing carbon dioxide and alcohol as by-products.

Ficelle. A French bread, as long as a baguette but only half the thickness.

Folding. A technique used to strengthen the gluten in a dough without overkneading it, by lifting it from the dough-rising container and placing it back down in a new position midway through fermentation.

Fresh yeast. Commercial yeast that hasn't been fully dried but is packaged instead in moist cakes. Fresh yeast (also known as compressed yeast) has a much shorter shelf life than dried yeast (it loses potency a few weeks after it is packaged).

Gelatinization. What happens to starch molecules in flour when they come in contact with water and are heated: They swell and then gel, solidifying and setting the structure of the bread.

Germ. The portion of the wheat kernel highest in healthy oils and nutrients, from which the roots of a new wheat plant emerge when the kernel is planted.

Gliadin. The protein contained in flour that links with glutenin to form gluten; gliadin is responsible for a dough's extensibility.

Glutelin. A protein present in small quantities in wheat flour, but in larger quantities in rye flour.

Gluten. The protein web formed by the gliadin and glutenin in wheat flour when they link together. Gluten gives dough its structure, expanding as the gases produced during fermentation expand so that the dough rises.

Glutenin. The protein contained in flour that links with gliadin to form gluten. Glutenin is responsible for a dough's elasticity.

Hard wheat. A class of wheat that is relatively high in protein and when milled into flour is good for bread.

Hydration. The amount of water relative to flour in bread dough.

Instant yeast. Commercial dried yeast that does not require rehydration before being mixed into dough. Choose instant yeast for bread machine baking, where all of the ingredients are simply added to the bread pan with no opportunity for hydrating the yeast ahead of time.

Kamut. An ancient grain originating in Egypt that is now grown, in very limited quantities, in the United States and occasionally used in bread baking.

Kneading. The vigorous working of the dough, either by hand or machine, to distribute the dough's ingredients evenly and to develop its gluten structure.

Lactic acid. Another type of acid produced by lactobacilli during fermentation (see **acetic acid**), lactic acid favors warmer conditions and a loose pre-ferment such as a sponge or poolish or a liquid sourdough starter.

Lactobacilli. Friendly bacteria that produce flavorful lactic and acetic acids during long (at least 8 hours) fermentation of bread dough or a sourdough starter.

Lame. A traditional French instrument for scoring loaves, with a handle and a razor-sharp blade.

Levain. The French term for a sourdough starter, a levain is usually stiff and doughlike, but it can also refer to a liquid sourdough.

Miche. A large, round, rustic loaf, such as those made famous by Lionel Poilâne in France.

Oven spring. The rapid rise of bread dough during the first few minutes of baking.

Pâte fermentée. A stiff dough pre-ferment that, unlike a sponge, poolish, or biga, usually contains salt.

Peel. A flat, handled paddle, made of wood or metal, that is used to slide loaves in and out of the oven.

Pentosan. A type of carbohydrate molecule present in large quantities in rye flour that is responsible for the stickiness of rye dough and rye bread.

Poolish. The French term for a loose, batterlike pre-ferment.

Pre-ferment. A percentage of a dough's flour, water, and yeast mixed together at least several hours and up to several days before the dough is mixed, which is then added to the dough to "age" it and give it more flavor without the risk of overfermenting it.

Pre-shaping. When dough is gently shaped into rough rounds or rectangles and allowed to rest briefly before shaping, to make shaping easier.

Proof box. A sealed chamber, with strict temperature and humidity controls, for proofing bread consistently.

Proofing. The period of a bread dough's second rise, after bulk fermentation and shaping.

Pumpernickel. Coarsely ground whole rye flour.

Rapid-rise yeast. Dry yeast that has been packaged with enzymes and other yeast foods in order to hasten fermentation.

Refreshing the starter. Keeping the active yeast in your sourdough starter alive and healthy by giving it fresh flour and water once a week.

Retarding. Refrigerating the dough either before or after it is shaped to slow down fermentation in order to allow flavorful acids, produced by lactobacilli, to build.

Sauerteig. The German term for sourdough starter, usually made with rye flour and usually considerably more sour than a starter made primarily with wheat flour.

Scoring. Using a razor blade, sharp knife, or lame to make cuts in the dough just before baking to allow steam to escape and the dough to rise in an attractive way.

Semolina. Durum wheat, coarsely milled for pasta making and finely milled to make sunny-looking yellow loaves.

Slashing. Another term for scoring.

Soaker. A mixture of whole grains and seeds, presoaked for several hours to overnight to release enzymes, which aid in fermentation by converting flour's starches into sugars.

Soft wheat. Lower-protein wheat.

Sourdough bread. Bread raised with wild, as opposed to commercially raised and packaged, yeast.

Sourdough starter. Wild yeast, cultivated in a mixture of flour and water, used instead of or along with commercial yeast to raise bread.

Spelt. A lower-protein variety of wheat, well tolerated by many people who are sensitive to gluten, and used to make lower-gluten wheat breads.

Sponge. The English term for a wet pre-ferment made with flour, water, and commercial yeast.

Spring wheat. Wheat planted in the spring and harvested in the summer, usually high in protein and good for bread.

Starch. The carbohydrates found in wheat and other grains that, when broken down by enzymes into sugars, provide food for yeast.

Starch retrogradation. The process by which, during baking and as the bread cools, water molecules inside the bread migrate to the crust and evaporate, leaving the interior of the bread moist, but not spongy or doughy, and the exterior crisp.

Straight dough. A bread dough mixed in one step, with no pre-ferment or sourdough starter, in which commercial yeast is added directly to the dough. Also known as **direct dough**.

Triticale. A wheat-rye hybrid grain, developed in Scotland in the nineteenth century to grow in climates and soil where wheat doesn't thrive.

Whole wheat. Whole-wheat flour contains the entire milled wheat kernel — germ, bran, and endosperm — as opposed to white wheat flour, which consists primarily of the starchy endosperm.

Windowpane test. Stretching a small piece of kneaded dough to see if it will form a translucent membrane, performed to see if it has been kneaded adequately and has developed enough gluten to rise high. Useful primarily for wetter doughs. Relatively dry doughs will be unable to stretch so thin without tearing.

Winter wheat. Wheat planted in the autumn that grows all through the winter and is harvested in the late spring or early summer.

Yeast. Single-celled microorganisms that produce carbon dioxide (along with alcohol) as they feed on starches in bread dough, causing the dough to rise as it ferments and bakes. Yeast can remain dormant for years, becoming active when moistened with water. This is why properly stored packaged yeast can raise bread after years and why wild yeast that lies dormant in sacks of flour will become active when the flour is combined with water and allowed to stand at room temperature.

Resources for the Bread Baker

Baking with professional-quality ingredients and equipment has never been easier, since online shopping puts everything from brioche pans to organic kamut flour at your fingertips. Here is a list of my favorite purveyors of baking equipment and ingredients, in case you are in the market for a baker's peel, a bench scraper, or French sea salt in bulk.

Baking Supplies and Ingredients

Bluebird Grain Farms

888-232-0331

www.bluebirdgrainfarms.com

One of the only sources for organic emmer flour in this country, Bluebird Grain Farms is also worth checking out for its wheat flours, including hard white and hard red, if you'd like to explore the differences, and its whole grains, including rye berries and three kinds of wheat berries.

Bob's Red Mill

800-349-2173

www.bobsredmill.com

This widely stocked brand of organic flours is available in many supermarkets and most natural foods stores, but if you can't find it, you can order kamut, triticale, spelt, semolina, three kinds of rye, and many other types of flour directly.

Breadtopia

800-469-7989

www.breadtopia.com

This online store doesn't sell many ingredients, but it sells every imaginable piece of equipment that a home bread baker might need, including bannetons, peels, Kevlar oven mitts, instant-read thermometers, grain mills, bread boxes and storage bags to keep your loaves fresh, and a couple of bread knives selected by expert buyers.

Cooking.com

800-663-8810

www.cooking.com

This online cookware store runs frequent specials on pricey items such as KitchenAid stand mixers and Zojirushi bread machines. You will also find a good selection of baking stones, pizza wheels, and digital scales.

Giusto's Vita-Grain Flours

888-884-1940

http://giustos.com

Based in San Francisco, Giusto's has long been the choice of many of northern California's best professional artisan bakers, including Steve Sullivan of Acme Bread Company. Recently, Giusto's has begun to package its carefully milled flours in smaller quantities for the home baker. If you would like to duplicate Acme's award-winning baguettes, order a bag of Giusto's Baker's Choice Unbleached Bread Flour.

Hodgson Mill

800-347-0105

www.hodgsonmill.com

Another popular purveyor of organic and stone-ground flour and meal.

King Arthur Flour Company

800-827-6836

www.kingarthurflour.com

I get all of my flour from King Arthur. I'm convinced that their organic all-purpose flour has helped me produce the best bread I've ever made. I've also bought rye flour, semolina flour, and cocoa powder from them. This is the site I visit to order precut sheets of parchment paper, without which I wouldn't be able to bake bread. And I've ordered a lot of the other bread-baking equipment I own from The Baker's Catalogue, including dough-rising containers, instant-read thermometers, and a bench scraper that I've been using for almost 20 years. Not only is this online baker's supply company a one-stop source for ingredients and equipment, but it is also a great source for bread recipes, developed by the company's bakers in their renowned kitchen.

Lehman's

888-438-5346

www.lehmans.com

This is the best source for grain mills, both electric and old-fashioned hand-cranked varieties. Lehman's is the exclusive dealer for the Cadillac of mills, the Diamant, a cast-iron hand-cranked model that is, according to their catalog copy, "equally at home in the farmer's barn cracking bushels of corn for livestock or in the baker's kitchen milling fine flour for delicate pastries."

Nuts Online

800-558-6887

www.nutsonline.com

If you like to bake with nuts, you can find great prices on large bags to keep in the freezer. I especially like the blanched hazelnuts, which don't need to be skinned before using in Whole-Wheat and Honey Boule with Hazelnuts (page 222). Difficult-to-find dried fruits such as dried blueberries, boysenberries, and gooseberries could be fun to use in bread. And there's a big choice of candied fruit and zest for creative panettone in the bread machine.

Pleasant Hill Grain

800-321-1073

www.pleasanthillgrain.com

Not only does this online store sell flour, but it also sells a variety of whole grains along with a large selection of home grain mills, if you are inclined to mill your own flour one of these days.

Salt Traders

800-641-7258

www.salttraders.com

Purveyors of sea salts and other fine salts from around the world, many sold in bulk for economy and convenience.

SaltWorks, Inc.

800-353-7258

www.saltworks.us

This Seattle-based company provides fine sea salt to restaurants and gourmet markets and also sells smaller quantities to retail customers online.

Sourdoughs International

208-382-4828

www.sourdo.com

Dr. Ed Wood is a trained pathologist who began studying sourdough cultures while working in a hospital in Riyadh, Saudi Arabia. His hobby became a passion, some might even say an obsession. Over the years, he traveled the world, collecting wild yeast cultures, which he brought home and stored in his refrigerator. In addition to traveling to the Great Pyramids with the National Geographic Society to re-create ancient Egyptian bread, he has written a book, *World Sourdoughs from Antiquity*, and has started a small business selling some of his dehydrated sourdoughs, including cultures from Finland, Australia, Italy, South Africa, and, of course, Egypt.

Williams-Sonoma

877-812-6235

www.williams-sonoma.com

This well-known chain sells top-quality appliances such as KitchenAid mixers and Cui-sinart bread machines, as well as wonderful Goldtouch loaf pans and French bread pans, which I highly recommend for their nonstick surfaces.

Suggested Reading

Bread is a vast and complicated subject, and an entire library could be filled with helpful and interesting books on the subject. I own dozens of bread books, and every single one has given me tips, techniques, and recipe ideas that have expanded my bread-baking knowledge and ability. Once you've baked a few of your own loaves, you will surely want to read about other bakers' ideas and experiences, try new recipes, and expand your baking knowledge. If you are looking for a place to start, here is a list of books I turn to time after time for information on every aspect of home bread baking.

Baking Science

Corriher, Shirley O. *BakeWise: The Hows and Whys of Successful Baking with Over 200 Magnificent Recipes.* New York: Scribner, 2008

Corriher is a food scientist with a knack for explaining complex chemical reactions in an elegant and understandable way. If you are having trouble understanding how gluten develops before you read her chapter on bread, you won't have any problem afterward.

Figonia, Paula. *How Baking Works: Exploring the Fundamentals of Baking Science,* 2nd ed. Hoboken, NJ: Wiley, 2007

Although this book is written for cooking school students gravitating toward a career in baking, there is much here for the home bread baker, including an especially comprehensive discussion of flour and other bread ingredients.

Wood, Ed. *World Sourdoughs from Antiquity,* rev. ed. Berkeley, CA: Ten Speed Press, 1996
This highly readable book by a trained pathologist traces sourdough from ancient Egyptian times and pays homage to Egyptian baking techniques with some interesting recipes.

General Bread Books

Bertinet, Richard. *Dough: Simple Contemporary Bread.* London: Kyle Books, 2005
If you are interested in, or confused about, the importance of proper kneading, you might take a look at Bertinet's book, which contains a very helpful and detailed discussion/demonstration of how he stretches and slaps the dough in order to incorporate air into it as well as develop gluten. Bertinet's breads are bubbly, with a large, uneven crumb, due to the care he takes with kneading.

Calvel, Raymond. *The Taste of Bread.* Gaithersburg, MD: Aspen, 2001
A French professor of baking who taught Julia Child how to make a baguette, Calvel was an advocate of autolyse and gentle kneading. If you can afford this costly translation of the French classic, and if you can manage to find a copy, you will own what is to many professional artisans a biblical text on the science of bread baking.

Clayton, Bernard. *Bernard Clayton's New Complete Book of Breads,* 30th anniversary ed. New York: Simon & Schuster, 2003
If you had a bread book on your shelf in the 1970s, chances are it was *Bernard Clayton's Complete Book of Breads.* For this new and revised edition, Clayton updated the original recipes and added 100 new ones. This isn't the most scientific or rigorous bread book out there, but for simplicity and breadth of recipes it can't be beat.

Hamelman, Jeffrey. *Bread: A Baker's Book of Techniques and Recipes.* Hoboken, NJ: Wiley, 2004
Jeffrey Hamelman runs the bread program at King Arthur Flour, and his knowledge of all types of breads — straight doughs, breads made with pre-ferments, sourdough loaves — is encyclopedic. This book has a split personality, addressing the professional baker and the home baker at the same time. Sometimes Hamelman's technical language is difficult to decipher, but the wealth of information he delivers is well worth the effort.

Oppenneer, Betsy. *The Bread Book.* New York: HarperCollins, 1994
This is one of the first books on bread that I owned, and it's one that I still turn to for commonsense advice and no-fuss recipes.

Ortiz, Joe. *The Village Baker.* Berkley, CA: Ten Speed Press, 1993
Joe Ortiz was a pioneer, becoming a village baker in the European style before most people had ever considered European breads. His recipes are elegantly simple, and his account of starting his business is fascinating.

Reinhart, Peter. *Crust and Crumb.* Berkeley, CA: Ten Speed Press, 2006

In this classic book, Reinhart does a wonderful job of explaining why a slow fermentation makes superior bread and how to use pre-ferments and sourdough starters to extend fermentation. His recipes are so detailed and careful that they guarantee success.

Van Over, Charles. *The Best Bread Ever: Great Homemade Bread Using Your Food Processor.* New York: Broadway Books, 1997

This is a great book to have if you don't have a stand mixer and would like to use your food processor to knead dough.

Artisan and Sourdough Baking

Glezer, Maggie. *Artisan Baking Across America.* New York: Artisan, 2000

This book profiles some of the best artisan bakers working in the United States today and prints some of the recipes I covet most, such as the rustic baguettes from Berkeley's legendary Acme Bread Company.

Leader, Daniel, and Judith Blahnik. *Bread Alone.* New York: William Morrow, 1993

One of the books that ignited the home baking movement, *Bread Alone* remains a favorite because of its easy-to-follow recipes and the author's obvious passion for quality bread.

Leader, Daniel, and Lauren Chattman. *Local Breads.* New York: W. W. Norton, 2007

This long awaited follow-up to *Bread Alone* is a fascinating travelogue through some of Europe's best bakeries and a wonderfully practical manual that shows American home bakers how to easily bake authentic European artisan breads at home.

Silverton, Nancy, and Laurie Ochoa. *Nancy Silverton's Breads from the La Brea Bakery.* New York: Villard Books, 1996

This is a sometimes daunting but always fascinating book of recipes to help you re-create breads developed by Los Angeles's premier baking authority.

Wing, Daniel, and Alan Scott. *The Bread Builders.* White River Junction, VT: Chelsea Green, 1999

Considered a classic by fanatical home bakers, this isn't a recipe book, but a detailed and informed discussion of how to craft wild yeast breads. The second half of the book explores masonry ovens — the different types that professional artisans use as well as custom home ovens for the baker who is dreaming of building an oven of his or her own.

Baking with Whole Grains

Hensperger, Beth. *The Pleasure of Whole-Grain Breads.* San Franciso: Chronicle Books, 1999

Hensperger takes a more low-key approach to the subject in this beautifully photographed book of recipes that includes breads made with amaranth, buckwheat, teff, soy flour, and other unusual ingredients.

Reinhart, Peter. *Peter Reinhart's Whole Grain Breads: New Techniques, Extraordinary Flavor.* Berkeley, CA: Ten Speed Press, 2007

Reinhart brings his expertise to bear on whole-grain baking. Anyone who has baked a bricklike loaf of bitter whole-wheat bread will appreciate his techniques, aimed at getting the best flavor and highest rise using whole-grain flours. There is plenty of technical and scientific information to go along with the excellent recipes. Reinhart's thesis is that delayed fermentation results in the best whole-grain breads, so the recipes are predominantly two-stage breads employing yeasted pre-ferments.

No-Knead Bread Books

Baggett, Nancy. *Kneadlessly Simple.* Hoboken, NJ: Wiley, 2009

Baggett uses a technique similar to Leahy's, often baking bread in a cast-iron pot to support very wet doughs and encourage crust development. But her tone and perspective are distinct. She comes at the subject less from a professional artisan's point of view and more from the home baker's position. Baking from this book is like learning how to make no-knead bread from a trusted and experienced neighbor.

Hertzberg, Jeff, and Zoe François. *Artisan Bread in Five Minutes a Day: The Discovery That Revolutionizes Home Baking.* New York: Thomas Dunne, 2007

Although no-knead bread has been around for a very long time, this was the first book on the market to capitalize on the technique. Some may find the method — making large batches of dough, cutting it into

pieces, and refrigerating it for up to 2 weeks before baking — inconvenient. But others will love the way the recipes provide an easy system for making bread regularly.

Leahy, Jim, and Rick Flaste. *My Bread: The Revolutionary No-Work, No-Knead Method.* New York: W. W. Norton, 2009

The baker responsible for the no-knead craze explains the science behind this type of ultraslow fermented bread. Leahy is a respected artisan baker, and his excellent and well-tested recipes for all sorts of no-knead doughs (pizza, rye, apple bread) reflect the seriousness and integrity of his project.

Reinhart, Peter. *Peter Reinhart's Artisan Breads Every Day.* Berkeley, CA: Ten Speed Press, 2009

The newest book by expert baker and teacher Peter Reinhart isn't strictly a no-knead bread book, but it is filled with simple recipes and considerably less technical information than his previous books. It's a good introduction to this important authority's work as well as an introduction to home bread baking in general.

Flatbreads

Alford, Jeffrey, and Naomi Duguid. *Flatbreads & Flavors.* New York: William Morrow, 1995

A classic exploration of flatbreads from around the world, this is as much a travelogue as a bread book. Filled with recipes for yeasted and nonyeasted flatbreads, it is a fascinating study of how different cultures conjure myriad breads from the same few ingredients.

Helou, Anissa. *Savory Baking from the Mediterranean: Focaccias, Flatbreads, Rusks, Tarts, and Other Breads.* New York: William Morrow, 2007

This book, written by an expert on Mediterranean cooking, goes well beyond pizza to explore a wide variety of regional flatbreads that have become more and more popular in the United States recently.

Bread Machine Baking

Brody, Lora, and Millie Apter. *Bread Machine Baking: Perfect Every Time.* New York: William Morrow, 1993

Although this book is out of print and not so easy to find, it's worth seeking out for the variety of recipes they developed specifically for the bread machine.

Eckhardt, Linda West, and Diana Collingwood Butts. *Rustic European Breads from Your Bread Machine.* New York: Doubleday, 1995

These authors have done the work of adapting traditional recipes for bread machine baking.

Best Bread-Baking Websites

Although you can always turn to your baking library in search of new recipes or answers to questions about bread baking, sometimes it's nice to have an interactive source for bread-related information. Here are a few of my favorite bread websites, where you can go to hang around virtually with other bakers and even get into a conversation about your sourdough starter or your favorite pizza dough if you'd like.

Bakers' Websites

Many high-profile bread book authors and artisan bakers maintain active websites where they post new recipes and answer readers' questions. Here are some of the best.

Danlepard.com
Dan Lepard
www.danlepard.com
When I want to get a European perspective on what's new in bread, I visit British baker Dan Lepard's site. Browse through his archive of baking articles to get an idea of his witty and no-nonsense approach to home bread baking. His rundown of British artisan bakeries makes me want to hop on a flight to London and check out the thriving baking scene from Cornwall to Wales to Devonshire and beyond.

Real Baking with Rose Levy Beranbaum
Rose Levy Beranbaum
www.realbakingwithrose.com
What I love about Beranbaum's site is the way she answers readers' questions in a wonderfully friendly and opinionated way,

so friendly that you can often read extended back-and-forth correspondence between Beranbaum and her followers. These conversations are usually fascinating and always educational. I also value her recommendations on new bread books. She is picky, so if she likes a book you can be sure it is worth the cover price.

Peter Reinhart

www.peterreinhart.typepad.com

Keep up with this master baker by checking out his blog every once in a while. Not only will you be able to read about his works in progress (he blogs in detail about the testing that goes into the recipes for each new book), but you'll also get his schedule, in case he's visiting a cooking school near you soon.

The Baking Business

Home bakers can learn a lot from professional artisans whose livelihood depends on well-risen breads. Here are a couple of websites that provide access to some of the leaders and innovators in the baking business.

Modern Baking

www.modern-baking.com

The website for the trade magazine *Modern Baking,* this is primarily a resource for professionals, but it has many fascinating stories about important professional bakers along with recipes and advice about their favorite breads and baking techniques.

Stir the Pots

www.stirthepots.com

Jeremy Shapiro's blog about the food business is filled with interesting audio interviews with well-known artisans, including Jim Lahey (Sullivan Street Bakery), Daniel Leader (Bread Alone), Steve Sullivan (Acme Bread Company), Noel Comess (Tomcat Bakery), and Amy Scherber (Amy's Bread).

Online Baking Communities

If your gluten won't develop or your sourdough is on life support and you need someone to talk to, check out one of these online baking communities, where friendly strangers are always willing to share their knowledge or commiserate. The following are among the most active.

The Fresh Loaf

www.thefreshloaf.com

This is an online community for passionate home bakers, with recipes, tutorials, forums, and book reviews. I especially like the forums, where you can ask a question — "Why did my sourdough baguettes fail to rise in the oven when my starter was so active?" — and you'll get a dozen helpful comments almost instantly.

Sourdough Companion

www.sourdough.com

This is a website devoted to just sourdough baking, with recipes, forums, tutorials, and many helpful articles on the subject. I love the photo albums posted by members that are filled with their successes, and sometimes their all-too-relatable failures, with sourdough.

Wild Yeast

www.wildyeastblog.com

This popular bread-baking blog, written by a student in the professional bread and pastry program at the San Francisco Baking Institute, has a wonderful weekly feature called "YeastSpotting," for which readers send in photos of breads they've baked. When you are especially proud of something that's come out of your oven, it's a good way to brag.

Bread-Baking Classes

Take your interest in home bread baking to the next level by signing up for a bread-baking class at a nearby cooking school. Many schools that train professional bakers also have programs for passionate amateurs, taught by the same staff or by high-profile visiting bakers. Here are a few to check out.

The Baking Education Center

King Arthur Flour
Norwich, Vermont
800-652-3334
www.kingarthurflour.com/baking

America's oldest flour company is a mecca for home bakers. They offer many classes of interest to the home bread baker at their Vermont headquarters. If you can't get to Vermont, you can pick up a few tips from their resident bakers, who travel the country throughout the year, demonstrating baking techniques.

Bread Bakers Guild of America

707-935-1468
www.bbga.org

This northern California–based professional organization puts together workshops for amateurs. The classes are held at various cooking schools around the country and led by experts like King Arthur Flour's Jeffrey Hamelman.

Institute for Culinary Education

New York, New York
800-522-4610
www.iceculinary.com

This New York City school for professional chefs also offers numerous recreational bread-baking courses, including classes in pizza and bread science.

L'Academie de Cuisine

Bethesda, Maryland
800-664-2433
www.lacademie.com

This cooking school offers many classes of interest to home bread bakers, including workshops on flatbreads, baguettes, and brioche.

San Francisco Baking Institute

San Francisco, California
650-589-5784
www.sfbi.com

SFBI offers a variety of courses for the amateur, covering topics such as whole-grain breads, sourdough breads, artisan breads from a wood-fired oven, and artisan breads of Germany.

Artisan Bakeries to Visit

There's nothing like visiting a top-notch artisan bakery for inspiration and perhaps a few baking tips. Here are just a very few of the wonderful village-style bakeries to have opened in the past 25 years, as the artisan bread movement has caught fire in the United States. In your travels, you might think of stopping in at one of them to taste a new bread and even to chat with the baker about how it was crafted. If you can't manage a visit, some of the following bakeries will deliver bread overnight. And certainly seek out and support local bakeries that are doing their best to craft bread with love and care.

Bakery Nouveau

4737 California Avenue SW

Seattle, Washington

206-923-0534

www.bakerynouveau.com

In a city dotted with good bakeries, this one stands out as world class, consistently topping "Best of Seattle" lists while catering to the neighborhood and fostering community with friendliness and monthly charitable donations of bread and pastry to local nonprofit groups.

Bread Alone Bakery

Route 28

Boiceville, New York

800-769-3328

www.breadalone.com

Daniel Leader's was one of the first, and is still one of the best, artisan bakeries in this country.

Breadfarm

5766 Cains Court

Bow, Washington

360-766-4065

www.breadfarm.com

Committed to using local ingredients, this local bakery turns out breads named after the sources of their ingredients: Bow Hill Baguette, Tonasket Rye, Samish River Potato Bread.

The Bread Shack

1056 Center Street

Auburn, Maine

207-376-3090

www.thebreadshack.com

An off-the-beaten-path bakery owned by Dara Riemers, who has represented the United States in the World Cup of Bread.

Clear Flour Bread

178 Thorndike Street

Brookline, Massachusetts

617-739-0060

www.clearflourbread.com

This bakery produces an impressive menu of European-style breads using organic, stone-ground flours whenever possible.

The Model Bakery

1357 Main Street

St. Helena, California

707-963-8192

www.themodelbakery.com

An old-fashioned village bakery (it's been operating at this location for more than 80 years) with some very up-to-date sourdough-raised artisan breads.

Ninth Street Bakery

136 East Chapel Hill Street
Durham, North Carolina
866-801-6218
www.ninthstbakery.com

This North Carolina bakery is committed to using flour milled locally at Lindley Mills in nearby Saxapahaw.

Pearl Bakery

102 NW 9th Avenue
Portland, Oregon
503-827-0910
www.pearlbakery.com

Remarkable for its commitment to local ingredients, including flour milled from wheat grown in nearby Washington State.

Red Hen Bread

1623 N. Milwaukee Avenue
Chicago, Illinois
773-342-6823
www.redhenbread.com

Considered by many to be the best bakery in Chicago.

Standard Baking Company

Fore Street Restaurant
75 Commercial Street
Portland, Maine
207-773-2112
www.forestreet.biz

Owned by the perfectionists behind Portland's premier restaurant, Fore Street, this bakery produces some of the Northeast's finest sourdough baguettes, as well as amazing croissants and brioche.

Sullivan Street Bakery

533 West 47th Street
New York, New York
212-265-5580
www.sullivanstreetbakery.com

Although Jim Leahy recently became well known for his no-knead bread recipe, he's been baking acclaimed Italian-style sourdough breads in New York City since 1994.

Turtle Bread Company

4762 Chicago Avenue
South Minneapolis, Minnesota
612-823-7333
www.turtlebread.com

Head baker Solveig Tofte is one of the most prominent women bakers working in the United States today and is a member of the Bread Bakers Guild of America's Team USA, which competes with teams from around the world at the prestigious World Cup of Bread.

WheatFields Bakery Café

904 Vermont Street
Lawrence, Kansas
785-841-5553
www.wheatfieldsbakery.com

In the heart of America's breadbasket, WheatFields uses flour milled from heirloom wheat grown right in Lawrence to make many of its breads.

Index

Page references in **bold** indicate charts; page references in *italics* indicate illustrations.

matzoh, 189

measuring
    cups/spoons, 55, *55*
    ingredients, 65–66
    yields and, 102

milk, 34
    dry, 28
    scalded, myth of, 227
    yogurt, buttermilk or, 41

milling flour
    home-milled, 24–25, *25*
    how wheat becomes flour, 14–15

mixer. *See* stand mixer

mixing and kneading, 66–78. *See also* kneading dough

mixing bowls, 55, *55*

mixing methods, 67–69
    direct method, 67–68
    pre-ferment method, 68–69
    sourdough baking, 69

My Bread (Leahy), 76, 80

Naan
    on gas grill, 212
    Grilled Whole-Wheat Naan, *205,* 205–6

Navajo fry bread, 211

New Complete Book of Breads (Clayton), 80

No-Knead Roman Pizzas, 193–94

nonstick baking sheets, 60

nuts, dried fruit, olives, seeds, 36, 105

Oat flour, 22

Oatmeal Bread, Overnight, 254–55

oil. *See* fats/oil

"old dough," 133, 142

olives, seeds, nuts, dried fruit, 36, 106

Oppenneer, Betsy, 109

oven
    convection setting, 60–61
    tips for use of, 54

oven mitts, 55, *55*

oven spring, 90, 191–92

overbaking, 98

overfermenting dough, 127

Overnight English Muffins, 200–201

Overnight Oatmeal Bread, 254–55

overproofing, 96–97, *97*

Pain de mie, 41, 47, 142–43
    crust of, 150
    for Pullman loaf, 150–51

pain de mie pan. *See* Pullman loaf pan

Pancakes, Scallion, 204–5, *205*

Pane alla Cioccolata, 252–53

panettone, 260–61

panettone pan, 46–47, *47*

pan loaf, 89, *89*

Pan Loaf, Rye and Pumpkin Seed, 174–75

Pan Pizza with Tomatoes, Mozzarella, and Sausage, 112–13

parchment paper, 56, *56*

Parker House rolls, 98

pastry brush, 56, *56*

pâte fermentée, 133, *133,* 134
    baguette and, 151
    described, 70

"peggy tub" fermentation method, 109, *109*

Other Storey Titles You Will Enjoy

The Baking Answer Book, by Lauren Chattman.

Answers every question about common and specialty ingredients, the best equipment, and the science behind the magic of baking.

384 pages. Flexibind. ISBN 978-1-60342-439-4.

Cookie Craft, by Valerie Peterson & Janice Fryer.

Clear instruction, practical methods, and all the tips and tricks for beautifully decorated special occasion cookies.

168 pages. Hardcover. ISBN 978-1-58017-694-1.

Home Cheese Making, by Ricki Carroll.

A classic primer to making artisanal-quality cheeses and other dairy products, as well as cooking with cheese.

288 pages. Paper. ISBN 978-1-58017-464-0.

The Home Creamery, by Kathy Farrell-Kingsley.

Step-by-step instructions to guide home cooks in making fresh dairy products, including butter, yogurt, sour cream, and buttermilk.

220 pages. Paper. ISBN 978-1-60342-031-0.

Home Sausage Making,
by Susan Mahnke Peery & Charles G. Reavis.

The complete guide to making delicious, healthy, one-of-a-kind sausages.

288 pages. Paper. ISBN 978-1-58017-471-8.

These and other books from Storey Publishing are available wherever quality books are sold or by calling 1-800-441-5700.
Visit us at _www.storey.com_.